MADISON COUNTY, TENNESSEE,

TOMBSTONE INSCRIPTIONS

Transcribed by:

The Works Progress Administration
1937

With New Index by
Samuel Sistler

Janaway Publishing
2006

> *Notice*
>
> This book has been reproduced from carbon-copies of the original transcriptions of court records by the Works Progress Administration (WPA) in 1930s. In many instances, the resulting text is light, the documents are physically flawed, and foxing (or discoloration) occurs. The pages of this reprint have been digitally enhanced and, where possible, the flaws and markings eliminated in order to provide clarity of content and a pleasant reading experience.

Madison County, Tennessee, Tombstone Inscriptions

Originally transcribed by:

The Works Progress Administration (WPA)
1937

New Index
Copyright © 2004, Samuel Sistler

Reprinted by:

Janaway Publishing, Inc.
732 Kelsey Ct.
Santa Maria, CA 93454
(805) 925-1038
www.JanawayGenealogy.com

2006, 2012

ISBN: 978-1-59641-139-5

Made in the United States of America

MADISON COUNTY, TENNESSEE
TOMBSTONE INSCRIPTIONS

prepared by Ingram James and Mamie Jerome of the Works Progress Administration, 1937
with new index by Samuel Sistler, 1999

The transcript this book was printed from is a carbon copy typed on onion skin paper over 60 years ago. The print quality varied throughout the work--this would seem to be due to the wear on the carbon paper. We have made an effort to make all the print as legible as possible. This is a second generation copy of the original, and there will be a few places where the writing cannot be made out.

We would like to thank Jean Sugg and Chuck Sherrill of the TN State Library and Archives for their kind loan of the original book.

Byron Sistler & Associates

TENNESSEE

RECORDS OF MADISON COUNTY

TOMBSTONE INSCRIPTIONS

HISTORICAL RECORDS PROJECT

OFFICIAL PROJECT NO. 165-44-699

COPIED UNDER WORKS PROGRESS ADMINISTRATION

MRS. JOHN TROTWOOD MOORE

STATE LIBRARIAN & ARCHIBIST, SPONSOR

MRS. ELIZABETH D. COPPEDGE

STATE DIRECTOR OF WOMEN'S & PROFESSIONAL PROJECTS

MRS. PENELOPE JOHNSON ALLEN

STATE SUPERVISOR

MRS. KATHLEEN W. CARADINE

SUPERVISOR THIRD DISTRICT

1937

COPYIST - INGRAM JAMES

TYPIST - MAMIE JEROME

MADISON COUNTY

TOMBSTONE INSCRIPTIONS

CONTENTS

Riverside Cemetery, 1,69

Browns Church Cemetery, 70,107

Old Salem Cemetery, 108,112

Taylor Cemetery, 113,120

TOMBSTONE INSCRIPTIONS

RIVERSIDE CEMETERY

MADISON COUNTY

Riverside Cemetery is located on Mc Cory Street, Jackson, Tenn.
There are 228 unmarked graves.
Ingram James, Copyist.
April, 1937.

Jeff D. Bledsoe
1864 - 1901

Minna L. Bledsoe
1867 - 1932

Lelia May Bledsoe
Died 1892

Annie Myrtle, daughter
of J.M. & M.M. Irvine
Aug 26th, 1881
Sept 16th, 1884

Robert Jackson Allen
Feb 17, 1870
May 27, 1892

George Allen,
Sept 27, 1886
Nov. 18, 1891

Bessie Allen
July 19, 1884
Sept 14, 1886

Hamner Allen
Nov. 18, 1881
Sept 18, 1883

Robert Hill
 - 1825
Dec 17, 1883

Lena May Hill
July 13, 1865
Aug 1st, 1886

M.M. Bledsoe
(No date)

Mayme Day

Elijah P. Russell
Nov 9, 1855
July 5, 1902

Jos. S. Lee
Aug 9, 1865
Aug 31, 1903

Alice Talbot Laird
Died Sept 29, 1902

May Talbot Cunningham
1829 - 1853

Little Billie, Son of
 J. W. & H.E. Gaither
April 17, 1900
Oct. 31, 1901

John A., Husband
of M. A. Pringle
Sept 9, 1843
Sept 20, 1904

Charlie, Son
of J. A. & M. A. Pringle
Apr 24, 1871
Nov 2, 1909

(Riverside Cemetery p.2.)

Ernest McPherson Murray
Aug 18, 1883
Dec 26, 1935

Cornelius M. Murray
Oct 23, 1878
June 9, 1934

Eloise Macpherson Murray
Oct 9, 1853
Jan 25, 1929

Jeter James Murray
Aug 12, 1845
Oct 22, 1903

Jennie E. Campbell, wife
of W. D. Kierole
Oct 16, 1853
March 8, 1892

Little Oddie
Son of Hattie
Aug 15, 1867
Nov 11, 1875

R.S. McRee
1861 - 1913
Olivia - Wife of Jas. M. McRee

Thos. Copeland
Died Aug 30, 1880

George Broad
Feb 4, 1824
Aug 2, 1883
Mary Jane, wife of Geo. Broad
July 4, 1827
   -    1883

W. A. Graham
1860 - 1924

Julia L. Stephens
1838 - 1911

W. A. Graham
Sept 26, 1833
Mar 7, 1890

Wade W. Lyon
Mar 9, 183-
Apr 13, 18--

Mary Reid, wife of
Wade W. Lyon
Died Feb 1, 1905

Atwell Thompson
1864 - 1912

Katherine B. Witherspoon
1839 - 1881

Elvira Witherspoon, wife
of Wm. Witherspoon
1814 - 1879

Angie Hays, wife
of Ross Witherspoon
1850 - 1916

Capt. W. D. Dupree
Died April 17, 1901

Emma Bush, Wife of
Capt. W.D. Dupree
May 13, 1900

Lida, daughter of
W. D. & E. B. Dupree
Aug 1, 1861
Aug 22, 1882

Ernest H. Means
1888 - 1933

Thos. E. Gates
1877 - 1918

H. C. Irby
June 16, 1835
Feb 18, 1917

Elizabeth Irby
Sept 9th, 1838
Nov 13,   1920

(Riverside Cemetery p.3.

B. R. Person
Oct 23, 1810
Feb 24, 1881

Emily Greer Person
Nov 21, 1824
Oct 3, 1915

Hunter Gates
1870 - 1894

Emma Neill Gates
Died June 6, 1932

G. F. Neil
Died Feb 5, 1885

Alexander Person
1872 - 1877

Emma Munford
Died Aug 7th, 1933

Ben M. Person
1877 - 1934

Elnora S. Person
Nov 13, 1845
Aug 8, 1891

B. A. Person
1845 - 1930

Louanna M. Baird, wife
of R. L. Baird
May 3, 1875
May 11, 1926

H. C. Goode,
July 10, 1847
Sept 8, 1885

Mildred A. Roberts, wife
of R. F. Goode
1878 - 1899

A. M. Rushing
Died Jan 4, 1879

Joseph H. Evans, D. D.
1834 - 1912

Valena M. Standefer, Wife
1838 - 1918

William P. Towler
Aug 15, 1851
Mar 30, 1885

Frank B. Hamilton, Sr.
July 2, 1843
Mar 11, 1910

Geo. D. Hamilton
Jan 12, 1871
Aug 16, 1906

William W. Hamilton
Nov 12, 1876
Aug 5, 1901

Frank B. Hamilton, Jr.
Sept 9, 1880
Dec 12, 1929

Thos. A. Andrews
1866 - 1936

Martha Anderson Nance
Apr 18, 1867
Dec 22, 1906

Sallie E. Carter, Wife
No Date -

Mary A. Rush
Died March 16, 1897

J. W. Rush
1852 - 1895

Susan C. Rush
1863 - 1928

August W. Rush
1883 - 1884

Chas. B. Wilson
1887 - 1936

(Riverside Cemetery p.4)

Eliza P. Balch
1834 - 1912

David L. Balch
1831 - 1901

May Wilbon
1865 - 1910

Richard L. Balch
1860 - 1934

Jas. P. Bond   - Theo Bond
1866 - 1902   - 1900 - 1900.

Annie C. daughter
of J. J. Rice
No Date

Sarah A. Rice
April 3, 1844
Dec. 8, 1883

Capt. J. J. Rice
April 18, 1830
Dec 8,   1879

F. Spah
Nov 9, 1812
Nov 30, 1885

Lora Spah
1845 - 1917

Mary Spah, wife of
J. H. McMillan
May 14, 1843
Mar 31, 1926

John Harrison McMillan
April 2, 1832
 - - , 1900

Nancy Jane Wright
Died Dec 9, 1880
    Age 32 years

John Wright
Dec 31, 1847
Mar 22, 1881

Mina Belle Goode
No Date -

W.H. Conner
July 19, 1819
Sept 11, 1881

L.B. Shelton
Apr 8, 1834
Oct 11, 1896

Sarah Willie, Wife of
L.B. Shelton
Apr 17, '71
Aug 6, 1888

Ida, daughter of
L.B. & S. Shelton
Sept 6, 1866
May 16, 1882

Jennie Vieve L., Wife
of J.L. Diffee
Died Feb 13, 1892

Mary Ada Lyalls
Oct 24, 1853
Died April 19, 1892

Willie Corrin, son of Mary
& Robert Crabtree
Died July 25, 1888

Mrs. Mary C. Simmons
Died July 16, 1882

Matilda Corrin
Sept 5, 1853
Nov. 5, 1908

Little Pron
Jan 5, 1896
Sept., 1896

Little George
-No Date -

SONS OF GEO. & MINNIE MC CLOHN

(Riverside Cemetery p.5)

Benjamin C. Dunn
1815 - 1888

Annie E., wife of
D. H. Millender
June 5, 1848
July 25, 1883

Ateliah Dunn
1828 - 1887

Lucy Jobe
1855 - 1888

Annie M. Jobe
1876 - 1886

Elmore Dunn
1883 - 1884

Lucius C. Dunn
1853 - 1913

Hattie B., wife of
A. Robinson
Died Dec 18, 1881

Mary E. Daughter of
G.&M.J. Mc Natt
Sept 13, 1849
Oct 23, 1883

Mahuldah, Wife of R.P. Dunaway
- No date -

Dr. W. R. Cole,
Apr 20, 1834
June 10, 1906

Sarah E. Dunaway, wife of
Dr. W.R. Cole
Oct 19, 1855
Nov 8, 1919

Vanden Mc Kinnie
1898 - 1920

Kate A. Mc Kinnie
1876 - 1903

John R. Mc Kinnie
1849 - 1909

Daisy Dean, daughter of Betty A.
& A. Fariss
Died May 7, 1890

Mary Love, daughter of
Betty A. & A. Fariss

T. Thorp Fariss
1868 - 1894

William H. Fariss
1836 - 1899

Bettie A. Fariss
1841 - 1902

Elizabeth Whitlow
1836 - 1913

Nathan Whitlow
1826 - 1905

J. Walter Rogers
1882 - 1919

Bess, daughter W. Whitlow
& Kate J. Rogers

W. Whitlow Rogers
1878 - 1928

Alice, Wife of W.T. Rogers
1858 - 1919

Emma W. Carter
1830 - 1918

Floyd S. Carter
1832 - 1879

Elissa May
J. G. & M.G. Carter
Died Aug 15, 1887

J. G. Carter
1851 - 1916

Wife Margarette
1859 - 1934

Addie L., wife of
J. T. Higgason
Dec 5, 1850
Sept 8, 1904

(Riverside Cemetery p.6)

Mary A. Carter
1828 - 1907

John Fenner, Son of T.J.
& Fannie Emmons
Nov 11, 1887
Oct 10, 1888

T. G. Emmons
Nov 11, 1859
Nov 12, 1900

Mrs. A. A. Emmons
- No Date -

Eva Neal Schefold
1868 - 1921

Julia -
1899 - 1831

Mary A. Ritch,
1835 - 1924

-Three Unmarked Graves-
Sallie E., wife of Dr.J.F.Cobe
Oct 17, 1830
Oct 11, 1887

Willie G., Son of J.P.
& M. J. Lockard
Aug 10, 1885
Nov 30, 1886

J. T. Amis
June 29, 1844
Oct 22, 1922

Sue Noel, wife of J.T.Amis
Sept 22, 1846
Jan 17, 1917

Son - Robert S. Garrett
1890 - 1914

Nannie, wife of A.T.Garrett
1862 - 1935

A. T. Garrett
1870 - 1907

Infant -
March 29, 1894

Addie D.
1892 - 1894

Doma P., Wife of S.M. Dunn
Dec 26, 1891

Wm. P. Payne
Feb. 1826
Aug 25, 1885

John J. Temain
- No date -

J. J. Temain
Died March 1875

Addie V. daughter of J. J.
& S. J. Tenain
Died 1883.

Tabitha Brigham
Died Aug 16, 1902

Elise Mary, Daughter W.D.
& Mary Bradberry
Born Mar 9, 1881
Died Oct 6, 1889

Eliza, Mother of
Haniah Pope
- No date -

Willis Pope,
Mar 10, 1825
Dec 30, 1896

B. Ann Lackey
1820
June 1900

Haniah, Wife of Willis Pope
1844
Jan 26, 1914

(Riverside Cemetery p.7)

Mary Annie, Daughter of Willie
& Haniah Pope
Born July 28, 1860
Died 1880

Annie Lackey
   -   1842
Sept 15, 1912

C. J. Reid
Died April 16th, 1935

Anna, Wife of George Reid
1856 - 1902

Wiley W. Davis
Oct 12, 1828
July 14, 1883

Edward Owen
Mar 22, 1834
Dec 7, 1902

Bettie Owen
June 18, 1839
Feb 13, 1905

Eliza K., wife of Charles Owen
Aug 7, 1841
July 15, '77

Fay, Wife of F.A. Wilson
Mar 22, 1850
Feb 12, 1873

Comer May Wilson
Sept 18, 1871
Sept 22, 1872

Francis Marion Wilson
Feb 24, 1873
Oct 30, 1875

John Wakefield
1802
Feb 7, 1876

John A. White
 - - 1825
June 13, 1876

Loretta W., Wife of
Gen J. J. Brooks
1824 - 1892

Gen. J. J. Brooks
June 3, 1824
Sept 15, 1875

John T. Botts
Aug 8, 1845
Oct 2, 1893

Lyda T. Botts
1850 - 1834
  - Infant's Grave unmarked-
James M. Robbins
1865 - 1922

Margaret Mc Conicke Strothers
1800 - 1878

Samuel Lawrence Sparks
1867 - 1936

John Jay Williams
1818 - 1904

Eliza Strother Williams
1839 - 1919

Steelman
Chas.W. Died 1831
Maggie E.   "   1909

Infant Myrtle Bessie Steelman
Aug 8, 1892

Charles Byrd Steelman
Died Feb 13, 1895

Dr. J. W. Leonard
Aug 3, 1826
Sept 7, 1896

Sallie, daughter of S.H.
& S. C. Neff
1882 - 1895

Samuel H. Neff
Dec 10, 1839
Nov 25, 1887

(Riverside Cemetery p.8)

Ella Neff
1820 - 1857

Charlie David Neff
June 8, 1860
Sept 18, 1910

Sarah Elizabeth Neff
June 14, 1837
Aug 3, 1883

John Amos Neff
Dec 6, 1833
Nov 19, 1901

Rev. R. P. Sutton
Mar 19, 1836
June 1, 1886

John D. Son of J.J.
& A.R. Nicely
Mar 2, 1856
Feb 26, 1879

J. H. Gilbert
1865 - 1921

Edith Knight, Wife of Arney Henry
1875 - 1924

Fenner Henry
1847 - 1929

Frank Henry
- No date -

Dr. M. S. Neely
1833 - 1914

Lou Mc Clanahan, Wife of M. S. Neely
1841 - 1885

Minnie Neely Murdoch
1860 - 1927

Anna Bell Hicks, wife of E.L. James
Dec 22, 1859
Aug 5, 1889

Jeanette Hughes, Wife of
C. C. Mc Call
1865 - 1916

Lou Ellen, wife of J.S. Gunn
1867 - 1890

Elnora M. Snider, Wife
of D. W. Hughes
1885 - 1905

D. W. Hughes
June 15, 1836
Jan 30, 1889

Edward D., Son of
Rev. D.W. & J. Rowland
- No date -
-One lot with 7 Unmarked Graves-
Maggie L., Daughter of
Everett Jarman
Died Aug., 1882
   Age 22 yrs.

Willie Street Jarman
Jan 16, 1878
Feb 7, 1885
-Two Unmarked Infants' Graves.
Walter M. Shortt
1877 - 1928

John Keith
1838 - 1919

Charles S. Keith
- No date -

Thos. W. Keith
1866 - 1902

S. H. Neff
1861 - 1921

Lila May, wife of S.H. Neff
Jan 26, 1863
Dec 13, 1900

(Riverside Cemetery p.9)

Little Alfred, Son of Jas. B.
& Edith Jones
Mar 5, 1895
Oct 16, 1898

Jas. B. Jones
1861 - 1922

Rev. M. B. Faris
Aug 11, 1810
Sept 9, 1865

John T. Caviness
Died Feb. 1885

Mollie River, Wife of Ludes Nance
Oct 2, 1844
Jan 4, 1882

Fred Warren Crego
Dec 5, 1898
May 18, 1901

Emma March
July 7, 1833
Aug 9, 1909

Nannie Alexander
1852 - 1900

OUR CARRIS, daughter of J.P.
& Annie Kell Alexander
Aug 27, 1876
Died Aug 13, 1895

Fannie, Daughter of R.E.
& F. S. Hopper
Aug 19, 1871

One Mausoleum
"Wagner Gausman"
 No Names or Dates

W. H. Rush
June 16, 1812
Dec 24, 1876

Sarah A. Kershaw, wife of W.H.Rush
May 12, 1848
May 12, 1917

E. E. Briggs
1903 - 1906

J. A. Rush
1845 - 1915

M. E. Rush
1854 - 1881

M. O. Rush
1854 - 1890

Samuel Goodrich
Mar 24, 1861
Nov 29, 1889

Caroline (wife) of W.A. Bainhill
Apr 18, 1830
May 2, 1892

Rudolph Hofell
Aug 3, 1851
Apr 16, 1886

Ruby Louise
Aged 5 yrs. 120 days.

Michael F. Bonner
1836 - 1892

Rachael Branner
1844 - 1924

Chas. E. Kisber
May 17, 1861
Mar 25, 1927

Lottie, daughter of
H. C. Mackie
Aug 19, 1871
Jan 8, '72

Minnie, Daughter
- No date -

Harry, Son of H.C. Mackie
- No date -

Thos. E. Walsh
July 4, 1867
Mar 10, 1911

(Riverside Cemetery p. 10)

Thos. Nagle
Mar 6, 1829
Nov 25, 1904

Eliabeth Nagle
Apr 16, 1837
Feb 11, 1910

Mary Samuel Martin
Feb 15, 1826
July 25, 1901

I. W. Martin
Sept 12, 1826
Apr 26, 1910

Gideon Blackburn Harris
1829 - 1919

Walter Person
1868 - 1923

J. F. Snider
1848 - 1931

Mrs Fannie C. Parker
Mar 1, 1828
Mar 15, 1909

Wm. R. Theus
1855 - 1919
Mattie, Wife of W. R. Theus -

Martha A. Mallory
1826 - 1893

Callie King Parker
July 26, 1839
July - 1905

J. M. Parker
- No date -

Anna M. Parker
- No date -

Callie Parker Mallory
Jan 27, 1873
Feb 5, 1902

Jennie Parker Mallory
July 23, 1852
June 1, 1896

Martha Skinner Mallory
- No date -

Edmund Skinner Mallory
Sept 22, 1846
Aug 19, 1908

Joseph L. Pope
1877 - 1928

Samuel D. Mc Donald
1835 - 1908

Emma G. Mc Donald
1838 - 1909

Joseph W. McDonald, M.D.
1862 - 1900

John Taylor Barber, Jr.
Died June 26, 1902

Edward Ross Ingersoll
1901 - 1907

Duane Henry Ingersoll
Aug 4, 1890
June 23, 1904

Wm. H. Long
1856 - 1918

Ida K., wife of Wm. H. Long
1858 - 1916

J. A. Tomlinson
1819 - 1882

Frances, Wife of J. A. Tomlinson
1817 - 1888

Ike C. Tomlinson
Oct 6th, 1860
March 22, 1913

Sallie Pope Tomlinson
1866 - 1930

Mary J. Blair
Dec 4, 1831
June 28, 1909

(Riverside Cemetery p.11)

John B. Blair
Feb 8, 1832
Sept 3, 1848

John Morgan, Son of
J. F. and Anna Wright
Oct 22, 1900
July 5, 1901

Felix Wright
Jan 19, 1897
Aug 18, 1912
-One New Unmarked Grave-
James A. Collins
Sept 9, 1830
Mar 3, 1876
- One illegible stone-
Capt. Charles Collins
Aug 3rd, 1868
May 27, 1914

Mary Deleisseline Utly
Sept 19, 1869
June 1, 1919

Mary Elizabeth, daughter
of E. C. & M.C. Johnson
Sept 7, 1921
July 7, 1924

Marie Deleisseline, daughter
of E.C. & M.C. Johnson
Sept 30, 1917
Jan 23rd, 1918

Robert A. McBride
Died Jan 31, 1905

Henry H. McBride
Died March 16, 1881

Thos. N. Alexander
Jan 4, 1835
June 20, 1906

Edwin F. Alexander
Aug 18, 1838
Sept 28, 1926

J. F., Son of E, F. Alexander
May 8, 1871
July 29, 1899

Lilie Mae Wilie
Sept 14, 1880
Feb 29, 1908

W. R. Wilie
 (Date illegible)
-Two illegible stones-
Chas. Wilde
1834 - 1872

Lena Wilde
1869 - 1870

August Wilde
1851 - 1901

Mary Wilde
1843 - 1914

Chas. F. Wilde
1866 - 1923

Dan G. Caldwell
1859 - 1904

Lella R. Caldwell
Died Aug 18, 1836

Sophie Beatty Reid
Died June 5, 1905

Sophie G. Beatty, wife of G. Reid
Died May 6, 1889

Eula S. Miller
1859 - 1934
-Three illegible stones-
Ruth Robinson
- No date -

Ham Robinson
- No date

Horace Robinson
Died Apr 12, 1887

(Riverside Cemetery p.12)

Ham Robinson, Jr.
- No date -

Martha L., wife of W.W. Potts
Aug 20, 1855
Dec 22, 1876

Fannie J., wife of J.A. Wilson
Sept 11, 1860
Jan 22, 1881

OUR BABY
(No name - No date)

W. H. Watkins,
Jan 28, 1827
Dec 27, 1877

P. D. Cook
Died Sept 17, 1882
Aged 45 years

J. E. Cullen
Apr 28, 1869
Feb 15, 1925

Nicholis Arthur, Son of
P. J. & S.M. Gaffney
Nov 9, 1883
Aug 7, 1884

Charles B. Mc Cabe
1879 - 1895

Alleane Mc Cabe
1875 - 1895

Jas. G. Mc Cabe
1894 - 1895

Wm. G. Mc Cabe
1900 - 1901

Nora B. Mc Cabe
1877 - 1908

E. R. Mc Cabe
1875 - 1909

Elizabeth R. McCabe
1847 - 1904

J. G. Mc Cabe - L.E. Muse
1846 - 1899 - 1867 - 1892

Mary Lee Scott
1892 - 1925

Annie I. Johnston
1871 - 1930

J. R. Johnston
1871 - 1936

Mary E. Johnston
Died 1904

Dorothy L. Stedman
Died 1914

Walter G. Spence
Died Nov 11, 189__
Aged 29 yrs

Ella Spence Jester
Feb 28th, 1867
Jan 9, 1931

Sammie, Son of J.T. &
M. Baxter
Oct 3rd, 1895
Jan 6, 1896

Robert L. Dawson, Husband of
Mary E. Dawson
1869 - 1922

Margaretta, Dau. of R.L.
& M. E. Dawson
1902 - 1905

Eugene R. Dawson, Husband of
Effie M. Dawson
-No date -

Irene Mc Coy, Wife of
Geo. Vandenbrook
Died Oct 14, 1921

Newton Vandenbrook, U.S.N.
1896 - 1918

(Riverside Cemetery p.13)

P.L. Vandenbrook
1850 - 1934

J. J. Vandenbrook, Son.
1878 - 1927

Peter Lancaster
- No date -

J. D. Johnson
1856 - 1935

Frances Henry Estes
Died July 25, 1902
   Aged 5 mos.
Three Unmarked Graves
Jennie Boyce
1858 - 1916

Mary Boyce
1834 - 1915

Delia M. Bell
-No date -

Dr. W. H. Lane
1872 - 1915

Rev. P. W. Lane
Aug 19, 1860
Dec 29, 1904

Isaac, Son of Bishop Lane
1864 - 1889

Martha, dau. of Bishop Lane
1854 - 1855

Mary E. Lane
1886 - 1927

Frances Lane
1824 - 1895

Sadie L., Dau. of G.O.
& Anna Upton
Jan 31, 1921
Nov 9, 1927

J. W. Seward (Father)
1852 - 1902

M. E. Seward (Mother)
1853 - 1912

Katie, Wife of N.B. Williams
July 12, 1872
Nov 22, 1903

Will Buntin
1876 - 1915

Mary Holm Buntin
Aug 28, 1900
May 20, 1906

Irene Norton
Aug 28, 1889
June 28, 1908

Minerva Moore
July 21, 1818
May 15, 1891

William E. Giffee
Aug 27, 1878
Mar 1, 1916

Ernest Mc Ree
1880 - 1936

Wm. H. Mc Ree
1849 - 1893

Parrie W. Mc Ree, Wife
of Wm. H. Mc Ree
1848 - 1889
One Unmarked grave.
Lella Wade Utly, Wife of
W.T. Blackard
Aug 20, 1872
Mar 23, 1906

Wm. Thomas Blackard
Feb 19, 1866
Apr 3, 1916

(Riverside Cemetery p.14)

Willie P. Blackard
Dec 21, 1833
Mar 28, 1896
 -One illegible tablet-
J. O. Ray
Nov 1, 1837
 Mar 2nd, 1910

P. S. Spivey
1865 - 1889

R. B. Spivey
1856 - 1885

MOTHER
M.A.E. Spivey
1820 - 1900

Calvin J. Spivey
1815 - 1861

Sarah C. Robins
Died July 9, 1845

Dan H. Smith
Mar 2, 1824
Jan 16, 1901

William Walter Ramsey
May 10, 1864
Nov 30, 1927

W. W. Ramsey, Jr.
Dec 21, 1900
Sept 5, 1902
 -One illegible stone
J. W. N. Burkett
1854 - 1923

John Robbins Burkett
1891 - 1918
-Two illegible stones
Mr. H.P. Luckey, wife
of Samuel Luckey
Apr 5, 1815
Jan 5, 1888

Samuel Luckey - One illegible stone-
Oct 23, 1801
Mar 8, 1870

Robert W. Haynes, Adj. 62nd N.C.
Inf. C.S.A.
1840 - 1905

Sarah W. Gill, wife
of Samuel H. Gill
May 4, 1880
Oct 1, 1936

MY SISTER
Rogelia E. Anderson
Died Aug 28, 1899
 Aged 66 yrs.

(One stone marked "Anderson"
(the rest illegible)

Wm. E. Dunaway
1841 - 1918

Lula, Wife of Wm.E.Dunaway
1860 - 1910

Rev. Wm. M. Dunaway
Jan 2, 1811
Aug 22nd, 1872

Ellen Dunaway Anderson
1889 - 1900

James W. Anderson
1835 -
June 16, 1879

Benjamin Letcher, Son
of Jas. W.& Ellen
D. Anderson
- No date -

Wm. T. Anderson
1804 - 1870

Mahola Wisdom, Wife of
Wm. T. Anderson
1806 - 1890

Annie Fay, dau. of J. P.
& Annie Balch
June 5, 1894
Sept 15, 1895

(Riverside Cemetery p.15)

Terrell Bond, Son of
J.P. & Annie Balch
Oct 24, 1891
Feb 9, 1919

Ellen Bond, Wife of
Hu C. Anderson
1854 - 1918

Little Florence, dau.
of Dr. F.H. & D.H. Hamilton
Dec 10, 1873
June 6, 1876

Deneta H., Wife of
Dr. F.B. Hamilton
Dec 2, 1850
Jan 5, 1884
-One Unmarked Grave-
Annette Walsh, Wife of
Robert S. McClaran
Jan 30, 1878

Teliatha J., Wife of
W. K. Walsh
May 15, 1828
Jan 30, 1878

W. K. Walsh
1813 - 1880

Benjamin R. Harris, M.D.
Feb 5, 1825
Nov 11, 1891

Ellen Anderson, Wife of
B. R. Harris
Mar 14, 1837
Jan 4, 1897

Ophelia, dau. of Dr. B.R.
& Ellen Harris, wife of
Jno. Theus
Dec 22, 1869
Sept 16, 1892

Jno. Womack Theus
Oct 4, 1862
May 31, 1893

Carrie Lucile, dau. of J.F.
& J. A. McKinney, and wife
of J. W. Conger
July 1, 1862
May 2, 1883

Horace W. Conger
May 5, 1876
June 4, 1930

Maggie H. Johnson
Died Aug 8, 1886

Rowena Conger, wife
of R. M. Shoffner
Sept 26, 1887
Jan 27, 1916

Hallie, Son of V. S.
& J. B. Conger
July 23, 1879
Dec 30, 1879

Virginia S. Conger, Wife.
Feb 1, 1851
Feb 8, 1928

J. B. Conger
May 8, 1851
Sept 20, 1917

Jas. T. Phillips
- No date -
- Two Unmarked Grave
Leula, wife of J.A. Thompson
May 9, 1868
Aug 29, 1911

Annie Ruth, dau. of J.A.
& L.I. Thompson
Nov 14, 1902
June 14, 1904

Evalyn Dorothy, dau of J.A. &
L. S. Thompson
Sept 28, 1909
July 15, 1928

Nellie Robinson Snow
June 7, 1818
Dec 5, 1894

(Riverside Cemetery p.16)

Fletcher J. Snow
Apr 23, 1838
July 7, 1908

Polly B. Snow
Oct 14, 1807
June 12, 1883

M. B. Spencer
1837 - 1906

Nell Spencer, wife of
Dr. Joe Cason
June 20, 1870
July 17, 1892

George B. Spencer
1867 - 1906

Will Branson Spencer
1882 - 1915

*Nancy Ann Spencer, wife of
Mark B. Spencer, Sr.
1809 - 1897*

Infant Son of R.H. &
Nell B. Bond
Mar 6, 1915

Sampson Royster, Son of C. G.
& K. J. Bond
Jan 28, 1878
Feb 14, 1882

Mary Jane, dau. of C.G.
& K. J. Bond
Dec 4, 1873
Dec 10, 1873

Allen Campbell
Died Dec 18, 1934

Allen Campbell, Jr.
Sept 13, 1902
Aug. 2, 1924

Katherine J. Royster, wife
of Chester G. Bond
June 24, 1851
Oct 4, 1916

Margaret H. Chester
1858 - 1905

R. H. Chester
Apr 8, 1829
Nov 24, 1921

Mary J. Long, wife of
R. H. Chester
June 20, 1832
July 10, 1900

W. L. Chester, M. D.
Aug 15, 1854
July 26, 1909

Sallie Chester
Nov 23, 1856
Feb 19, 1913

Kate Chester Harris
1882 - 1907

Joseph Hammerly
July 21, 1816
Apr 11, 1878

Virginia B. Hammerly
Jan 21, 1821
Aug 4, 1906

Mary Frances Chappell
Aug 29, 1848
Feb 8, 1929

Wm. Henry Chappell
Jan 14, 1869
Dec 26, 1893

Kate Hammerly Hooser
1885 - 1931

Ada F. Hammerly
1856 - 1922

Henry Hammerly
1844 - 1918

William Arthur Dugger
1856 - 1935

-3 Unmarked Graves - 1 illegible stone-
R. W. Hall
Mar 10, 1813
Oct 4, 1890

(Riverside Cemetery p.17)

(Hall Family cont'd)
Martha C., consort of R.W.Hall
Feb 25, 1825
Nov 2, 1888
Willie Ewen, Son of R.W.& M.C.Hall
1861 - 1889
J. R. Wilbon
Apr 7, 1848
Sept 18, 1892
- One Unmarked Grave - One illegible stone.

Elisa Ann Boon
Jan 14, 1814
Jan 14, 1891
Mary W. Brown
Sept 9, 1839
Sept 20, 1900
Laura Ann, dau.of Jas.M.& M.W.Brown
1855 - 1875.

- Four illegible stones -

Benjamin H. Brown
Apr 7, 1873
Aug 5, 1902
Lloyd M., Son of H. M.& M.L.Clayton
Fannie May, dau. of M.N.& C.L.Carter
  - One illegible stone
Mary L., wife of H. M. Clayton
Sept 4, 1860
May 5, 1901
Hamilton M. Clayton
May 31, 1897
Nov 19, 1920

Nathaniel G. David
May 19, 1827
Mar 21, 1869
Walter T. Rook, Sr.
Dec 12, 1864
Nov 22, 1935
  -One new grave unmarked-

Z.N. Wright,
Died May 5, 1886
   Aged 38
Christiana Hogsett Wright
Aug 28, 1853
Oct 30, 1936

J. W. Mercer
Oct 27, 1845
May 29, 1913
Rebecca Friley, wife of
J. W. Mercer
May 1, 1885
May 29, 1917
Garnett W. Mercer
Aug 30, 1879
Apr 19, 1929
Harry Mercer
July 16, 1888
Jan 10, 1891
Vida L. Featherston, dau.of
T. J. Featherston
July 3, 1887
Dec 8, 1922

Elizabeth Helena Parkman, wife
of J. H. Trimble
Feb 8, 1873
Jan 5, 1916

- One illegible tomb.-
- One unmarked grave -

Jessie L. Chester
1863 - 1921
Robert I. Chester
1855 - 1929

Chas. H. Conner
Feb. 16, 1887
Oct 16, 1932

Tella, wife of Isham Lewis.

Will Stringfellow
1832 --1882
Virgie E., wife of C.F.
Stringfellow
1907 - 1926

Elvira Witherspoon-wife of
Jas.H. Price
1872 - 1917

-One Unmarked Grave -
T.S. Stringfellow
Feb 17, 1857-
June 24, 1924

(Riverside Cemetery p. 18)

W. H. Hill,
1858 - 1923

Elizabeth Whitaker,
1898 - 1909

Flora Whitaker
1885 - 1899

Lillie Williams, Wife of L. W. Whitaker.

J. B. Cooper
1855 - 1923

Lucille, dau of
J. B. & Sarah Cooper
1900 - 1919

D. T. Pope, Jr.
Dec 25, 1882
Feb 26, 1923

David T. Pope
1844 - 1914

Ellen Baker, wife of Louis Baker
1871 - 1913
-One Unmarked Grave-
P. C. Callahan
1851 - 1916

Catherine P., wife of
P.C. Callahan
1866 - 1913

Dennis Murphy, Company M. 1st N.C. Inf. Spanish American War
- No date -

W. E. V. Luker
Dec 29, 1879
Dec 9, 1912

Walter E., Son of W.E. & V.Bettie Luker
Nov 14, 1900
Feb 22, 1912

Wm. V., Son of W.E. & Bettie Luker
Dec 27, 1911
Jan 7, 1912

Robert B. Allen
Dec 28, 1905
Mar 18, 1931

MOTHER
Betty Conner
1867 - 1935
-Two Unmarked Graves-
John H. Manor
July 28, 1872
Nov 6, 1908

Dr. C. A. Manly
Oct 16, 1834
Aug 20, 1910

Sarah F. Manly
1849 - 1935

Horace B. Manly   -One lot 16
1868 - 1931   -unmarked Graves-

Gilbert Christian Anderson
C.S.A., Son of Robert Henry
& Isabella Christian Anderson
Nov 14, 1846
May 20, 1920

Martha, dau. of W.A.& E.A. Turner, wife of Gilbert Anderson
Jan 8, 1855
Aug 29, 1893

Mrs. Ellen M., Wife of
G. L. Christian
Died Sept 12, 1862
-One illegible stone-
Emily, Wife of Rev. R. Wilson
Feb 28, 1832
Mar 23, 1895

(Riverside Cemetery p.19)

G. L. Christian
Aug 29, 18____
Oct 23, 1886
-- One illegible stone-One unmarked grave-

W. M. Mc Cutcheon
Died July 16, 1861
 -One Unmarked Grave

B. F. Noel
April 15, 1857
Jan 12, 1900

Laura C. Pyles
1833 - 1907

Addison & Mary Pyles
- No date -

Martha, wife of A. Pyles
1810 - 1873

Wallace C. Pyles
Born 1811
(Date of death illegible)

Willie C. Pyles
1841 - 1916

BABY
(No name - no date)

Joe Will Tyson
Mar 5, 1852
Feb 6, 1910

OUR BABY
(No name - no date)

Joseph Benjamin Hicks
Aug 15, 1857
Feb 15, 1931
-One illegible stone-
Lendepum DeWest Murrell
1888 - 1920

Mrs. Martha M., wife of
Rev. David Cochran
-No date -

John T. Cochran
Died 1891

Rev. D. Cochran
(Illegible dates) -One illegible
                    -stone   -
 George Murrell
  (Illegible dates)

Sallie Murrell
Died 1856

Henry Still, Son of R.L.
& Leila Murrell
Died 1882

Margot Friar
(No date legible)

Barney M. Fryer
Aug 9, 1856
Aug 27, 1880
-One Unmarked Grave-
Mary L., dau. of J.W.
& M.A. Foster
Dec 26, 1860
July 28, 1862

Virginia E. dau of J.W.
& M. A. Foster
Died Jan 18, 1869

Thos.A., Son of J. W.
& M. A. Foster
Died Mar 16, 1869

Samuel E. Reavis
Dec 14, 1871
June 8, 1910
-Five Illegible stones-
MY FATHER
Thos. G. Reavis
Aug.15, 1802
Aug 15, 1858

William H. Mayo
June 1, 1855
Sept 6, 1927

(Riverside Cemetery p.20)

Margaret M. Mayo
Nov 15, 1859
Aug 29, 1927.
Charlie H. Mayo
Aug 23, 1881
June 27, 1902
"TO MY WIF"
 (Illegible)

Kate, wife of W.M. Bradly
& dau. of J. A. &.McMarks
Mar 28, 1858
Nov 16, 1879

W. H. Ulrich
-(No date)

Thos. Henderson
June 5, 1819
May 19, 1877

Capt. Wm.E. Butler, Jr.
TENN. ARTY.CORPS,C.S.A.

Sue Pat Henderson, Wife
of Wm.E. Butler, Jr.
Apr.25, 1854
July 5, 1909

"OUR MOTHER"
Mary Ormond Henderson
Died Jan 1st, 1888
-One lot 7 unmarked Graves-
Thos. D., Son of J.L. &
Annie E. Pearson
June 11, 1888
July 23, 1889
-Two unmarked graves-
John L. Pearson
1832 - 1860

Elizabeth P. Hutcherson
1814 - 1895

Mary E., Wife of E. Jorden
Died Dec 11, 1833

Lizzie A., dau. of Wm.P.
& Mary K. Howard
1880 - 1888
-One illegible stone-

Elizabeth A., Wife of
Wm.R. Howard
Born July 8, 1839

Katie A., wife of Wm. F.,
& E. A. Howard
Nov 27, 1857
July 29, 1879

Maud Celeste, Wife of O.R. Staley
July 18, 1856
Sept 2, 1895

L. C. Hammond
1870 - 1902

Josie

Dora

Wade

M.M. Hammond
1820 - 1893
Margaret, his wife
1830 - 1892

Jeanette Campbell, Wife of
Ben Tyson
Died Feb 6, 1919

Frances Watkins Campbell
May 31, 1834
Mar 16, 1908

Maria Womack Campbell
July 31, 1841
Jan 19, 1898

Frances Watkins Campbell
Feb 22, 1879
Dec 20, 1900

Charles Randolph Symons
Jan 8, 1855
May 14, 1907

Annie Neilson Symons
Nov 14, 1890
Sept.16, 1902

(Riverside Cemetery p.21)

Elizabeth Lee, Wife of
Dr. J. G. Womack
Nov 14, 1867
Oct 9, 1921

Dr. James Green Womack
July 25, 1818
Dec 26, 1874

William Stewart White
Dec 28, 1833
Apr 13, 1910

Callie P. Gates
1867 - 1869

Edgar A. Gates
1873 - 1879

James Gates
1862 - 1884

Norman Gates
1875 - 1909

Narcisa Newsum, Wife
of B. F. Gates
1831 - 1892

Wm. G. Estes
1874 - 1874

Emma H. Gates
1901 - 1902

Benjamin F. Gates
1817 - 1889

Elizabeth J. Roper, Wife
of B. F. Gates
1823 - 1858

Mildred A. Roper (Aunt Millie)
1829 - 1889

Elizabeth R. Gates
1852 - 1873

Mary C. Gates
1854 - 1873

Elizabeth T. Cooke
1830 - 1885

Robert Gates
1840 - 1915

Caledonia Jane Jester, wife
of Robert Gates
1828 - 1850

Virginia Day, Wife
of Jno. S. Fenner
Died Mar 21, 1909

Jno. S. Fenner
Feb 25, 1835
Died Nov 24, 1888
-One lot with 4 unmarked graves-
Martha Day, dau of
Jno. S. & Virginia Fenner
1867 - 1915
-Six Plain Stones -
Isabella, Wife of Robert
Henderson
Nov 26, 1841
Sept 10, 1882

Cora Belle Anderson
    Aged 22 years

MY MOTHER

Charlie Edwin

Robert Patton

Lizzie Lee

OUR FATHER
P.C. McCowat
1819 - 1902

Frances Jane, Wife of
P. C. McCowat

Fannie, youngest daughter
of P.C. & F.J. McCowat
and wife of J. W. Tyson

(Riverside Cemetery p. 22)

OUR BROTHER
T. R. Mc Cowat
1855 - 1909
- Four unmarked graves-
B. F. Sneed
Died Apr 22, 1890
   Aged 29 years

Helen, Beloved wife
of B. J. Sneed
1826 - 1905
- Four unmarked graves-
Mary Sybert, wife of
H. H. Curtis
Died Nov 8, 1888

Horace Horatio Curtis
Died May 26, 1902

Charles S. Curtis
Died March 20, 1885

  Robt. Mann

Minnie C. Anderson
   Aged 22 yrs.

C. E. O'Connor
July 24, 1855
Oct 17, 1897

Nettie Russell
Wife of C. E. O'Connor
1864 - 1934

Hortense Eugenia, dau.
of Milton Winham
1865 - 1927

Annie O'Connor
Wife of James O'Conner
Mar 1st, 1831
Feb 3, 1908

Fannie E., dau. of Dr.
& Mrs. R. W. Fleming, wife
of W. J. O'Connor
Oct 19, 1862
Jan 5, 1896

Little Horace, Son of
James & Anne O'Connor
Dec 12, 1861
Sept 23, 1862

Irene, dau. of James
& Anne O'Connor
Jan 21, 1865
Jan 21, 1865

Ida, dau. of James
& Anne O'Connor
Dec 31, 1865
Dec 31, 1865

May, dau. of James
& Anne O'Connor
May 10, 1854
July 4, 1858

Ida May, dau. of James
& Anne O'Connor, wife of
Dr. J. T. Herron
1858 - 1885
- Four illegible tablets
Mrs. J. T. Williamson
Aug 27, 1839
May 24, 1905

J. J. Williamson, Sr.
June 27, 1868
Oct 7, 1922
- Four unmarked graves-
John F. Newsom
1827 - 1884

Susan M. Newsom
1832 - 1857

Mother-Beulah Thornton
1868 - 1908

Brother - Frank Thornton
1889 - 1912

Joel R. Chappell
Feb 28, 1819
Feb 20, 1876

(Riverside Cemetery p.23)

Martha Chappel, wife of Charles Nelson
July 18, 1816
  Oct 13, 1898

Bettie, Wife of J. B. Hunt
and dau. of J.G.& A. Chappell
Born Sept 11, 1840
Died Feb 12, 1862

Nannie E., dau. of J.R.
& T. E. Hurt
Died July 9, 1862

William, David Neff,
Oct 4, 1846
Mar 8, 1897

Liddie Maud, Dau.
of M. D. & M. A. Neff
Born Mar 13, 1877
Died Sept 22, 1885

M. I. Neff
Dec 25, 1874
Nov 5, 1909

Jas. D. Neff
1873 - 1929

Elizabeth, dau. of Albert
& Nora Muse
Sept 27, 1912
Sept 7, 1927

William Collier, Son of Albert
& Nora Muse
Jan 15, 1875
Died Nov 17, 1895

William C. Muse
Mar 7, 1861
Apr 30, 1892

Theresa Edrington, Wife of
Thos. G. Muse
Mar 4, 1837
June 8, 1912

Thos. G. Muse
Jan 23, 1834
Nov 29, 1892

E. H. Mc Colpin
Nov 10, 1847
Aug 15, 1915

Rebecca Cason McColpin
July 7, 1852
Sept 29, 1926

Thos. D. Cason
1862 - 1936

Hays Brown
Sept 12, 1859
Sept 17, 1904

Thirty Five Stones
Marked "C.S.A."
  Numbered - one to thirty
  five, inclusive.

Warner Mc Coy Blackard
Feb 22, 1886
Nov 20, 1905

Two illegible Infant Tablets

Arleen P. Henderson
Oct 9, 1890
July 17, 1913

John Young
Born Dec 28, 1823
Died Sept 20, 1884

May J., wife of John Young
Jan 22, 1825
  (No death date)

Lousa J., dau. of John &
M. J. Young
1855 - 1881

Alice M., wife of John M.J. Vann
  (Date not legible)

One illegible tablet.

Four unmarked graves.

One Infant Tablet illegible.

(Riverside Cemetery p. 24)

Robert R. Russell,
Mar 10, 1878
Aug 11, 1899

Jess Russell
Nov 15, 1831
May 10, 1898

Sarah H., wife of Jesse Russell
Feb 1, 1817
Sept 7, 1892

Three unmarked graves

Chas. A. Bond
Nov 27, 1821
July 7, 1852

Mary Cartmell, wife of John D. Bond
1830 - 1915

John D. Bond
1820 - 1894

Nanie D. Cole
1836 - 1911

One Infant Tablet illegible

Four unmarked graves

Sarah C. Key
1835 - 1914

George Thomas, Son of Sarah
& D. H. King
Aug 1, 1859
Feb 17, 1860

D. H. King
Feb 14, 1835
Oct 14, 1892

Mary, wife of John Read
Died Feb 12, 1875

John J. D. Read
Aug 21, 1812
June 17, 1833

John Read
Nov 26, 1851
June 23, 1865

Howell A. Hunt
Feb 16, 1872
Nov 20, 1894

One Table illegible

13 Unmarked Graves

One Illegible Tablet

Dr. Jas. T. Jones
1846 - 1915

Bell Gates, wife of J.T. Jones
May 12, 1852
June 16, 1915

Dr. Gates M. Jones
Oct 9, 1897
    Aged 24

William Ashley Ingram
1871 - 1923

Mary J. Ingram
Nov 7, 1880
June 9, 1925

Samuel E. Brown
Died Dec 29, 1881

Matilda, wife of S. E. Brown
Mar 18, 1833
Aug 9, 1900

MOTHER -
Irene Cozart

Two Unmarked Graves

One Illegible Tablet

P. B. Wadley
July 16, 1854
Oct 1, 1886

(Riverside Cemetery p.25)

Layton A. Russell
Dec 25, 1882
Dec 22, 1909

Irene Claiborne Russell
1895 - 1933

Chas. Thweat Russell
1871 - 1932

Martha J., Wife of J.Russell, Jr.
Died 1852

Pearl Mc Cann Russell
Aug 2nd, 1883
Jan 30, 1914

Job Umphlett
Feb 21, 1827
July 19, 1905

Miriam S., Wife of Job Umphlett
Sept 16, 1832
Oct 10, 1899

Hamilla H., dau. of Job.&
M. S. Umphlett
May 1, 1866
Aug 25, 1868

Rachael W., wife of Job Umphlett
Aug 26, 1833
Oct 6, 1855

Daisy Collins
Died 1806

One illegible tablet

Millie B. Martin
May 11, 1906
Nov 17, 1907

Lewis Collins, Son of J.&.M.S.Umphlett
Born Dec 6, 1869
Died July 1, 1888

Lucy E. Umphlett -B.J.& E.Hawthorne
Died Dec 1, 1868
   (As it is on tombstone)

Isabella Yancy
1855 - 1934

Amanda, wife of J.T.Beveridge
Oct 31, 1880
Jan 1, 1913

J. T. Beveridge
Mar 11, 1831
Dec 22, 1898

Ann W., Wife of Thos.Beveridge
Nov 12, 1791
May 3, 1876

Three illegible tablets

F. W. Yancy
Died Sept 19, 1861

Susan R., wife of F.W.Yancy
Born Sept 7, 1823
Died Dec 30, 1899

Robt. J. Yancy
July 24, 1868
Nov 28, 1917

Robt. Haskins Ford
Aug 3, 1855
May 13, 1901

Three illegible markers

Martha A. Hayly,
Aug 28, 1828
Nov 18, 1917

Three unmarked graves

Thos. W. Newton
Apr 5, 1868
June 21, 1922

One plain stone

Four unmarked graves

J. P. Newton, Jr., Son of J.D.
& Eunice Newton
1893 - 1895

(Riverside Cemetery p.26)

Eunice T., wife of J.D.Newton
Born Aug 1869
Died July 16, 1910

J. D. Newton
Died April 8, 1929

Mrs. Rosamond
Consort of Samuel Neely
Dec 27, 1791
June 26, 1857

Samuel Neely
Died Aug. 25, 1867

Rev. Collin Mc Kinney
1808 - 1878

Matilda Plumer Shepard
Wife of Rev. Collin Mc Kinney
1808 - 1878

Wm. Plumer, Son of C.& M.P. McKinney
Died Mar 13, 1853

Rev. Robt. Nall, D.D.
Oct 17, 1805
Dec 28, 1885

Elizabeth Woods, dau. of Jas. Hodge, D.D.

Beloved wife of Rev. Nall, D.D.
Dec 8, 1811
Feb 16, 1885

Rev. Jas. Hodge Nall
1837 - 1915

Anna S. Mc Mahon,
Beloved wife of J. H. Nall, D.D.
June 5, 1837
Oct. 13, 1890

Annie A. Martin, wife of W.H.Barnes
Born July 16, 1843
Died June 17, 1901

Six unmarked graves.

W.P. Howard
Dec 6, 1838
July 13, 1906

R. E. Howard
Aug 26, 1873
May 3, 1911

Richard Leroy, Son of R.E. & B. B. Howard
Born June 15, 1902
Died July 15, 1903

Five plain stone markers - No lettering.

Henry Mason
Mar 29, 1813
May 3, 1853

Ten unmarked graves

One illegible tablet

Don Cameron
Dec. 17, 1814
Oct 2, 1895

Margaret, Wife of Don Cameron
July 31, 1896
Apr 13, 1925

J. A. Janes
July 17, 1908

Four illegible tablets

David A. Dalton
1864 - 1889

Four unmarked graves

Milton B. Boyd,
Sept 11, 1819
Dec 11, 1855

"Boyd"
(Balance illegible)

26

(Riverside Cemetery p.27)

Charlie, Son of J. A. & M. A. Robertson
May 23, 1850
June 30, 1856

John T. Hicks,
Oct 28, 1831
June 5, 1877

Little Mazie, dau.
of G. W. & S. A. Cundiff
Born Oct 3, 1887
Died Nov 3, 1896

Geo. Lea Cundiff
(No date)

Herman J. Vandenbrook
1876 - 1908

Rebecca Vandenbrook
1901 - 1910

S. W. Tucker
Oct 21, 1852
Mar 8, 1889

Susanah Gates
Mar 11, 1823
Aug 29, 1893

- Three unmarked slabs -

- One illegible marker -

Blance James
   (No dates)

Mary Gates
   (No dates)

Wm. Word Gates
1848 - 1927

Carolyn P. Gates
1849 - 1920

Hewitt P. Gates
1875 - 1914

Carolyn H. Gates, Dau. of
1912 - 1914.   (W.W. Gates

(Riverside Cemetery p.28)

Hattie Gannaway

Gertrude de Gourgy

Percy Crutcher

Kate Snider
1856 - 1860

One illegible flat slab

Anna Eliza, Consort of Thomas
Henderson and only daughter of
Samuel & Anna Lancaster
Born Aug 9, 1827
Died Aug 1, 1850

Anselum Lynch Lancaster
1830 - 1850

Janie Lancaster, wife of
John H. Gary
1856 - 1900

Anne T. Lancaster
1858 - 1859

Christine, Wife of John L. Lancaster
1833 - 1860

Nat E. Lancaster
1847 - 1872

John Lynch Lancaster
Aug 27, 1824
May 18, 1875

Henriette Snider Lancaster
Dec 29, 1840
Jan 17, 1908

George L. Lancaster
1862 - 1880

J. E. Ryley
May 3, 1856
Dec 19, 1920

Anna Terrell, Wife
of Samuel Lancaster, dau.
of John & Anna Lynch
Oct 21, 1858
Apr 13, 1901

Samuel Lancaster
Apr 13, 1799
Mar 2, 1859

Infant, Son of John
& Eleanor Lancaster
Mar 2, 1859
Aug 28, 1902

Ernest R. Parham
Sept. 14, 1872
Mar., 5, 1921

Infant dau. of J. L. &
R. H. Williams, Dorothy,
Died June 9, 1882

Chas. H. Williams
1884 - 1917

John L. Williams, Sr.
1848 - 1921

Emma Williams Fleming
1846 - 1876

One illegible broken tablet

Etta
Dau. of F. E. & Ella Bond
Died Sept 8, 1885
  Aged 2 years

W. B. Hawkins
June 22, 1828
Oct 2, 1861

Sarah, wife of Giles Hawkins
Nov. 1807
Feb. 2, 1873

(Riverside Cemetery p.29)

Giles Hawkins
Jan 20, 1801
June 19, 1869

Mary Eunice, dau. of C.D.N.
& T. T. Campbell
Born Jan 10, 1859
Died May 29, 1860

One illegible broken tablet

Six unmarked graves

Sophia F., Wife of D.E.McGraw
Born Nov. 16, 1840
Died Jan 2, 1872

Infant Son of J.L.& Ruth Siler
Mar 20, 1891
 June 22, 1891

H. C. Mc Cutcheon
1818 - 1873

Mary E. Mc Cutchen
1829 - 1872

W. T. Mc Cutchen
1847 - 1878

Anna Mc Cutchen
1848 - 1906

Eunice E. Mc Cutchen
1850 - 1907

Fannie B. Mc Cutchen
1853 - 1935

Thos. Butler
1848 - 1916

Eugenia B. Butler
1851 - 1919

H. H. Pegues

J. T. Pegues

Mary A. Pegues

Carolyn D. Hewitt
Born July 5, 1805
Died Aug 29,1849

Four unmarked graves

One unmarked slab

Rev. A. W. Jones, D. D.
Dec 28, 1815
Sept 13,1892

Mary E. Jones, wife
of Rev. A. W. Jones
1815 - 1871

Amanda C., wife of A. W. Jones
Died June 5, 1886

Ida B., dau. of A. W. & A.B.Jones
Died Aug 16, 1882

Ira B. Son of G.C. & L.L.Jones
Died Feb 15, 1887

John E. Jones
Died Mar 6, 1857

Eddie C. Son of Amos W.&
Amanda C. Jones
Oct 11, 1866(Died)

Harriett A., dau.of
John & Harriett Mann

James L. Elrod
1855 - 1856

Dollie Vernon, wife of Jas.Elrod
& dau. of Wm.& Elizabeth Long
Dec 25, 1831
May 10, 1858

Wm. Harrison Long
  -   1803
May 4, 1867

Elizabeth J. Long
1805 - 1872

(Riverside Cemetery p.30)

Robt. A. Treadwell, C.S.A. Tenn Cav.
1831 - 1911

Eliza Jane, wife of John P. Pryor
1827 - 1876

Thos. C. Long
1830 - 1843

Edward, husband of Isabella Benz
Born Dec 25, 1862
Died June 19, 1897

Chas. C. Son of E.& I. Benz
July 28, 1893
August 16, 1900

Robert K. Dempster
Mar 18, 1844
May, 1922

James, Son of Gilbert
& Alice Dempster
Jan 11, 1875
Apr 9, 1892

Alice, wife of
Gilbert Dempster
1847 - 1917

G. Dempster
July, 1841
June, 1905

Robert Kerr Dempster
May 21, 1876
June 26, 1922

One unmarked grave

Merle Lawler, wife of T.A. Fail
1893 - 1915

W.T. Fail
1844 - 1918

Mattie, wife of W.T. Fail
Died Dec 9, 1891

Alice Gibson Menzies
1867 - 1910

Rosalie, dau. of W.B.
& A. E. Menzies
Died Nov 22, 1893

One unmarked grave

Baby Eleanor, dau. of
B. D. & R. M. Snider
Sept 19, 1891
Aug 30, 1933

Mary Roxie Snider (Daughter)
1893 - 1926

Mother, Roxie M. Snider
1853 - 1926

Father, B.O. Snider
1851 - 1928

Ralph Burgan Anderson
Died July 31, 1891

Mary Janes, wife of R.S. Clayton
1868 - 1925

4 new unmarked graves

Frank De Courcey
April 5, 1844
July 17, 1894

One unmarked grave

Father, B.T. Clayton
Oct 27, 1828
Mar 16, 1902

Rebecca S. Clayton
Jan 13, 1840
Sept 24, 1912

Myron Ira Best
Apr 21, 1852
Aug 1, 1924

(Riverside Cemetery p.31)

Myrtle Irene Best
Feb 12, 1894
Dec 16, 1898

Mabel Ella Best
Dec 27, 1890
Dec 14, 1898

Benjamin Rowe
Sept. 1828
Oct 27, 1907

George, Son of E. & C. Rowe
Died Dec 29, 1903

Peter, Son of E. & C. Rowe,
Died Mar 17, 1904

A. N. Naylor
Died Dec 21, 1893
   Age 31 years

Four unmarked graves

One unmarked grave

Ted, Son of E. L. & K.S. James
Born Oct 30, 1892
Died Mar 1, 1894

Alice M. Ingram, Wife of
John M. Greer
Died Feb. 19, 1925

Rose S. Smalley
1839 - 1917

John S. Smalley
1834 - 1895

Smalley
Died Feb 1, 1878
   Age 9 yrs. 1 mo. 20

Four unmarked tablets

Lucy H. Rhodes

May L. Rhodes

Leah Rhodes Locke

Lucy A. Rhodes

David Rhodes Locke

John W. Buford, Sr.
Lt.Col.9th Tenn.Regt.C.S.A.
Aug 24, 1836
Dec 27, 1897

William Abner Mc Geahee
Sept 7, 1885
Apr 15, 1920

Laura Dimond, wife of W.M.May
Nov 25, 1855
Mar 19, 1924

W. M. May
Mar 1, 1856
July 24, 1901

Joseph Johanas Losier
1857 - 1917

Joseph Earl Lasier
1886 - 1916

Vina May Rose, wife of
Joseph L. Losier
Born June 26, 1863
Died Aug 5, 1896

Joseph Cameron, Son of
Emma Camerson & Joseph J. Losier
Mar 27, 1902
June 25, 1903

Baby "Lindsey"

Brother "Elrod"

Father "Barr"

Mother "Barr"

Brother James Elrod
May 10, 1833
Nov 1, 1905

(Riverside Cemetery p.32)

Pattie L. Bates
1849 - 1925

Charles Tappen Bates
Died Feb 11, 1895

Sister "Bates"

W. W. Gates
1812 - 1891

Ann M. Gates
1821 - 1911

Walter C. Nance, Jr.
1883 - 1933

Walter C. Nance
Nov 18, 1854
Jan 27, 1885

Mary E. Collett
Mar 30, 1849
Mar 22, 1860

Rev. Word Early, Son of Dr.E.G.
& Mary Slater
Aug 23rd, 1855
Sept 4th, 1876

Richard H. Bostick
1850 - 1912

Phie Chester, Wife of
Richard H. Bostick
1860 - 1923

Dr. John Chester
May 18, 1827
June 4, 1877

Robert I., Jr., Son of Dr. John Chester
Born Apr. 22, 1853
Died Apr. 27, 1871

Three Infant Tablets (No names)
Sons of Jno. I. Chester

R. A. Briggs   J.W.Briggs
1843 - 1919   Nov 7, 1868 - Nov 30, 1895.
I.H.Briggs
1843 - 1927   Two plain unmarked stones
               One unmarked grave

Fannie Whitfield, dau. of J.P.
& Amelia Collins

Susan A., wife of Dr.A.Jackson
& dau of Jas. Freeman
Oct 7, 1816
Mar 1, 1849

Meville F. Gamewell
Nov 9, 1847
Sept.11, 1873

Thos. Vincent
Aug 22, 1846
Aug 22, 1881

Thos. W. Gamewell
Died April 1, 1885

One plain Tablet

Two unmarked graves

Abie Dew, dau. of M. & F.C.
Parker
Died April 17, 1850

Louisa Ann, dau. of J.M. &
C. K. Parker
Died Oct 5, 1819

Cally, dau. of J.M.
& C. K. Parker
Died July 6, 1851

S. J. Smith
Apr 12, 1810
Mar 3, 1847

Emeline, his wife
Jan 18, 1822
Jan 12, 1883

Walter Henry, Son of Walter
& Bessie Beal
1909 - 1912

Mary Margaret, dau. of
Joseph & Mattie Harrington
1916 - 1918

(Riverside Cemetery p. 33)

MOTHER
Mattie D. Bell
1850 - 1917

FATHER
James C. Bell
1849 - 1911

M.O. Fullerton
May 7, 1883
Aug 18, 1914

Elvira Bruce, Wife of
John H. Tomlin
Died May 16, 1910

John L. H. Tomlin
1824 - 1905

Amanda Caroline, Wife
of John L. H. Tomlin
& dau. of Benj.& Eliza A. Elder
Dec 1, 1827
Aug 12, 1851

Son of J. M. & M. L. Houston
Dec 12, 1870
Feb 28, 1871

Three unmarked graves

Carl de Vineyard
1875 - 1918

David Hampton
June 17, 1808
Sept 2, 1882

Harriett H., wife of David
Hampton
1812 - 1856

D. Fletcher Mc Clintock
Sept 10, 1843
Sept 13, 1906

Kate Harper
Sept 4, 1856
Apr 6, 1935

Daisy Mc Clintock
Died 1894

Robert P. Harper
1868 - 1908

Josephine Harper
1854 - 1864

Jesse H. Harper
1826 - 1905

Sarah E., his wife
1832 - 1913

Gen. Wm. T. Haskell

Willie Rogers Polk
Mar 1, 1855
Mar 20, 1907

J. J. Polk
Died Aug 25, 1894

John Ead.

Two illegible tablets

Lillian Pearl, dau of W.J.
& Nannie Hunt
Feb 22, 1885
July 8, 1885

Two illegible tablets

Sarah Norvell
 (Date illegible)

Thos. G. Norvell
1800 - 1875

John Annie, Wife of J.M. McGill
1862 - 1885

Hattie F., Their Dau.
1883 - 1886

John G., Son of J.B. &
Susan D. Norvell
Born June 23, 1813
Died Jan 6, 1863

(Riverside Cemetery p. 34)

Susan D., Wife of John Norvell
June 16, 1802
Sept 25, 1864

John Norvell
Sept 24, 1876
July 9, 1878

Five Unmarked graves

MOTHER GLASS

Richard Henry Dashiel
Jan 14, 1855
Nov 7, 1923

A. T. Dashiel

Eliza Jane, wife of
R. R. Dashiel
Born Oct 2, 1826
Died June 26, 1899

Mary Elizabeth, dau. of F.E. Joyner
Died Aug. 3, 1876

John G. Goff
Died Oct 11, 1876
   56 years of age

One unmarked grave

One unmarked brick vault

Fanny Connally, Wife of
Thomas D. Connally
1813 - 1819

William E., Youngest Son of
Martin & Jemima Cartmell
1844 - 1862

Mary Jane, Wife of Robert
H. Cartmell
1831 - 1865

Lizzie Cartmell, dau. of R.H.
& M. J. Cartmell
1853 - 1899

Jemima A. Sharp, wife
of Martin Cartmell
Feb 13, 1809
Dec 26, 1891

Martin Cartmell
Nov 3, 1797
July 4, 1864

Sarah Dean, dau. of
Martin & Margaret Cartmell
Aug 2, 1822
Nov 20, 1838

Margaret Helen, dau. of
Martin & Jemima Cartmell
 Apr 17, 1835 - Sept 18, 1842.

Infant Son of R.H. &
M. J. Cartmell
1852 - 1852

Infant Son of R. H. &
M. J. Cartmell
1851 - 1851

Infant Son of R. H. &
M., J. Cartmell
1865 - 1865

Infant son of R.H. &
M. J. Cartmell
1861 - 1861

One unmarked grave

Richard Ridgly Dashiel
Aug 18, 1816
May 17, 1907

Annie Ridgley Dashiel
Dec 21, 1852
Dec 20, 1924

Infant Son of W.S. &
Annie D. Campbell
Died Mar 5, 1853

John W. Campbell
Died June 30, 1871
   75 years

(Riverside Cemetery p.35)

Jane Eliza, Wife of John W. Campbell
 (Date illegible)

A. M. Campbell

Alexander Campbell
July 5, 1879
Feb 19, 1887

Katherine, dau. of John W.
& Emma A. Campbell
July 6, 1890
Oct 17, 1895

Infant dau. of Preston B.
& Jane E. Scott

Campbell Allen Mc Intosh
Aug 7, 1878
Oct 2, 1926

Wiley Robert McIntosh
June 18, 1850
May 20, 1927

Annie Allen, dau. of A.W.
& A.D. Campbell, wife of
Wiley R. McIntosh
April 12, 1860
Jan 29, 1909

One Mausoleum - R.A. Allison - A.F. Dudly

Dogia S. Patterson
Died 1919

Morton Patterson
1854 - 1912

Malinda Robinson
May 4, 1820
Feb 9, 1894

Henry W. Shelton
Oct 13, 1813
Jan 11, 1893

Thos. C. Reavis, Husband of
Alice A. Reavis
Dec 26, 1866
July 27, 1927

Reavis, Alice A.,
Wife of T.C. Reavis
Sept 22, 1868
April 25, 1926

Albert Reavis
Died Nov 7, 1892
 Age 2 yrs.

Martha Elizabeth Burgess Day
Apr 10, 1855
July 12, 1914

Alice, wife of Dr. W.F. Rachelle
Sept 24, 1863
Oct 12, 1907

Emma, wife of J.D. Day
Dec 2, 1857
Aug 31, 1889

A. D. Day
Aug 21, 1854
Feb 28, 1920

Ella Ragland, Wife of Dr. S.H.
Chester
Mar 8, 1855
June 2, 1910

Dr. S. H. Chester
Feb 24, 1840
June 10, 1893

Wm. R. Chester
1799 - 1854

Richard Chester
Died 1826

 -(Name Illegible) Brown
 Consort of James Brown
Nov 13, 1809
Sept 23, 1833

(Riverside Cemetery p. 36)

James Lee
Died November 12, 1835
   Age 25

Ida Alderson
June 27, 1852
Sept 24, 1879

Mary A. Alderson
1847 - 1927

T. B. Alderson
1838 - 1898
   Private Co. B.
   Forrest Reg. Tenn. Cav. C.S.A.

William C. Alderson
Feb 12, 1885
Apr 28, 1885

Annie J. Alderson
1877 - 1920

Richard Blount
Mar 11, 1823
Feb 30, 1855

John Jacob,
Died 1836
   Aged 48 years

Mary Louisa
Died Feb 11, 1813

Dorthala Bradford
   (Dates illegible

Frances Hall, Wife of W. A. Marks
1860 - 1924

John H. Clark
1814 - 1885

Sallie Clark, wife of
W. H. Nourse
Feb 5, 1885
   Aged 22 yrs.

Charles Clark
   Age 5 mos.

Will C.
1892 - 1894

Mary Lou
1894 - 1909

Georgia Lee Nourse
1868 - 1923

Pearl Nourse, wife of C. E. Johnson

BILL, MY SON
July 25, 1932
June 17, 1934

F. C. Stutts
1876 - 1936

Mary Lou, dau. of J. W.
& M. O. Haggard
Aug 28, 1928
Jan 12, 1932

One plot of 25 unmarked graves.

Mary Oglesby
Died May 8, 1882

William A. Mc Lean
1884 - 1918

John Mc Lean
1874 - 1918

Lizzie Mc Lean, wife of
Michael Mulvey
1866 - 1916

Michael Mulvey
1861 - 1915

Thomas J., Son of J.
& Margaret Mc Lean

(Riverside Cemetery p.37)

Margaret Digan Mc Lean
1836 - 1901

Michael J. Mc Lean
1828 - 1877

Margaret A. dau. of
Michael J. &Margaret Mc Lean
1863 - 1873

Five Unmarked graves.

Mary Quinn

Mrs. Iva Rollins, Wife of
J.P. Rogers
Mar 2, 1868
Sept 25, 1904

Seven Plain Stones -
No names - no dates.

Pansy Harris, Wife
of Vernon Edenton
May 9, 1875
Feb 11, 1902

Three Plain Stones

Lucy M., wife of W.E. Green
Mar 4, 1831
May 4, 1874

Minnie, Wife of F.W. Zeiser
Dec 9, 1866
July 22, 1889

Frances B., Wife of
Thos. Clark
Oct 29, 1824
July 17, 1888

Thos. Clark
May 24, 1821
Sept 12, 1900

Thos. Clark, Son of
J. G. & A. M. Pybas
Sept 8, 1875
Nov. 1, 1875

Elizabeth Dixon
Died Feb. 27, 1863

Fannie Clark Person
Dec 24, 1851
Mar 13, 1925

Theophilies Lacy Kendrick
Sept 27, 1848
June 28, 1885

Sue Clark Marks
Jan 14, 1866
Aug 5, 1935

Thos. P. Clark
July 23, 1846
Aug 12, 1870

Calvin, Son of Thos. Clark
Oct 2, 1856
Oct 15, 1857

Elizabeth Patterson Clark
Oct 5, 1862
Aug 8, 1863

Richard, Son of Thomas
& Marion Henderson
Died Sept 2, 1857

Thos. Clark, Son of Thomas
& Marion Henderson
Born Mar 25, 1856
Died Sept 6, 1857

Marion, Wife of
Thos. Henderson
Feb 27, 1829
Oct 21, 1858

Edward P. Clark
Apr 20, 1855
Mar 10, 1915

Thos. A. Henderson
Sept 2, 1842
Oct 18, 1867

(Riverside Cemetery p.38)

Eliza, wife of Calvin Henderson
Born Aug 25, 1822
Died June 11, 1887

Calvin Henderson
Died Oct 11, 1842
    Aged 29 yrs.

Martha Outerbridge
1826 - 1846

James Patterson
Jan 15, 1838
Sept 19, 1908

Drucilla J., Wife
of Allen L. Patterson
Dec 18, 1800
Feb 28, 1839

Allen L. Patterson
Mar 8, 1792
Sept 28, 1857

John Kemp, Son of Allen L.
& Drucilla J. Patterson
Aug 5, 1818
Sept 16, 1832

Lucille P., dau. of A.L.
& D. J. Patterson
Born Aug 20, 1833
Died May 20, 1836

Thomas H. Clark
Oct 17, 1853
Aug 5, 1915

Eliza Lyon
Jan 17, 1820
Mar 7, 1840

Mrs. M.D. Lyon
July 1st, 1886
Sept 15, 1905

Samuel W. Lyon
Sept 9, 1828
May 31, 1872

One illegible Tablet

J. G. Cisco
Apr 25, 1844
Apr 24, 1922

Georgie Pursley, wife of
J.G. Cisco
Aug 2, 1853
Apr 1, 1894

Bertie Cisco
May 12, 1928

Eliza Ann, wife of
G.N. Harris
Mar 17, 1821
Nov 2nd, 1849

Lizzie G., wife of
B. L. Rozell
Aug 30, 1830
Sept 15, 1887

Dr. B. L. Rozell
Aug 5, 1818
Aug 13, 1903

Joseph, L., Son of J. M.
& George M. McClathery
Died Sept 7, 1886
    Aged 5 mos.

Malinda R. Matthews
Sept 20, 1833
Mar. 15, 1899

Alsia Goforth
Jan 16, 1804
Feb 8, 1878

Lee Goforth
July 10, 1851
Aug 10, 1873

Nannie J., wife of
Sam York

Nancy E., Dau. of Sam York
Died July 29, 1857

(Riverside Cemetery p.39)

Cathurine, dau. of Peter
& Ellen Kelly
Jan 14, 1863
May 14, 1863

Mary Ann, dau. of Peter
& Ellen Kelly
Apr 26, 1864
Aug 31, 1868

Catherine, wife of John Touhey
Died Nov 20, 1864
    Aged 20

Kittie L., dau. of Jno. &
Catherine Touhey
Oct 15, 1861
Jan 7, 1865

Martha S., wife of E. G.
Tarkington
Died May 24, 1869

Nathaniel N. Bivens

One Lot - Three Unmarked Graves.

Three illegible tablets -
One Broken Tablet

Isabella, Wife of Jas. F. Habaway
Died Sept 20, 1877
    Aged 48 yrs.

C. I. Rawlings
Aug 6, 1818
Mar 9, 1879

James Todd Hogsett, Sr.
1816 - 1900
Jemima S. Hogsett
1823 - 1855
Chas Todd, Jr., Hogsett
1850 - 1888
Jno. Arnold Hogsett
1851 - 1857
Mary Ann Hogsett
1855 - 1856
June Hogsett Lemon
1800 - 1892

Dr. Stanford A. Still
Died 1860

Four Infants Graves
  (No dates or names)

James F. Still
1856 - 1914

Fannie Harper, his wife
1858 - 1918

William L. Howlett
1886 - 1919

Ann Eliza, wife of
W. R. Howlett

Arrington B. Hicks
Sept 5, 1889
Mar 16, 1915

J. R. Hicks
July 28, 1820
Sept 29, 1862

John Magrane
Died April 1, 1873
    Age 36

William Eugene, Son of
J. G. & Martha Sharp
Died Dec 20, 1848
    2 yrs. 48 days

W. B. Marshall
Died May 1863
    Age 60 years

Albert Searcy
Died a Confederate late
Soldier during the war.

L. B. Bailey
Mar 4, 1853
Oct 8, 1898

M. Frances Jones
May 5, 1904
Aug 18, 1905

(Riverside Cemetery p.40)

Henry Jones
June 29, 1893
Apr   3, 1901

Josephine, wife of
W.T. Jones
July 2, 1861
May 27, 1899

W. T. Jones
Aug 24, 1856
Apr 3, 1919

John J. Beck
1826 - 1899

Wilhelmine Beck
1827 - 1900

Clara Beck
1866 - 1927

Johnnie Holloway
Born & Died 1902

R. G. Stegall
May 11, 1841
May 3, 1917

Susan Cockrill, his wife,
Dec 11, 1845
June 22, 1894

Willie D.H., Son of J.A. &
M. A. McClanahan
Apr 7, 1875 - Dec 28, 1877
Nannie Louisa McClanahan
May 6, 1872 - Jan 5, 1898
Nelson McClanahan
May 15, 1824 - May 6, 1851
Samuel McClanahan (No date)
(Two Unmarked Graves)
C.E. McClanahan, dau. of Jas. M. Lift
 - 1865.
Sorma Jeanette, dau of Samuel
& Laura Mc Clanahan
Oct 18, 1867 - June 22, 1870
Charles Robert, Infant Son of Samuel
& Laura McClanahan
 Born & Died 1859

Julian Marcus Brooks
Mar 29, 1885
Mar 24, 1918

Infant dau. of J.M. &
W. A. Brooks
Died 1911

Francis S., Son of A. S.
& Maude Richardson
Feb 1, 1900
May 23, 1900

L. B. Mc Carley
1849 - 1881
Sarah Mc Cabe McCarley
wife of J. J. Snow
Died August 11, 1928

James D. Morgan
1855 - 1916

W. N. Harris
1843 - 1913
Thos. Harris
Mary Harris

William Payne Turley
July 12, 1846
Feb 14, 1926

John Clark Cochran
1826 - 1849
Louisa W. Concord of
Samuel Mc Clanahan.

(Riverside Cemetery p.41)

Stephen Gray Clark
1891 - 1891

Annie Louise, dau. of J. K.
& M. L. Stephens
1853 - 1918

Mary Louisa Miller, wife
of James Kemp Stephen
Aug 2, 1832
Dec 19, 1891

James Kemp Stephen
Oct 9, 1826
Aug 10, 1877

Sarah Eliza, Wife of
Daniel M. Stephen

Laura O'Connor Chester
1852 - 1921

Rob I. Chester
July 31, 1793
Jan 14, 1892

1 Grave Marked J.P. C.

Capt. Wm. Butler Chester
1833 - 1887

Bettie S., wife of T.N.E. Epperson
1849 - 1932

Thos. N. Epperson
Oct 11, 1847
Feb 28, 1910

E. M. Nichol
1821 - 1875

One hundred plain tablets
letteredC.S.A.
Numbered one to one hundred and six

MaryAnn & Sarah, children of Patrick
& Hanna Joyce

Hannah, Wife of Patrick Joyce
Died Oct 7, 1896

Sarah California
daughter of Hamner

Lew Morgan, dau. of
J. W. & C. A. Boyd
Born 1816
Died (No date)

1 illegible stone

"Kit"
Died 1865

William
Died 1858

Eliza Ann, Wife of Samuel
L. Collins -1835-1873
Samuel L.Collins
Oct 27,1834-Dec 30,1903.

Viola Mc Cabe, Wife of
S. L. Collins
June 10, 1853
Jan 8, 1909

Samuel L. Collins
May 20, 1884
Aug 24, 1902

Martha J. Lively
Born Mar 19,1842
Died (No date)

Ethel B., Wife of Albert G.
Zaricor
1889 - 1910

Juanita, daughter of A.G.
& E.B. Zaricor
1908 - 1909

Five Unmarked Sunken Graves

Milly Dickson
Died Jan 22, 1888

Catherine R. Bogue
Died 1888

(Riverside Cemetery p. 42)

Anna B. daughter of
P. M. Gripp

One Unmarked Brick Bordered Grave

Lunda McBuckner

Infant daughter of W.B. &
Nora Chester
Died 1918

One Illegible Shaft

W. F. Alexander, Jr.
1876 - 1900

Elizabeth Alexander
Died Aug 11, 1868

W. H. Alexander
1871 - 1874

Mary Thelma Ware
dau. of W. S. & E.A. Ware
Died 1897

Mary Hughes Alexander
1850 - 1918

W. F. Alexander
1845 - 1915

Capt. W. M. Alexander
1809 - 1877

E. Alexander
1812 - 1868

M. W. Caldwell
1841 - 1863

L. J. Alexander
1839 - 1845

F. M. Enloe
1836 - 1898

Mildred Bertie, dau. of W.D. &
R. B. Smith
Feb 2, 1901
Dec 31, 1902

Phoeba T. Parker
Died Dec., 1902

Two Illegible Stones

Little Etta Lunsford
Died Oct 15, 1880

Sallie B. Cates
Born Feb 3, 1857
Died Dec 1, 1905

Willie B. Benton
July 18, 1852
Aug 5, 1923

Isaac O. Benton
Aug 2, 1851
July 24, 1902

Fred Stetzel
1869 - 1926

Baby Stetzel
-    1916

Katherine Allois. Dau. of
F. & M. E. Stetzel
May 26, 1906
Feb 6, 1908

John D. Worrell
Dec 12, 1870
April 9, 1903

J. Frank Taylor
1873 - 1927

Henry G. Smith
Oct 29, 1843
Dec 5, 1905

Blanche, Daughter of
H. G. & B. J. Smith
Feb 19, 1881
July 11, 1884
Julia, Dau. of H. G.
& B. J. Smith
July 15, 1882
Oct 27, 1897

(Riverside Cemetery p.43)

Samuel, Consort of Mattie Collins
Aug 19, 1883
    Aged 36 yrs and 6 mos.

Landon A. Collins
   (date not legible)

Willie Scott, Son of Mr. & Mrs. M. A. Kincaid
Sept 30, 1896
May 15, 1897

Artif B.T.A. Hinton
CO.L.27 U.S.Inf.
 (Impossible to read)

Eugene, Son of T. D. & N. R. Windrom
1884 - 1885

Florence E., Dau. of T.D. & N.R. Windrom
1882 - 1883

Rich, Son of T.D. & N.R. Windrom
1880 - 1882

Thomas D. Windrom
1837 - 1915

Nancy R. Windrom
1860 - 1933

R. H. Stringer, Wife of J. B. Jester
Born at Norwich Norfolk Co. England
Nov 22, 1851
Feb 20, 1889

Charles Kunz,
Oct 17, 1835
April 26, 1895

Elizabeth Kunz
Feb 6, 1840
Dec 29, 1884

Phoebe J. Miller, Wife of A.F. Franklin
1847 - 1914

A. F. Franklin
1847 - 1926

E. C. Powers
1861 - 1901

J. G. Neudorfer
1860 - 1931

Andrew Murray Mc Millin
March 8, 1882
July 26, 1904

Little Murray
1899 - 1903

Frances Lee Moore
May 30, 1890

Laura M. Gates
1839 - 1897

Thomas M. Gates
1838 - 1922

John Ford Person
June 30, 1882
Jan 5, 1909

Mother Person
FATHER
Rush Person
June 9, 1852
March 21, 1928

Mildred, Wife of
Thos. Taylor
May 21, 18____
Oct. 15, 1885

William Taylor
Dec 9, 1817
(Not legible)

R. B. Williams
May 27, 1814
Jan 13, 1891
Frank - (Not legible)
W. F. Campbell
1836 - 1913

(Riverside Cemetery p.44)

Elizabeth, Wife of W.T. Campbell
1846 - 1881

Jane M., wife of J. H. Williams
Jan 20, 1879
    Aged 62 yrs.

FATHER
J. C. Smith, Sr.
1846 - 1911

Emma, His wife
1854 - 1919
(SISTER
Katie De May, Dau. of
J. C. & & Emma Smith
1885 - 1900

Nellie D. Wright
  (Not legible at all)

C.N. Harris
April 10, 1858
April 28, 1926

Fannie S., Wife of C.N. Harris
Jan 10, 1858
Aug 29, 1898

Charlie, Son of C.N. & F.S. Harris
Nov 7, 1882
Feb 20, 1885

C. N. Harris
  (Not legible)

Georgie Belle, Wife of R.G. Leland
Dau. of C. N. & F. S. Harris
July 10, 1856
Feb 14, 1880

Robert E., Son of Ira & Alice Lee
Jan 17, 1871
Mar 17, 1886

  - Lee
Sept 1, 1863
June 2, 1882

Alice, Wife of Ira Lee,
Born in Union Co., S.C.
Dec 6, 1853
Feb 11, 1890

Lena P., dau. of R. A. Lee
Oct 8, 1875
Apr 2, 1898

Lizzie, Wife of D. E. Jeter
July 22, 1868
    Aged 52 yrs.

Unmarked Infant Grave

Geo. Angel
Jan 1, 1847
Dec 7, 1880

Katie Bell Wilson
Wife of W.W. Spence
Aug 7, 1857
Nov 13, 1889

Locke Brown
Sept 11, 1822
April 19, 1880

Unmarked Grave
    O.
Margaret/Stockton
Dec. 9, 1872
Jan 2, 1890

Helen Haysels Stockton
Sept 18, 1844
April 24, 1900

William H. Dutler
Oct 12, 1851
March 23, 1889

Little Donald
Nov 28, 1881
Feb 11, 1882
MOTHER
Minnie C. Brittle
1859 - 1902
FATHER
James M. Brittle
1845 - 1927
-Unmarked Grave -

(Riverside Cemetery p.45)

W. T. Tinkle
1839 - 1912
Elizabeth Tinkle
1849 - 1923
Amos Tinkle
1869 - 1882
John B. Tinkle
1881 - 1883
Pratt Tinkle
1872 - 1885
Ben Rose
1887 - 1907

David B. Hawks
Nov 16, 1852
Aug 30, 1886

Elizabeth, Wife of D. B. Hawks
Dec.16, 1849
Dec 2, 1911

Unmarked grave

J. T. Burge
Aug 10, 1856
July 27, 1887

Nelly Bly Simpson, wife
of Samuel James Creevy
1858 - 1922

James M. Dugan
June 21, 1862
June 19, 1889
George Martin Dugan
1835 - 1913
Ada Shinkle Dugan
1836 - 1916
Reese Hill Dugan
1874 - 1896
James Montgomery Dugan
1862 - 1889
G. M. Dugan (Not legible)
A. S. Dugan   "   "

Maud May. Dau. of L.D.&
S. E. Langley
July 25, 1877
Aug 2, 1896
Sarah Elizabeth Langley
Jan 15, 1855
Apr 17, 1925
Mary Janice, Dau.of
Lewis & Bessie Black
Feb 15, 1924
Ada A. Rooks, Wife of P.A.
Rooks
Jan 16, 1880
Dec 23, 1915

Catharina, Daughter of
M. & D. Steiger
Sept 20, 1806
Nov. 30, 1897

Parthenia Frances Lancaster
1849 - 1922
Robert Henry Lancaster
1875 - 1887
Martha W. Dalton
1827 - 1899
William G. Dalton
1825 - 1897

T. J. Carter
March 22, 1859
Nov. 10, 1889
Iona C. Carter
Aug 14, 1881
Dec 15, 1915
 Lenora L. Carter
Feb 16, 1861
Sept 16, 1920

Lizzie S., Wife of G.B. James
Dec 13, 1861
Dec 16, 1886
Jessie, Daughter of G.B.
& Lizzie James
Oct 10, 1881
July 1, 1882
D. Lacy Exxx
Oct 22, 1869
April 25, 1926

(Riverside Cemetery p. 46)

D.L. Kimbrough
June 23, 1841
April 30, 1896
Sarah P. Kimbrough
Nov 19, 1844
Apr 12, 1911
Annie D., Wife of R.A. Kimbrough
Sept 5, 1871
July 6, 1897
Daisy V. Kimbrough
July 10, 1881
July 19, 1925
Amos B. Kimbrough
Sept 15, 1872
June 4, 1904
Lemia, Wife of
R.G. Kimbrough
Feb 6, 1818
Feb 12, 1899

Jennie Crawford Wilson
1854 - 1887
Thomas T. Wilson
March 9, 1851, married
to Jennie L. Crawford Apr 4, 1880
and married to Addie L. Cathey
June 19, 1888
Died Sept 4, 1904.
Addie Cathey Wilson
1861 - 1934.
Little Jennie, Dau. of T. T.
& Jennie Wilson
Jan 28, 1867
June 6, 1887.
Little Vernon, Son of
T. T. & Addie L. Wilson
Jan 2, 1891
Feb 1, 1891

Dossie Voss
Jan 30, 1867
Feb 13, 1915
Lizzie, his wife
Feb 28, 1867
July 25, 1913

Miss S.E. Bledsoe   --Susan Bledsoe
Oct 12, 1842   1852 - 1887
Apr 21, 1906
H.M. Bledsoe   George Bledsoe
Feb 7, 1878   1845 - 1914
July 26, 1909

U.P. Heavner
Born in North Carolina
March 23, 1847
Died Dec 22, 1913
Susan Elvira, Wife of
U.P. Heavner
Born in Russell Co. Ky.
July 22, 1840
Nov 24, 1903

Jonnie, Wife of E.L. Long
Dec 28, 1886
Nov 4, 1909

Addie Euphemia, Dau. of
J. H. & L.J. Seaborn
Jan 24, 1874

George H. Deer
Died Aug 8, 1916

Zillah Ann, wife of L. Long
Dec 10, 1860
Jan 28, 1888

Keith Moffat, Sr.
1856 - 1921
Mother
1835 - 1895
Sister
1858 - 1906
Keith Moffat
1892 - 1910
Nettie Moffat
1885 - 1888
Eva May Moffat
1891 - 1892

Children of Pinckney Elgin
and Emma Laura Walker
Albert Joel - Jesse Wells
1887 - 1887 - 1889 - 1890
Earl   - Joel
1890 - 1890 - 1897 - 1899
Dorie Oneida - 1906 - 1908
1902 - 1904 -
Grandson-James Walker Ross,
1906 - 1908
Carl
1901 - 1907.

(Riverside Cemetery p.47)

Lucy, Daughter of Lee & Rachel Beatty
July 1, 1893
Nov 8, 1899

Mary A., wife of Arthur G. Norwood
May 17, 1901
    Aged 31 years

Robert H. Wallace
Oct 8, 1866
Feb 24, 1931

George Gorham
Died 1916
Docia Gorham
Died 1926
Dent Gorham
Died 1899
Harry Gorham
Died 1899

John P. Balch
Feb 8, 1859
Feb 21, 1935
Mrs. Fay Stribling
May 14, 1831
Oct 25, 1911
Ariadne Fay, Dau. of
W.H. & Allene Hawkins
Aug 26, 1880
Oct 17, 1897

Nancy McDonald Perry
Oct 15, 1810
Feb 15, 1895
David J., Son of D.J.
& L. A. Perry
May 10, 1883
Aug 19, 1900
Lucy A. Perry
Jan 28, 1848
Feb 28, 1907
William Thomas Perry
Mar 21, 1877
Oct 18, 1903

Ballew, Joseph
1832 - 1913
Ballew, Paralee
1833 - 1882
Ballew, Martha
1837 - 1915

Caroline Baker
March 11, 1840
Sept 15, 1911
 Christian Kunz
 March 17, 1845
 May 1, 1904
Jacob, Son of Caroline Baker
Dec 1, 1869
Mar 30, 1888
Chris Lawrence, Son of
Fannie and Chris Baker
Apr 13, 1907
May 16, 1909

H. F. Smith
1837 - 1914
Margaret Bell (his wife)
1846 - 1916
Edna Louise Thompson
Sept 22, 1875
July 14, 1904

J. A. Perry
Feb 11, 1863
Feb 6, 1920
B. F. Bond
Aug 26, 1871
May 18, 1889
Sarah, wife of R.W. Bond
Nov 26, 1837
Oct 14, 1877
R. W. Bond
Sept 19, 1828
Dec 8, 1911

Robert O. Hicks
1860 - 1900

William Meriwether
Born Sept 7, 1877
Died Jan 2, 1883
Judith Ann Collins
Dec 30, 1840
Nov 7, 1893
Fannie Etta Meriwether
Aug 27, 1869
Oct 14, 1893
Mary Meriwether
  "OUR MA MA"
- Unmarked Grave.

(Riverside Cemetery p.48)

Edwin Snipes
Jan 2, 1912
Mar 1, 1929

R. C. Brown
1872 - 1904
Ora L. Richardson, Wife
of R. C. Brown
1880 - 1906
Elizabeth, Dau. of Robert F.
& Sarah R. Brown
Jan 8, 1867
May 7, 1894
Sarah R., Wife of Robert F. Brown
Mar 20, 1842
Dec 18, 1875
Robert F. Brown
July 3, 1834
Sept 9, 1884

Robert T. Hamilton
1849 - 1913

Wife of Dr. J. W. Collins
Nov 13, 1835
Jan 25, 1884

Three Tombs not legible.

Ethel Hamilton
1878 - 1895
Cora H. Hamilton
1854 - 1909
  -Unmarked Grave-
Thomas H. Temple
1847 - 1916
Hattie Temple
1879 - 1936
Son of T.H. & Lillie Temple
Nov 10, 1886
   (Date of death not legible)

Several Unmarked Graves.

Edna Wheeler, Wife of E.G. Parish
1882 - 1925
E.G. Parish
1868 - 1925
Infant Son of E.G.& Lou Lee Parish
Jan 23, 1897

Henry, Son of Mark
& Elizabeth Dannatt
Aug 15, 1850

Pinckney, Elgin Walker
1858 - 1927
Emma Laura Walker
1864 - 1927

-Unmarked Grave-

M. A. Lyerla
1853 - 19
D. A. Lyerla
 - Son of D.A.& M. A. Lyerla
Jan 19, 1871
July 9, 1882
Lena, Dau. of D.A. &
M. A. Lyerla
Jan 13, 18 -
Apr 27, 1883
Bonnie, Dau. of D.A.
& M. A. Lyerla
Aug 1, 1881
Apr 8, 1871
Arthur C. Lyerla
1871
1906
Ivo C. Meroney
1876 -1904

William N. Collins
Dec. 25, 1848
Apr 10, 1891
Elizabeth Thompson Collins
Oscar F. Collins
John T. Thompson
Dec 14, 1819
June 17, 1892
Virginia A. Thompson
Aug 28, 1830
Dec 10, 1882
Emma V. Thompson-Aug 16, 1856
              Oct 29, 1875

- Infant Son of E.M. & Lucile Parish
- Jan. 11, 1925
- Lou Lee Parish
- 1871 - 1899

****

(Riverside Cemetery p.49)

Lillie D. Thompson
July 14, 1862
Oct 25, 1882
William O. Thompson
April 11, 1868
Jan 22, 1897
S. Sanford Shelton
Feb 17, 1856
Mar 2, 1899

A. W. Ransom
1839 - 1882
Emma B., His wife
1849 - 1926
Neff Shelton
  (Not legible)

Russell, D. G.
  (No date)
Caroline A., wife of D.G. Russell
Oct 31, 1841
Mar 16, 1895
David Russell, Jr.
  (No Date)
Bessie Russell
  (No Dates)
Annie Russell (No date)
Willie D.   "   "
Abbie Lillian "   "
Carrie A.   "   "

- Bond (Not legible
    Kelly "   "
- Several Unmarked Graves)

Susan E., Wife of T. W. Adamson
Dec. 5, 1853
Nov. 30, 1881
Frederick William Adamson
1850 - 1909
Dr. Benj. G. Adamson
June 30, 1875
July 24, 1912
Elizabeth Larkin Adamson
Jan 8, 1811
Feb 11, 1871
Greenberry Adamson
June 22, 1807
Jan 31, 1876
Capt. J.T. Mc Cutchen-1831 - 1912
Mrs. Annie T. Mc Cutchen-1848-1909.

Nannie Jane Mayo, wife of
Sidney S. Bond
July 28, 1859
Feb 22, 1895
-Two Infants Graves not legible-

Blanche C. Davis, Wife of C.C.
Duncan
Jan 25, 1871
June 23, 1905
Elizabeth, Wife of C. A. Duncan
Apr 2, 1822
Aug 17, 1871
Crawford A. Duncan
Oct. 12, 1814
Mar 7, 1882

C. A. Chandler
Feb. 15, 1836
Apr 3, 1905

M. A. De Jarratt
Feb 6, 1806
   Aged 72 years

Edgar Chandler
July 26, 1897
   Aged 35 years

Clara Chandler Matthews
Daughter of Edgar & Belle
Chandler
1888 - 1915

Rev. Benj. A. Hayes
Apr 23, 1818
Dec 1, 1904
Tennessee Newsom, wife of
Rev. Benj. A. Hayes
Sept 7, 1828
May 35, 1911
John Taylor Hayes, Son
of Rev. B.A. & T.N. Hayes
Oct 1, 1855
Mar 10, 1893
Dr. Newt. Newsom, Son of Rev. B.A.
& T. N. Hayes
Oct 6, 1849
Oct 26, 1901

(Riverside Cemetery p.50)

John A. Arrington, D.D.S.
1841 - 1910
Sallie H. Arrington
1852 - 1916

Charlie W., Son of W. W.
& Pattie Poll
Born Oct 15, 1874
Died - (Stone too deep in ground).

David Illingworth, Son
Died July 14, 1874
    Aged 25 years

Harry Martin, Son of David
& Mary Illingworth
Born Aug 13, 1874
Died June 9, 1878
  - Holloway (Not legible)
Edna D., Wife of J. C. Ozment
Dec 11, 1826
May 10, 1897
Mary Walstrum Martin, wife
of R.D. Anderson
July 30, 1852
Nov 30, 1892

Mary Susan, Dau. of J. K.
& Lillie A. Wright
June 26, 1888
Oct 8, 1891
James Kelly, Son of J. K.
& Lillie A. Wright
March 12, 1891
July 17, 1891
Isaac Pleasant, Son of J. K.
& Lillie A. Wright
Sept. 12, 1886
Aug 21, 1895

- Unmarked Graves -

J. R. Wilkinson
1843 - 1915
Sarah Elizabeth Wilkinson
1850 - 1921
Saida Lee,
Daughter of J. R. & S. E. Wilkinson.
Oct 14, 1853 - July 23, 1885

W. B. Moss
March 14, 1860
Sept 10, 1903
Little Ladell, Dau. of
W.B. & A.C. Moss
May 26, 1889
Nov 19, 1890
Little Mabelle, Dau. of W.B.
& A. C. Moss
Jan 10, 1885
Oct 18, 1887

S. D. Barnett
April 6, 1878
    Aged 46 years

- One Unmarked Grave -

J. D. Hackney
1890 - 1902

Mary, Dau. of T.D.
& H. B. Rowland
Feb 14, 1901
July 16, 1902
Infant of T.D. &
H. B. Rowland (Blank)
  (One not legible)

Mary Dado
Oct 20, 1876
March 11, 1878
Josie Dado Sprague
Oct 30, 1874
Feb 24, 1892
Frank F. Reavis
1863 - 1916
Amelia Reavis
Died June 17, 1928
Josephine Dado
Died Mar 15, 1928
John Dado
Born Feb 5, 1847
Died Dec 27, 1904

Edwin M. Seymour
1832 - 1919

James Rivers, Son of J.S.
& Lena King
1898 - 1901

(Riverside Cemetery p. 51)

William S. Warfield
Died June 23, 1935
   Aged 67 years
- Five Unmarked Graves-

Elizabeth -
   - 1853
Dec 25, 1889

William P. Conklin
Mar 18, 1871
July 6, 1936
Vir. Alexander Conklin
1850 - 1927
Nannie B. Newby
Aug 22, 1857
July 9, 1908
Mary K. Henry
May 24, 1829
July 7, 1904
Pleasant Daniel Williams
May 27, 1807
Mar 28, 1876

Charlie, Son of W. A. &
Della Hillman
Feb 25, 1882
Mar 20, 1883
-One Unmarked Grave-
William Augusta Hillman
April 21, ---
April 30, 1925
W. A. Hillman
1849 - 1901
Della Smith
1851 - 1925

Thos. J. Hunt   - J.D. Hunt
1858 - 1930   - 1867 - 1934.
Mollie James Hunt
1863 - 1931   -
Bennie R., Son of T.J.&
Mollie Hunt
Aug 15, 19___
   - - 1920
Baby Laurange   - May Hirsch, wife
June Hunt   - of J.D. Hunt
George F. Kelly   - 1867 - 1913.
1832 - 1905
Ella W. Kelly
1840 - 1917

Fannie K., wife of
John R. Hicks,
1837 - 1900
- One marked "EDDIE" (No date)

Ada Byron, Wife of J.H.Hirsch
1839 - 1900

Jacob Henry Hirsch
Nov 7, 1839
June 26, 1916

Milton B. Hurt
Aug 31, 1846
Sept 13, 1914
Annie Meriwether, wife of
M. B. Hurt
Jan 21, 1854
Sept 12, 1911
Rebecca, Dau. of M. B.
& A. M. Hurt
Apr 12, 1887
Feb 9, 1908
Eliza Allen Hurt
Dec 18, 1880
May 16, 1881
James Meriwether Hurt
Sept. 20, 1877
Feb 8, 1878
Mrs. E. A. Meriwether,
Apr 29, 1831
April 12, 1881
James Meriwether
Aug 20, 1855
Oct 12, 1877
Thomas Meriwether
Apr 29, 1858
Oct 9, 1882
Ann, Daughter of J. L. & L. K.
Wisdom
Feb 19, 1886
Nov 23, 1891

Elte May (Hurt), wife
of Walter P. James
Dec 17, 1876
Oct 4, 1918
Robert Emmet James
Sept 3, 1881
Dec 19, 1884
W.P.James, --Elnora James
Nov 12,1841--Feb 15,1846
July 19,1899-Died Mar 8,1925.

(Riverside Cemetery p.52)

John T. Taylor
Dec 11, 1844
Nov 26, 1904
Mary E. Ventress, wife
of Jno. T. Taylor
July 10, 1851
Jan 25, 1885

Tommie, Son of Jno. T. &
Mary E. Taylor
December 15, 1885
April 25, 1892
Walter H. Taylor
June 14, 1872
Aug. 14, 1881
L. E. Talbot
Co.D. 3 Tenn. Cav.C.S.A.
1847 - 1919
-One Infant's Tomb not dates.-

D. R. Staley
1854 - 1930
Lottie D. Dau. of Lula F. Pearcy
Sept 23, 1884
June 4, 1892
Adey Kershaw
June 11, 1867
Mar 11, 1895
William H. Pearcy
June 11, 1885
   Aged 30 years

Polk Bishop
Dec 14, 1848
May 6, 1916

Elisabeth Davidson
Feb. 1824
Jan. 1902
Benjamin Davidson
Dec. 1822
Mar 1881

Mrs. Louise Snider
Jan 23, 1825
Dec 6, 1904
 - One Tombstone illegible -
 - Two Unmarked Graves -

W.G.P. & S. J. Timberlake
 (No date)
W.P. & S. J. Timberlake
 (No date)
Elizabeth Ann, Infant of
G. R. & E. G. Timberlake
Born Mar 16, -
Died - 18, 1918
 - Two new Unmarked Graves -

Thomas Lyndon Caldwell
1857 - 1879
William Addison Caldwell
Oct 1, 1817
Mar 10, 1878
Mrs. Richie Donnell Caldwell
Apr 25, 1825
Aug 1, 1889
Robert Samuel Caldwell, Son
of W. A. & R. D. Caldwell
Mar 20, 1852
June 22, 1905
Fannie M. Caldwell
1862 - 1883
 - One Tomb Illegible -

Charles O. Grizzard
1872 - 1934
Sophia R. Williams, wife of
J. M. Cartmell
March 11, 1843
March 17, 1871
 - One Unmarked Grave -
A. D. Cartmell Jones
1884 - 1920
Fannie Augusta Held, wife of
J. M. Cartmell
Died Aug 16, 1911
Carroll Peirce Hoffman
Jan 12, 1872
Jan 20, 1901
Marie Lou Cartmell, wife
of C. P. Hoffman
Dec 12, 1872
April 27, 1894
 - One marked "OUR BABY"

(Riverside Cemetery p. 53)

John Bolton O'Neal Sullivan
May 10, 1865
July 18, 1927

W. T. Scruggs,
1851 -- 1919
Cora Weatherly Scruggs
Dec 11, 1858
Oct 16, 1927
J. M. Orbio Weatherly
July 22, 1828
Apr 18, 1872

Rosa Barbara Eppinger
June 4, 1842
Nov 24, 1902
Louis Eppinger
Born - 1837
Died Jan 31, 1887
Joseph H. Eppinger
Dec 6, 1861
Mar 8, 1886
  - Two Tombstones illegible -
  - Eight Unmarked Graves -

Bessie, daughter of S.R.& A.Conger
Dec 20, 1819
Jan 9, 1881
S. R. Conger
Oct 13, 1852
Oct 13, 1918
Annie C., Wife of S.R.Conger
Died 1871.
  - One Infant's Tomb illegible -
  - One Tomb illegible
Cora C., Dau. of P. D.W.
& B. J. Conger and
wife of A. B. Langford
Aug 4, 1844
April 26, 1899

Virgie, Dau. of J.G.& Sallie Childs
May 14, 1872
Jan 9, 1895
  - One Stone illegible -
Dr. J.I. Taylor
1851 - 1900
Leura Clapp Taylor
1858 - 1924
William A. Sanders
Dec 10, 1879 - Dec 23, 1913.

Fannie Taylor, Wife of Rev.
S.C. Caldwell
July 26, 1853
June 24, 1880
Dr. John Ingram
Died June 11, 1883
John A. Greer
Feb 27, 1827
Feb 7, 1903
Louisa Ingram, Wife of
John A. Greer
1832 - 1900
Lydia, Wife of James A.
Johnston & Daughter of
Dr. John Ingram
Died March 22, 1891
John I. Johnston
Died Sept 11, 1882
Ingram Johnston
  Aged 10 years

W. T. Nelson
1846 - 1905
Mrs W.T.Nelson
1852 - 1934
Ann Ingram, wife of
Matthias De Berry
Born August 16, 1829
Died Sept.   7, 1902
Mattie De Berry, Wife of
W. T. Nelson
January 25, 1850
May   10, 1872

William Stuart Moore,Jr.
Oct 5, 1888
Dec 3, 1900
William Stuart Moore
Aug 5, 1851
July 19, 1898

Menard Kennerly Bowen
Sept 10, 1858
April 9, 1899

Allen De Berry
July, 1801
July 1877
Annie Tarver, Wife of Allen
De Berry
May 3, 1832 - Apr 14, 1915.

(Riverside Cemetery p.54)

David Meriwether
1862 - 1921
J. H. Hunter
1846 - 1928
J. H. Hunter, Jr.
1898 - 1899
Mamie Merither
1877 - 1878
Lydia A. Meriwether
1839 - 1903
M. D. Meriwether
1835 - 1913

H. C. Parsons
1875 - 1929
Alberta M. Parsons
1922 - 1923
C. R. Hotchkiss
1865 - 1927

W. P. Robertson
1838 - 1917
Louanna Harris, Wife of W.P. Robertson
Oct 29, 1848
Jan 7, 1899
Mamie, Dau. of W.P. & Louanna Robertson
July 14, 1869
Aug 7, 1872
  - Two Tombs Unmarked -
  - Several Unmarked Graves -

Robert James Ruffin
Nov 8, 1832
July 17, 1900
Malissa A. Williamson, wife of
Robert J. Ruffin
August 6, 1834
January 16, 1895
James W. Chester (Father)
1845 - 1913
Mary R. Chester (Mother)
1861 - 1919
Thomas David Ruffin
April 16, 1863
April 17, 1907

J. B., Husband of M.J.Michie
Died Aug.16, 1873
    Aged 41 years

Little Jodie, Son of J.B.
& M. J. Michie
January 2, 1874
Died October 2, 1874
Charlie O., Son of
J. B. & M. J. Michie
Aug 31, 1858
Aug 16, 1897
Horace H., Son of J.B.
& M. J. Michie
January 8, 1871
September 23, 1878
 -Three Tombs illegible -
James Eaton Bright (Father)
1836 - 1907
Josephine Saunders Bright (Mother)
1845 - 1902

Daniel Warren Getty
Aug 12, 1837
Aug 23, 1878
 - One Unmarked Grave -

Addie Brooks, wife of
J. H. Long
Born Dec 3, 1875
Died Oct 15, 1914

Lizzie Leighton, Daughter
of J. H. & Addie B. Long
Died July 29, 1915
   Aged 9 mos. 27 days

James H. Long
March 11, 1845
March 20, 1928
   C.S.A. 1861-1865.

Clay Virginia, wife of
J. H. Long
Died Aug 9, 1898

mother Sarah Acton Brooks
June 9, 1825
June 21, 1895

father Rev. Jno. Brooks
July 12, 1810 *b. Ireland*
Oct 22, 1880

(Riverside Cemetery p.55)

Laura, Wife of Louis J. Brooks
Nov 29, 1859
Sept 21, 1891

Mary Louise, Dau. of
J. and Laura Brooks
Oct 27, 1884
Aug 17, 1886

John R. Alston
March 6, 1847
Oct 26, 1885

Mattie, Wife of Rev. E.B. McNeil
Mar 10, 1850
April 7, 1920

Percy R., Son of Rev. E.B.
& Jessie Mc Neil   - *Rev. Edw. Benton McNeil)
Nov 30, 1883   - Aug 13, 1837-Aug 2, 1902)
Feb 27, 1909   -   )
Dr. Eaton K. McNeil   -
Oct 9, 1868   - Jessie A.K., wife of   )
Mar 5, 1922   - E. B. McNeil   )
Mat Lacy Tate   - Mar 10, 1850-Apr 7, 1920)
 (AUNTIE)
1869 - 1934
Earl Taylor Mc Neil, Son of
Rev. E.B. & Mattie McNeil
Apr 21, 1889
June, 1889

L. D. Davis
Apr 16, 1866
Mar 15, 1904
Unie Epperson
 (No Dates)
George R. Reid
1844 - 1904
Rhoda - Wife of George R. Reid
1841 - 1899

W. C. Bray
1863 - 1928

Philip, Son of J.B. &
Mary Jackson
Apr 30, 1903
May 31, 1909

Mollie T. Henry, wife
of A. H. Hill
Oct 23, 1863
Feb 22, 1891
 —One Tomb Broken)

Minnie H. Hill (Sister)
Sept 1, 1861
Oct 29, 1887
Mary A. Hill (Mother)
Dec 20, 1834
June 15, 1891

James K. Landis
1838 - 1910
Martha D. Landis
1841 - 1903
Chas. W. Landis
1859 - 1905
T. T. Mason (Father).
Oct 11, 1830
Aug 24, 1886
Elvira A. Mason (Mother)
Sept 17, 1837
Aug 16, 1877
George (Illegible)
Mary   "
(Another Illegible)

Sarah Bell Briggs,
1909 - 1926
John Thomas Rush
1874 - 1933
Emma L., wife of G. H.
Ramsey
Aug 4, 1864
 Aged 26 years
W. W. Myler
Nov 6, 1866
 Aged 35 yrs. 6 mos.

Emma G. Ramsey (No dates)
Greenville H. Ramsey
1836-1907
Mrs. M.L. Ramsey
1836-1904
James W. Woollard
Mar 4, 1832
Dec 17, 1907

(Riverside Cemetery p. 56)

Rev. N. O. Blake
　(No Date)
Julia R. Woollard
1835 - 1905
W. W. M.
　± Several Unmarked Graves-

Monument illegible
Mrs. R.G. Malone
Aug 22, 1837
Apr 9, 1869
Little Fannie
Apr 2, 1860
July 22, 1869
Willis B. Malone
1860 - 1923
　- Five Unmarked Graves -

William Hale Darr
May 15, 1888
Apr 6, 1906
Leslie E. Darr
July 16, 1885
Aug 10, 1887
Sons of J. M. & A.G. Darr
　- One illegible -

Pope Edwards
1894 - 1935
　- One Grave unmarked -
Jack Edwards
1867 - 1915 (Father)
John D. Edwards
1890 - 1897 (Brother)
William R., Consort of Marie D. Smith
July 8, 1850
June 15, 1889
S. W. Edwards
1833 - 1915
Sarah Edwards
1832 - 1916
Eliza Edwards
1863 - 1881
　Two marked "E.E. & E. F."

Elizabeth, Dau. of R.A.& Fannie Reavis
Mar 27, 1869
Oct 5, 1871
　- Dau. of R.A. & Fannie Reavis
1870 - 1878

Maggie Johnson, wife
of J.S. Swayne
Married June 5, 1888
Died June 1, 1904
　FATHER
　(No date)
　MOTHER
　(No date)
J. S. Swayne
July 9, 1832
March 5, 1903
Luella & Merritt Swayne
"PAPA'S & MAMA'S DARLINGS"
Mildred Medora, wife
of J. S. Swayne
Died Oct 25, 1882
Luella
　(No date)

Joe H. Williams
-7 Unmarked Graves-

Lewis Dodds-Sep.5,1829--June 9, 1876,-
Sarah J., wife of L. Dodds
1861 - 1880
J. Laura Dodds
Died 1890
　-Several Graves unmarked-

A.H. Ellington
1843 - 1919
Nannie P., his wife,
1847 - 1891
One broken stone
One illegible

Elizabeth H. Howard
1868 - 1916
Sarah H. Hughes
Died Aug 20, 1894
　Aged 54 yrs.
George G. Hughes
　(No date)
Thomas Gratton Hughes, Jr.
Dec 11, 1915
Jan 28, 1916
Elizabeth Epperson
Jan 1, 1827
Sept 12, 1870
　-Two Grave Unmarked

(Riverside Cemetery p.57)

J. M. Reavis
Died Sept. 15, 1889
Mrs. J.M. Reavis
Died Oct 19, 1915
J. H. Reavis (Infant)
Died 1868
T. C. Gaston
Died Feb 22, 1918
Alice Reavis, Wife of
T.C. Gaston
Died Oct 6, 1915
Robert A. Reavis
Sept 30, 1848
May 1, 1912
Fannie E. Reavis (MOTHER)
1851 - 1922
Maggie M. Jackson, Dau. of
R. A. & S.E. Reavis
April 30, 1875
May 10, 1886
Robert, Son of R.A. & S.E. Reavis
Feb 15, 1896
   Aged 19 years
Fannie, Dau. of R.A. & S. E. Reavis
  (Dates illegible)

Infant Son of Chas.& Nina Hanebuth
Died Aug 11, 1899.
Infant Son of Chas. & Nina Hanebuth
Died Aug 7, 1900.
Nina Collins Hanebuth
Sept 14, 1877
June 1, 1935
Bena Hanebuth
1852 - 1917
Charles Hanebuth
May 3, 1843
Aug 10, 1915

Ben J. Howard
Dec 31, 1859
July 11, 1917
Nina E. Howard
April 6, 1862
June 2, 1934
B. J. Howard, Jr.
Aug 1, 1886
Feb 27, 1906
John W. Howard
May 29, 1884
Nov 2, 1914

(Howard con't'd)
-One Stone illegible
Several unmarked Graves.

     AKIN
J. M. Akin
July 20, 1850
Oct 20, 1887
J. H. Mason
(No Dates)
Buna Akin
March 1, 1877
Oct. 30, 1881
G. N. Brosius
  (Too deep in ground to read)
 -Unmarked Grave-
J. H. White
1844 - 1909

John R. Woolfolk
Aug 9, 1819
Feb 8, 1867

Nell Robertson, Wife of
T. W. Pope
Oct 21, 1882
Mar 3, 1933
William B. Pope
May 2, 1862
Feb 13, 1924
James E. Pope
Oct 5, 1868
April 21, 1910

Alice L., wife of Thomas Tate
Oct 3, 1850
June 26, 1904
Thomas Tate
Jan 6, 1841
Dec 15, 1911

Maria Gilkins, wife of
Jagoe Fulmer
Feb 27, 1852-July 17, 1889
- Dau. of Jagoe Fulmer
1883
    Aged 2 years.

(Riverside Cemetery p.58)

DUKE

Mrs. Sadie B., Consort of Jack Glass
1844 - 1865
Emma Burdette, Wife of Hugh C. Anderson
October 12, 1863
March 22, 1892
Hugh C. Anderson
1851 - 1915
Mary, dau. of Hugh & Lena M. Anderson
October 26, 1888
November 8, 1907
Little Lena
July 8, 1898
August 4, 1898
John H. Duke,
1830 - 1910
Susan W. Duke
1841 - 1925
Ella D. Cathey
1861 - 1883

Thomas J. Spragins
Aug 26, 1850
Apr 15, 1927
Mary S. Brown, His Wife
Oct 29, 1849
Sept 30, 1933
Bertha, Dau. of T. J. & M.S. Spragins
June 10, 1886
Sept 24, 1901
Clarence, Son of T.J. & M.S. Spragins
July 23, 1881
Feb 17, 1884

Elisha H. G. Brown, Son of
Robert & Susana Brown
August 10, 1845
April 5, 1868
Elisha W. Brown
Oct 28, 1861
June 16, 1876
Robert Brown   - Sarah M. Brown
March 25, 1804   - 1858 - 1900
Jan 7, 1892
Susan L. Brown   - William F. Brown
Jan 23, 1808   - Oct 10, 1843
May 29, 1896   - May 28, 1918

James R., Son of
B. R. Morenas
Captain of French Marines
Jan 14, 1863
Nov 7, 1900
  MOTHER
1846 - 1927

Anne Bess, Dau. of J.M.
& Minnie McCutcheon
Died 1886
   Aged 5 years
Little Fred (Infant).

J. M. Donald Morrill
April 21, 1827
Sept 30, 1862
Harrison G. Thomson
Oct 2, 1893
   Aged 36 years, 11 mos.
- Several Unmarked Graves -

James Hughes
Dec 21, 1811
Sept 27, 1870
Martha W. Parham, Wife
of James Hughes
Jan 8, 1889
   Aged 72 years
T. L. Hughes
   Aged 36 years
B. O. Hughes
   Aged 32 years
Nellie (illegible)
   -Eight Unmarked Graves-

Belle G., Wife of W.A. Graham
December 29, 1861
March 5, 1889

(Riverside Cemetery p.59)

LORENZO GOODELL'S FAMILY
John D. Hurt
1839 - 1885
  - Hurt (illegible
FATHER - Lorenzo Goodell
1817 - 1875
MOTHER - Laura Clark Goodell
1830 - 1869
Infant Son
1867 - 1867
Infant Son
1859 - 1859
Infant Daughter
1866 - 1867
Fannie A. Goodell
1854 - 1858
Lorenzo D. Goodell
1852 - 1856
Oren Goodell
1848 - 1866

William L. Anderson
Died April 1, 1890
   Aged 66 years
Nancy Johnson Anderson
Several Unmarked Graves

Mary Ann Dodd
1842 - 1921

Alice Mc Alexander, wife of
John A. Hadeway
June 28, 1853
Nov 3, 1884
- Several Unmarked Graves

Dreb Law, Sterling Scotland, Soldier C.S.A.
1810 - 1876
John Mc Coy Manor
Nov 27, 1899
Jan 6, 1903

Charles William Hamline
Died Dec 29, 1904
   Aged 44 years

Charles Suthers
1853 (illegible)

Rev. B.H. Hubbard
  (Dates illegible)
Mary Jane Martin, wife
of Rev. B.H. Hubbard, D.D.
Nov 19, 1809
Mar 23, 1887
Louisa Dorothea Swan
Aug 3, 1838
Dec 28, 1900
- Unmarked Grave
Edna Louise Russell
May 18, 1898
Aug 1, 1899
A.S. Russell
1868 - 1935
-One stone illegible

W. Holland
1834 - 1902
Harriet E. Holland
1847 - 1933
Hattie B. Holland
1890 - 1906
-Three Stone Illegible -
- Several Unmarked -

J. B. Long,
July 25, 1828
April 8, 1875
Anna McGee Long, wife
of J.B. Long
June 18, 1835
  Aged 53 years
Jennie W. Long
-Several Unmarked Graves-

Charles Edward Lewis
Aug 7, 1868
Feb 21, 1916
-Several Unmarked Graves -

Joshua Boyce
March 4, 1834
Apr 5, 1918
Martha Boyce
1827
June 6, 1905

(Riverside Cemetery p.60)

W. J. Murphy
April 21, 1860
Dec 28, 1905
Georgia B. Gates
1845 - 1930
John W. Gates
1841 - 1904
Carrie P. Gates
1888 - 1892
William W. Gates
1876 - 1878

Thomas H. Drake
1835 - 1916
Louisa M. Drake
1845 - 1916
John Miller Drake
Aug 23, 1868
Feb 20, 1932

N. M. Duncan
1855 - 1896
John M. Carmack
Oct 16, 1883 (Too deep in ground).

W. P. Miller
Sept 24, 1842
Oct 14, 1913
John S. Miller
1816 - 1894
Sarah Phipps, Wife
of John S. Miller
Jan 31, 1822
Nov 25, 1880
Sallie Phipps Miller
Aug 24, 1855
May 14, 1858
John Horace Miller
July 11, 1851
Apr 5, 1852
Pitser Miller
Mar 30, 1840
Nov 2, 1862
Alice Miller
1848 - 1928

A. T. Pegues
Feb 17, 1859
Aug 4, 1911
- Several Unmarked Graves -

Sion W. Boon
Mar 4, 1830
July 22, 1905
Mary Lou Boon
Jan 18, 1836
July 3, 1879
Robert Reese, Son of J. W.
& Mary E. Boon
Apr 17, 1907
Died Apr 27, 1909
Maggie Louise, Dau. of J.W.
& M. E. Boon
Died May 12, 1893
    Aged 4 years
- Several Unmarked Graves -

Charles G. Brooks
Feb 22, 1850
Apr 23, 1872
Bernard Mitchell
Died May 28, 1859
    Aged 70 years

William S. Callaway
Sept 11, 1811
Sept 17, 1880
E. M. wife of W. S. Callaway
April 30, 1812
June 29, 1875
John, Son of W. S. & E.M.
Callaway
March 12, 1841
May 3, 1871
James Hubbard Callaway
Feb 26, 1853
Dec 6, 1861
Mattie, Daughter of W.& E.
Callaway
Died May 16, 1860
    Aged 2 years

Milton Brown Gilmore
April 27, 1866
Feb 27, 1906
Henry Brown Gilmore
Jan 8, 1868
May 25, 1897
Dr. John Taylor Gilmore
Dec 7, 1835
Elizabeth Jane Gilmore
Aug 22, 1840
Sept 8, 1908

(Riverside Cemetery p.61)

Mary, Infant Dau.
of J. T. & L. J. Gilmore
John Taylor, Son
of J. T. & L.J. Gilmore
Born August 23, 1869
Died March 1, 1871
 -One marked A.J.B.-

William Stoddert Brown, Infant
Son of Milton & Sarah
F. Brown
Dec 30, 1838
Aug 8, 1839
Infant Daughter of James A.
& Annie Heard
Died Feb 10, 1871
Milton I. Brown
July 23, 1837
Jan 27, 1911
Alex I. Brown
Nov 1, 1835
Apr 15, 1864
Milton Brown
Feb 28, 1804
May 14, 1883
Sarah E., Wife of Hon. Milton Brown
Dec 22, 1817
May 10, 1876
Clifton Dancy
August 1838
January 1898
Sarah Brown Dancy
Dec 6, 1846
Sept 20, 1933
Stoddert Caruthers
Feb 21, 1845
Dec 20, 1904
Ella Brown Caruthers
Aug 31, 1853
July 7, 1931
Hervey Brown
April 13, 1870
   Aged 53 years
Martha Lenora Brown, wife
of Hervey Brown
Sept 15, 1826
July 7, 1900
Little Fannie, Dau.
of Hervey & Martha Brown
Died Oct 6, 1862
- Infant Son
- Died November 13, 1819

E.B. Jones
March 21, 1866
April 1, 1910
John B. Owens
Nov 28, 1848
Mar 25, 1899
- Two Unmarked Graves-

Sarah S. Wood
1841 - 1900
J. A., Jr., Son of J.A.
& Georgia Maxwell
Born & Died July 14, 1906
- Three Unmarked Graves -

Erie S. Hosford
Aug 28, 1834
Oct 19, 1893
Lucile E. Hosford
July 28, 1838
Jan 8, 1895
Erie S. Hosford, Jr.
Dec 30, 1867
Aug 9, 1896
Willie W. Hosford
June 23, 1860
June 22, 1862

Joseph H. Sewell
1847 - 1900
His Wife, Mary A. Hampton
1849 - 1917
- Several Unmarked Graves-

J. J. Carpenter, Sr.
Virginia Louise Carpenter
Sarah Rebecca Carpenter
John Collins Carpenter
Maria Taylor Carpenter
Annie Laura Carpenter
David Mc Alpin McCutcheon
Lewis Carpenter
   - Unmarked Grave -

(Riverside Cemetery p.62.)

James R. Taylor
Feb 2, 1809
Nov 19, 1871
Sarah Mc Clanahan Taylor
J. J. Taylor   (Illegible)

Sallie R. Payne
Aug 26, 1881
   Aged 25 years

Isaac Taylor Hall
Susan Taylor Hall
Rev. A. J. Hall
   (No dates)
Laura G., Wife of J.B.
Scharmahorn, Daughter of
J. R. & Sallie Taylor
March 6, 1836
August 27, 1881

Birdie Lua, Daughter of J.& Lua
Worrill
July 1, 1876
Nov 1, 1877
Martha Baker, wife of
Col. John Baker
July 28, 1807
Jan 9,   1866

Walter Fenner, Son of J.S.
& Maud Johnson
Sept 12, 1890
Jan 7, 1899
Julius Adams Johnson
April 24, 1889
Sept   9, 1932
Major Medical Corps, U.S.A.
J. S. Johnson
Feb 12, 1859
Aug 25, 1932
Mary Howson Johnson
Sept 1, 1820
March 5, 1900
Dr. Julius Johnson
April 5, 1819
Aug 14, 1880

Malissa E., Wife of Robt.C.Moore
December 25, 1831
September 9, 1850

Lottis, Wife of
Thomas E. Bessenburg
Feb 12, 1869
Jan 28, 1897
Mary Stoddard Bessenburg
Oct 8, 1861
Feb 3, 1864
Mrs. D.F. Bessenburg
May 28, 1825
Mar 25, 1887
- Several Unmarked Graves -

Absolem De Berry Hurt
March 3, 1844
July 30, 1888
Fannie Guthrie Hurt
March 18, 1844
Aug   15, 1888
Dr. R. B. Nelson
1882 - 1914
- Several Unmarked Graves
George W. Taylor(Bro)
July 14, 1832
Jan 18, 1862
Andrew Guthrie
Feb 25, 1856
   Aged 44 years
William Henry, Son of
Andrew & Mary A. Guthrie
Nov 14, 1852
July 28, 1857
Mrs. Mary A. Cobb
July 18, 1821
Apr 6, 1902
J. B. Cobb
Died Oct 20, 1884

Joseph E. Martin-Priest & Doctor
May 23, 1840
Dec 28, 1900
James Junius Vaulx
Aug 20, 1838
Dec 12, 1913
Margaret Garsides, wife of
James J. Vaulx
1848 - 1928
Margaret Akin Boyd, Daughter
of James & Eliza B. Vaulx
Dec 15, 1827
Sept 17, 1856

(Riverside Cemetery p.63)

Margaret Ann Vaulx
Julia Vaulx
Jane Vaulx
Susan Vaulx

Louis I. & D. J. Snidell
Jan 22, 1825
Apr 8, 1848
    Aged 23 years

Elizabeth H., wife of
Horace Bledsoe
June 14, 1812
Died Dec 28, 1895
Horace G. Bledsoe
-SOLDIER OF THE MEXICAN WAR-
Born Oct 31, 1810
Died Feb 10, 1891

Emily Perkins, Daughter of
James & E. D. Murrell
July 10, 1850
July 8, 1851
 - Four Unmarked Graves -

Alice, Daughter of Hon.A.W.U.Totten
Died April 28, 1873

Ora Hayley, Wife of W.P.Wildberger
Aug 7, 1861
Nov 5, 1887
Mrs.N.E. Hayley   - James T. Hayley -
Mar 21, 1836   - Nov 4, 1898 -
May 3, 1913   - Age 69 yrs. -
Isabella G., Wife of J.D.McClellan, Jr.
Died Oct 28, 1857
James D. Mc Clellan
Oct 16, 1808
Feb 18, 1892
M. F. & J. R. Withers
  - Three Unmarked Graves -

Judge Thomas McCorry
1872 - 1923
Henry McCorry
Company G, 19 Tennessee Cav. C.S.A.
1845 - 1904

Corina A., Wife of H.W.
McCorry, Esq.
Sept 9, 1821
June 19, 1850
 -Three Unmarked Graves -
William, Infant son of
Corina & H.W.McCorry, Esqr.
Born Apr 11, 1812
Died Apr 18. 1815

James, Son of Joseph B.
& Virginia Freeman
Oct 17, 1850
Jan 12, 1853
Frances Alice, Dau. of J. A.
& Frances E. Caruthers
Died December 18___
Thomas, Son of J.A. &
Frances E. Caruthers
Died June - (Illegible)
Lucy Howard, Dau. of T.J.
& M. J. Caruthers
Feb 5, 1871
Dec 7, 1871
Middleton, Son of Middleton
& S. P. Hays
Feb 20, 1871
Jan 21, 1888
Frances Eliza Mc Corry, Wife
of James Caruthers
Mar 5, 1808
Mar 4, 1859
James Caruthers
Mar 1, 1795
Mar 17, 1863
  CHILDREN OF
 JAMES & FRANCES ELIZA CARUTHERS
Thomas
Aug 31, 1825
June 8, 1826
William
Oct 3, 1827
Mar 24, 1864
Virginia
Nov 11, 1829
Mar 5, 1861
Laura E.
May 25, 1831
Feb 23, 1889

(Riverside Cemetery p.64)

(Children of James & Frances
(Eliza Caruthers Continued.
James
June 1, 1833
Nov 29, 1864
Frances A.
Dec 21, 1835
* Dec 14, 1840
Penelope Marie   -*Susan M., -
Sept 22, 1880   - Sept 11, 1838 -
Feb 28, 1884   - June 13, 1888 -
A.W. Campbell, Jr.
July 5, 1874
Feb 19, 1907
Annie Dixon Allen, Wife of
Gen. A. W. Campbell
Born Sept 13, 1833
Died March 30, 1916
Alex W. Campbell
June 4, 1828
June 13, 1893
Louisa A. Campbell
April 12, 1811
July 25, 1892
Katharine Preston Mc Intosh
Mar 5, 1882
June 20, 1883
Louise Mc Intosh (Illegible)
Caro Madoline, Dau. of Annie A.,
& Wiley R. Mc Intosh
Jan 12, 1890
Feb 9, 1895

Evelyn Moody
Died Aug 19, 1910
Dolopes Moody Wilkerson
July 24, 1907
Apr   2, 1908
Van Ellis Moody
Died July 7, 1903

James Elrod
Jan 8, 1794
Sept 28, 1839
David Austin, Son of John T.
& Mary Oates
    Aged 17 mos.
Mary E., Wife of J. T. Oates
Nov 15, 1834
Aug 21, 1870
   -One Grave Unmarked-

Margaretta Robb
July 30, 1883
   Aged one year.

William Stoddert (Illegible)
 -One Stone Broken-
 -One Unmarked   -

Elinor McCorry, Dau. of
Thomas & Sallie Jones Parker
Mc Corry
Jan 16, 1824
Jan 8, 1894
Sallie I. Mc Corry
1780 - 1835
Thomas Mc Corry
1776 - 1835
Masidora Clark Mc Corry, Dau.
of Thomas & Sallie Parker McCorry
June 26, 1821
Jan 16, 1905
Corinna Ann McCorry, Dau. of
Henry Wood & Corinna A. Henderson
McCorry
April 20, 1850
Jan   10, 1921

R. E. Prewitt
1828 - 1913
Dicie Ann, His wife
1827 - 1918
  -Two Stones Illegible-
  -One Stone Broken   -

Robert Edgar, Jr., Son of
R. E. & Mabelle Cobb
April 3, 1903
Oct 26, 1903
William K. Cobb
Dec 23, 1847
May 14, 1930
Jo Henry
Apr 8, 1841
Mar 9, 1888
Stoddert
Feb 22, 1845
Dec 20, 1904
Sallie P.
April 5, 1848
April 3, 1890

(Riverside Cemetery p. 65)

Children of R.E.& Mabelle Cobb(Contd)
James Caruthers, Jr.
Susan Medora Caruthers
William Caruthers
March 21, 1881
   Aged 36 years

Willis Moore
Aug 1, 1835
Feb 14, 1918
Fannie C. Gordon, Wife of
Willis Moore
May 15, 1851
July 31, 1914
Sarah L. Gordon, Wife of Willis Moore
Jan 15, 1841
Mar 5, 1893
W. J. Moore
Aug 1, 1810
Mar 9, 1905
Harriet Moore
Died Sept 1, 1890
   Aged 76 years
Gilliam J., Son of
W.J. & H. Moore
Feb 12, 1844
June 14, 1874
Anderson J., Son of W.J.& Harriet Moore
1848 - 1871
Harriet A. Hale
Dec 24, 1800
Feb 7, 1870
Wiley Pope Hale
Adj. of Second Regiment of Tennessee
Volunteers, Son of Thomas & Harriet
A. Hale
September 21, 1821
April 25, 1847
Myron W., Son of J. G.
& Nannie D. Neudorfer
June 12, 1884
Sept. 25, 1885
  - One Broken Stone -
Robert Taylor
Wiley H. Taylor

Robert Stark
Dec 23, 1851
   Aged 57 yrs.
Emmaline, Wife of
Robert Starke
Jan 27, 1806
Aug 24, 1882
- One Stone illegible -
- One Infant Grave Unmarked-

Dr. Alexander Jackson
Feb 22, 1805
Jan 20, 1879

Joseph Dashiel Evans,
Son of Rev. J.H.
& V. M. Evans
May 10, 1868
June 8, 1888

Major William Campbell
Oct 17, 1776
Jan 11, 1842
P. P. Sterling
Died August 19, 1873
Col. Robert Sterling
Died Oct 6, 1864
Janie Porter Sterling, Wife
of Dr. I.W. Buddke
Born Mar 25, 1857
Died Nov 23, 1883

J. T. Gaither
1845 - 1899
William Edward Hutchings
1854 - 1932 -, Son of Louise
& Christopher Hutchings
Frances Hutchings, Daughter
1844 - 1932

Lenud, Dau. of F. D. &
L. A. Theus,
   Aged 10 years
- One illegible Stone -
Fannie Theus
1858 - 1878
F. D. Theus
1819 - 1888

(Riverside Cemetery p.66)

Lucy A. Theus
1884 - 1893

Mamie Theus, Wife of
T. J. Dupreee, Jr.
March 19, 1871
Sept 7, 1896
 - One Unmarked Stone
Dr. Henry L. Theus
1868
   Aged 60 years
Eliza Womack, Dau. of
James G. & Eliza Womack
Died Dec 7, 1845
   Aged 2 years
Edward Croft Theus
Died Jan 19, 1846
William R. Theus
Eliza L. Theus
F. D. Theus
  (No dates)
Lucy A. Theus
Dr. Henry Theus
Howard Croft Theus
Died Jan 19, 1846
Maxey, Son of F.D.Theus&L.A.Theus.
   Aged 2 years
Eliza Lenud Campbell
July 21, 1854
   Aged 11 years
Eliza Love Theus
Sept 2, 1792
Aug.14, 1868
J. Maxey Theus
 (No dates)

Lucinda Brooks, Wife of A. Jobe
1804 - 1841
Andrew Jobe
Feb 4, 1800
Aug 28, 1870

Mary W. Jacks, Wife of
Dr. A. Jackson
November 22, 1811
May   23, 1841

Capt. Middleton Hays
1843 - 1926
Sallie Parker Caruthers Hays
1848 - 1890
Elinor Virginia Hays
1886 - 1909
 - One Stone Illegible -

Mrs Eliza Ann, Consort of
Dr. B. H. Ligon
Died October 31, 1834
   Aged 19 years

Eliza L. Theus, Daughter of
E.S. & Ann D. Campbell
July 8, 1840
Mar 3, 1841
Anne Deleisseline, Consort
of E. S. Campbell, M.D.
March 19, 1817
Feb   7, 1842
 - Several Unmarked Graves -

Lewis Groves
July 29, 1810
Jan 14, 1896
Frank, Son of A.N. & N.L.McCord
Dec 9, 1875
Died 1882

Susan, Wife of Thomas Beard
Nov 7, 1818
Jan 16, 1895
Charles Jarvos
   Aged 34 years
 - Several Unmarked Graves -

Edna May, Daughter of
J. H. & F.E. Ellis
Sept 6, 1892
Aged 10 years
Robert John Jeter
Nov 27, 1880
Dec 9, 1891

G. Haclitz
1889
   Aged 72 years
 - One Stone illegible-

(Riverside Cemetery p.67)

C. C. Grail
Died Jan 22, 1891
    Aged 58 years
- Several Unmarked Graves -

Green B. Husband of S.E. Tate
Oct 30, 1856
Apr 2, 1895

John M., Son of J. B. &
S.A. Moody
Sept 18, 1876
Sept 28, 1899

Franklin G. Callahan
Nov 3, 1907
Dec 2, 1908
Lilbern Ray Roach
Oct 29, 1898
Oct 18, 1900
Jessie B. Callahan
Oct 4, 1904
June 3rd, 1908
- Several Unmarked Graves -

Lavinia-Elzira-Susan Garrison
    (No Dates)

Mary A., Dau. of J. H. & Mary L.
Whitman
Feb 17, 1891
Dec 22, 1891
Henry Whitman
Feb 2, 1895
Feb 6, 1895
Lena Whitman
May 20, 1892
Aug 4, 1898
Bennie Whitman
Sept 4, 1889
May 7, 1899

Bryan B. Prothy
May 14, 1823
July 17, 1881

Florence Ione, Dau. of
Tracy & Bettie Robbins
- Several Unmarked Graves -

John C. Galbaugh
July 31, 1851
Nov 2, 1881
- Several Unmarked Graves -
- One illegible Stone -

Mary, Wife of J. P. Wooten
1864 - 1886
Mary - their Dau.
1883 - 1885

Alfred S. Poole
Nov 2, 1868
May 6, 1880
Sarah Annetta Poole
Oct 1, 1873
May 11, 1880

G. E. Macon
May 27, 1850
Apr 11, 1881
Jno. W. Gray
July 17, 1854
Aug 18, 1895
S. B. Davidson
Jan 22, 1852
Jan 2, 1870
-One illegible stone
Daughter of T.H. & J.E.Francis
Died May 16, 1878
- 1800 - 1876 (illegible)

Mrs. Almedia Ann Talbot, Wife
of Joseph H. Talbot, Esq.
March 5, 1807
Oct 10, 1835

-One Stone illegible
Joseph Greer, Son of Joseph
Sept 20, 1832
May 23, 1834
- Several Unmarked Graves -

L.E. Matheson
June 9, 1909
June 9, 1909

(Riverside Cemetery p.68)

M. S. Williams,
Dec 28, 1894
July 7, 1904
- One illegible Stone-

Our Father-Richard Jackson Hays
Mar 5, 1822
Feb 2, 1899
Our Mother-Sarah Ballou Hays
Died Aug 11, 1888
   Aged 60 years
Stokeley Donelson Hays
Apr 4, 1851
Dec 24, 1908
Stokeley Donelson, Son
of S. D. & G. S. Hays
May 29, 1891
Nov 18, 1893
Richard Hartwell, Son
of S.D. & G. S. Hays
1881 - 1883

Joseph Smith,
Feb 12, 1859
April 10, 1889
Dr. Julian R. Woolfolk
Nov.10, 1836
Jan 9, 1896
May C., Dau. of
Dr. J. R. & C. B. Woolfolk
1869 - 1928
Jessie J., Dau. of J. R.
& C. B. Woolfolk
1867 - 1869
  - One illegible Stone

Jessie Newton Seale
Died Nov 11, 1907
My Sister-Sophia Spratt Seale
Died Mar 9, 1908
Louise Parker Spratt
Died Nov 13, 1898
Henry Bishop Spratt
Died Jan 29, 1891
Etta Josephine Spratt
Died Sept 20, 1908
  - Five Graves Unmarked

C. S. Gaulding
(illegible)

A. J. Smith
June 9, 1830
Jan. 14, 1878

Sarah Goodwin
May 7, 1820
Jan 19, 1881

Mary E., Wife of
T. B. Kershaw
June 30, 1825
Aug 5, 1896
Thomas B. Kershaw,
Mar 9, 1821
Oct 30, 1877

Richard A. Stout
Sept 2, 1897
Mar 3, 1907
Albert French
Oct 3, 1861
Dec 27, 1906
Johnie, Son of W. R.
& L. L. Duncan
Feb 1, 1901
Apr 30, 1907
- , Son of W.R.
& L. L. Duncan
Sept 23, 1888
Apr 24, 1907

Mrs. I. F. Harris,
Died Dec 7, 1904
  Aged 54 years
Harmon Estelle, Dau.
of L. M. & L.T. Jaynes
Feb 18, 1901
Jan 11, 1904
James, Son of J. R.
& Elizabeth Cooksey
May 19, 1890
Feb 9, 1905

(Riverside Cemetery p. 69.)

Annie T. Prewett, Wife of
W. K. Cobb
July 6, 1848
June 30, 1919

William Ormond Butler
Oct 15, 1882
Feb 10, 1906
- Two Graves Unmarked -

Maria A. Biglow
Died Jan 11, 1822
Elijah L. Biglow
Died Jan 9, 1822
   Aged 21 years
Elijah Biglow
Died Aug 28, 1830
   Aged 31 years
Miss Mary Ann
Dau. of Amoziah Childs, Esq.
Died July 31, 1832

Lou Emma Cobb, Wife of S.J. Cobb
1855 - 1934
S. J. Cobb
1849 - 1916

D. Hammer King
June 6, 1890
June 11, 1932
  - One Unmarked Grave -

Mary E. Gaither
1849 - 1904
-Several Unmarked Graves

Anna Mae, Dau. of
S. I. & M. D. Lovett
May 28, 1892
May 5, 1911
Dollie Isabella, Dau.
of Anna Mae Kinsey
Born and Died May 10, 1911.

(End)

One Infant's Stone
    (illegible)

Cora P. Carpenter
July 28, 1898
Aug 24, 1905
John Lorenz
Died July 1, 1903
   Aged 44 years
- Several Unmarked Graves -

Mattie Elizabeth Zachary
July 4, 1891
July 19, 1904

J. E. Scott
May 2, 1881
Sept 3, 1904
- Several Unmarked Graves
Dr. G. R. White, Son
of N. White
Sept 8, 1860
Apr 2, 1894
Birdie, Wife of
Alex Mills,
May 12, 1885
Nov 8, 1903
 - Several Unmarked Graves -
Edie R., wife of
Genl. W. Davis
March 20, 1879
Oct 18, 1903
Several Unmarked Graves

J. K. Wilkinson
Died July 30, 1903

McMILLAN

(Editor's Note-)

John H. McMillan who is buried in Riverside Cemetery married first -
   Armeta Paralee Butler and had issue two children, viz:
      1. William Henry McMillan born 1864 and named for his uncle William Henry Butler
      2. Mary McMillan named for her grandmother Mary B. Butler.

John H. McMillan married as his second wife Mary Spah McMillan. No issue.

MADISON COUNTY

TOMBSTONE INSCRIPTIONS
BROWN'S CHURCH CEMETERY

Brown's Church Cemetery as it is known, is situated in the heart of one of the most thriving communities in Madison County. It is about six miles from Jackson.
To reach the cemetery, take the Memphis to Bristol Highway (No.1) going east out of Jackson, or in the direction of Nashville.
It is located approximately six miles out, and about a quarter of a mile off the highway, turning to the right, or due East.
There is a school nearby, and the cemetery lies near the Church which is of Methodist denomination (Rev.W.W. Henly, Pastor)
The following inscriptions are written as they appear according to rows, in consecutive order.   Unmarked graves 361.
Mary E. Stovall - Mary W. Beatty. Copyists.
June 15, 1938.

BUCHANAN
James Wilson Buchanan
Born June The 10, 1903,and
Died July The 18, 1908
Darling child is gone to
rest But never will be
forgotten.

3 unmarked graves.

(Lot begins)
PARISH
F. W. Parish
1845 - 1920
Elizabeth, His Wife
1848 - 1906
F.W.P.   E.J.P.

KEY
Lee Blackmon Key
1860 - 1934
    L. B. K.

BLACKMON
Mary E., Wife of B. Blackmon
Born Dec 24, 1828
Died July 25, 1895

Burrell Blackmon
Born Sept 18, 1824
Died Nov. 14, 1897

M.E.B.   B.B.
    AT REST
Dearest Parents thou hast
left us. Here thy loss we
deeply feel
But 'tis God who has bereft
us. He can all our sorrows
heal.
- - - - - - -

PHILLIPS
Ella I., Wife of
T. L. Phillips
Born Dec 11, 1851
Died Dec 14, 1909
Her spirit smiles from that
bright shore and softly
whispers weep no more.

Madison County
(Brown's Church Cemetery p.2)

PHILLIPS
Thomas L. Phillips
Dec 6, 1848
Dec 29, 1917
He is gone but his
light still shineth.
(End of lot)

(Begin lot)
BLACKMON-Charlie B.
1867 - 1934
FATHER

BLACKMON-Lenna V.
1879 - 1930
MOTHER

Helen
Aug 15, 1894
Apr. 1, 1904
Our loved one
BLACKMON.

MYERS
Gene Myers
Sept 19, 1927
Mar 11, 1933
Our Darling
G.M.
(End of lot)

4 Unmarked graves.

R. BRADY H.

2 Unmarked graves.

(Begin lot)
CROSNOE
J.W. Crosnoe
May 18, 1837
Nov 6, 1910
God knoweth best.
--
Malinda, Wife of J.W. Crosnoe
Jan 17, 1835
July 13, 1905
Thy Will be done.

CROSNOE
Gone Home
Addie, Dau. of J.W.
& M. Crosnoe
Born Dec 15, 1871
Died Jan 12, 1888
Remember friends, as you
pass by, As you are now
so once was I.
As I am now, so you must
be. Prepare for death
and follow me.

(Lot begins)
GARRETT
William T. Garrett
1864 - 1929
Fannie Blackmon, His Wife
1865 - 1922
FATHER   MOTHER

Infant Son of W.T.
& F. B. Garrett
1901
BROTHER.

Oma Garrett
1887 - 1888
BROTHER

(Infant grave, concrete slab
enclosed with no inscription)
(End of lot).

ANDERSON
Lucy A., Dau. of V.A.
& C.A. Rogers, wife of
W.T. Anderson
Born Nov 13, 1858
Died May 23, 1916.

W.T. Anderson
Born in Madison County
May 9, 1854
Died June 14, 1937
L.A.A   W.T.A.

3 Unmarked graves.

Madison County
(Brown's Church Cemetery p.3)

ONEAL
F. M. Oneal
Sept 16, 1843
Oct 22, 1911
Annie E., His Wife
May 7, 1850
Oct 15, 1911
There is no parting in heaven.

2 Unmarked graves.

SMITH
Catherine, Wife
of T. H. Smith
Born May 14, 1828
Died May 4, 1910
   C. S.

2 Unmarked graves.

CHILDRESS
John B. Childress
Died Sept 20, 1868
  Aged 21 yrs. 1 mo.& 24 days.

CLARK
Martha Ann, Consort
of E. A. Clark
Born Jan 1, 1835
Died Aug 7, 1869
She was. But words are
wanting to say what.
Think what a wife should be
and she was that.
She's gone she's left this
world of woe
For regions of eternal joys.

1 Unmarked grave.

Maj. E. A. Clark
Born at Charlotte, N. C.
Jan 21, 1826
Died in Louisville, Ky.
May 8, 1900
An honest man is the noblest
work of God.

JONES
Wm. T., Son of W. F.
& S. A. Jones
Born Feb 23, 1868
Died June 15, 18__
   W. T. J.

1 Unmarked grave

ANDERSON
Jane T. Anderson
Born Jan 29, 1806
Died Nov 23, 1880
She died as she lived
trusting in God.
   J. T. A.

LAND
Pattie E., Dau. of H.M.
& S.P. Land
Born Aug 24, 1870
Died Aug 7, 1876
Too good for earth
God called her home.

ANDERSON
Lillie M., Dau. of
S. H. & T. H. Anderson
Died May 17, 1878
  Aged 2 yrs.2 ms.25 ds.
   L. M. A.

Matilda W., Dau. of Jas.
& Nancy Fussell and wife
of J. J. Anderson.
Born Oct 23, 1824
Died May 13, 1889
Gone but not forgotten.
   M.W.A.

J. J. Anderson
Born In Madison Co.,Tenn.
March 31, 1824
Died Jan 27, 1879.
God gave, He took - He will
restore. He doeth all
things well.
   J. J. A.

2 Unmarked graves.

Madison County
(Brown's Church Cemetery p.4.)

ANDERSON
Lena B., dau. of S.H.
& H. T. Anderson
Died July 21, 1881
  Aged 2 ys. 1 mo. 6 ds.
Thou will never more be with
us - Such reflections make
us mourn - But we hope to
meet in Jesus where afflictions
never come

Elmer B., Son of S. H.
& H. T. Anderson
Born 1892
Died 1897
Our darling one hath gone before
To greet us on the blissful shore.
    E. B. A.

Children of J. W. & Flora
C. Anderson.
Minnie Maud
Born May 31, 1881
Died Oct 10, 1884

Our little twins
Born July 1
Died Aug 23, 1884

4 Unmarked graves.

(Lot begins)
    ANDERSON
Lizzie Anderson
1893 - 1935

    ANDERSON
Robert   ' Charlie
1898-1898 ' 1894-1895

F. C. Anderson
1863 - (No date)

1 Unmarked grave.
(Lot ends)

(Lot begins)
    CLARK
John Harvey Clark'Annie Land Clark
1864-1934   ' His Wife
           '1866 - 19____
J.H.C. - At Rest- A.L.C.

CLARK
John F. Clark
1822 - 1867
Mary J. Clark
1826 - 1906
Mary E. Clark
1859 - 1915
Loves last tribute.
(Lot ends)

Begins lot)
    WOOLFOLK
Farewell
G. N., Son of J. R.
& A. J. Woolfolk
Born Feb 16, 1858
Died Dec 27, 1887
Our darling one hath gone
before - to greet us on
the blissful shore.

Gone Home
J. C. Woolfolk
Born Nov 15, 1854
Died Oct 30, 1890

Neal Son of J. G.
& Jennie Woolfolk
Dec 16, 1889
Jan 22, 1898
    N. W.
(End of lot)

(Lot begins)
    RENSHAW
Rev. John Renshaw
Born Aug 16, 1785
Died Sept 28, 1864

Easter, Wife of
Rev. John Renshaw
Born Apr 15, 1805
Died Oct 1, 1864

Luna May, Dau. of
J. S. & S. E. Renshaw
Born Nov 18, 1875
Died May 2, 1910

Madison County
(Brown's Church Cemetery p.5)

RENSHAW
Anderson C. Renshaw
Born May 2, 1845
Died a prisoner of war
at Alton, Ill.
Oct 30, 1863

Elizabeth, Dau. of J. S.
& S. E. Renshaw
Born May 10, 1898
Died June 30, 1899.
End of lot)

BLACKMON
Erected by the
Woodmen of the World
John J. Blackmon
Born in Madison Co., Tenn.
Sept 3, 1845
Died Feb 5, 1902
   Aged 56 yrs. 5 m's& 2 D's.
Precious father he has left
us. Left us, yes, forever
more. But we hope to meet
our loved one on that bright
and happy shore.
Lonely the house and sad the
hours since our dear father has gone
But oh! a Brighter home than ours
In heaven is now his own.

Martha Francis Goodrich, Wife of
John J. Blackmon Born in Madison Co.
Tenn. Nov 27, 1842.
Died Dec 4, 1901
   Aged 59 yrs. & 7 Da's
Through all pain at times she smiled
a smile of heavenly birth. And when
the angels called her home, she
smiled farewell to earth. Heaven
retainth now our treasure, Earth, the
lonely casket keeps And the sunbeams
love to linger where our sweet sainted
mother sleeps?

Ora Cleveland, Dau. of John J. &
M. F. Blackmon
Born July 26, 1884
Died July 26, 1887
   Aged 3 Years.

GOODRICH
In my Father's house
are many mansions.
Mrs. M. M. Goodrich
Born June 2, 1812
Died Mar 6, 1878
   M. M. G.

J. P. Goodrich
Born Feb 14, 1845
Died Dec 5, 1879
   J.P.G.

2 Unmarked graves

HUTCHERSON
Infant dau. of L.W.
& F. M. Hutcherson
Died Feb 24, 1881

Samuel Elmore, Son of
L.W. & F.M. Hutcherson
Born June 23, 1882
Died July 7, 1882
   S.E.H.

SIMPSON
OUR MOTHER
E. L., Wife of S.C.
Simpson
Born Dec 3, 1833
Died May 13, 1885

1 Unmarked grave

ANDERSON
Ida Anderson, MOTHER
1858 - 1934

HICKS
Jule L.
Born Apr 6, 1867
Died Apr 24, 1928
FATHER
--
Jule Gideon, Son of
Jule & Maggie Hicks
Born Dec 18, 1890
Died Oct 20, 1900

Madison County
(Brown's Church Cemetery p.6)

HICKS
Florence, Dau. of J.L.
& Maggie Hicks
Born Dec 9, 1889
Died Aug 6, 1890
Earth hath one mortal less
Heaven one angel more.

Margarete Blackmon, Wife
of Jule L. Hicks
Born Nov 11, 1871
Died June 20, 1937

Lee Hicks
Born Madison Co. Tenn. 1864
Died 1938

(Lot begins)
JONES
John W.	Laura
1849 - 1914	1862-1936
FATHER	MOTHER
J.W.J.	L.J.

HULIHAN
Louisa J. Hulihan
1833 - 1901
AUNT
L.J.H.
(Lot ends)

9 Unmarked graves.

ANDERSON
Virgie L., Daugh. of James R.
& V. H. Anderson
Born Jan 21, 1873
Died Nov 4, 1873.

Virginia H., Wife of
James R. Anderson
Born (date illegible)
Died Mar. 3, 1873

James E., Son of
S. G. & N. Anderson
Born Sept 22, 1848
Died Jan 21, 1874
T'was hard to give thee up, but
Thy Will O! God be done.

LAWRENCE
Little Herbert, Son of E.
& L. D. Lawrence
Born Jan 21, 1871
Died Oct 8, 1875

Little Fanny, Dau. of E.
& L. D. Lawrence
Born Oct 19, 1865
Died Apr 2, 1866

1 Unmarked grave

REID
W. A. Reid
Born Nov 22, 1848
Died Sept 8, 1869
Aged 20 yrs. 9 m's 17 d's
Two hours before his
death he sweetly sung the
song "A crown of glory
bright by faith I see in
yonder realms of light.

Lot begins)
COLLINS
John J. Collins
Born June 22, 1844
Died Oct 19, 1912

Mary L. Collins
Born Sept 16, 1844
Died Nov 28, 1900

Julia A. Collins
Born Feb 8, 1842
Died Dec 2, 1878

Callie Mae Collins
May 16, 1867
Jan 18, 1870

John E. Collins
Apr 28, 1872
June 3, 1872

Fannie L. Collins

Luna E. Collins
Nov 10, 1878
Dec 8, 1878.
(End of lot)

Madison County
(Brown's Church Cemetery p.7)

ANDERSON
Infant Dau. of S.C.
& M. F. Anderson
Born June 5, 1877
Died June 7, 1877

8 Unmarked graves.

WEAKES
J. R. Weakes
Oct 31, 1845
July 30, 1905
Gone but not forgotten
    J.R.W.

WEEKS
Horace, Son of J.R. & M.A. Weeks
Born Sept 10, 1870
Died Aug 14, 1890

Ada, Dau. of J.R.&M.A. Weeks
Born July 6, 1873
Died Sept 30, 1873

HOPPER
Mary A., Daughter of
Daniel & Lucinda Hopper
Born Mar 26, 1850
Died Sept. 23, 1873

2 Unmarked graves

BURRUS
Thomas, Son of S.& S. Burrus
Died Dec 1, 1865
   Aged 4 yr's 2 m's 15 days

HOPPER
Daniel Hopper
Born May 28, 1812
Died May 18, 1889
Call not back the dear
departed - anchored safe
where storms are o'er -
On the border land we left
him - soon to meet and
part no more.

Lucinda, Consort of Daniel Hopper
Born Feb 7, 1822
Died Feb 5, 1885.

HOPPER
We loved him
Daniel B., Son of W. M.
& R. E. Hopper
Born Apr 29, 1884
Died Oct 5, 1885
(End of lot).

STEWART
SON
J.M. Stewart
Born Oct 4, 1848
Died Oct 5, 1936
MOTHER
Mary A. Stewart
Born July 25, 1921
Died Apr 29, 1874

JACKSON
Harriet Wilson Goodrich,
Wife of W.H. Jackson
Born Feb 1, 1817
Died Mar 19, 1890

Sarah E., Dau. of W.H.
& H.W. Jackson
Born Jan 13, 1836
Died Dec 21, 1884
   Aged 47 yrs.& 11 m's.

John Z. Jackson
Aug 9, 1837
May 6, 1876
   J A C K S O N

HOPPER
Wilson Barzilla Hopper
Born Apr 27, 1872
Died Oct 16, 1892

HOPPER
Dolphus L.   ' Mary Lou
1870 - 19____ ' 1872 - 1937
  D.L.H.   ' M.L.H.

Lot begins)
STEMM
Wm. D. Stemm
July 4, 1857
Apr 13, 1902
Servant of God, well done.

Madison County
(Brown's Church Cemetery p.8)

STEMM
Susan Rebekah, Wife
of Wm. Duncan Stemm
Feb 14, 1857
MOTHER: One who loved us
longest and best.

STEMM
Dewitt Stemm
Aug 15, 1885
June 16, 1910
(End of lot).

JOHNSON
Rev. Henry Clay Johnson
Jan 6, 1864
Dec 19, 1916

(Lot begins)
BARKER
Susan, His Wife' Frank
1871 - 1935 ' 1870-1930
   MOTHER   FATHER

2 small unmarked graves
(Completes this lot)

(Lot begins)
THOMPSON
MOTHER
Ellen Sneed Thompson
Feb 14, 1847
May 22, 1934

FATHER
W. H. H. Thompson
Apr 22, 1840
Oct 3, 1910
  At Rest

John Edgar, Son of
W. H. & E. Thompson
Born July 25, 1873
Died May 1, 1898
 T H O M P S O N

AT REST
Elizabeth Thompson
Born Oct 21, 1800
Died July 3, 1883
 T H O M P S O N
(Lot ends)

GRAVETTE
Mary Lou Gravette
Born Sept 23, 1901
Died Mar 26, 1903

1 Unmarked grave

BARNES
Laural, Wife of
T. J. Barnes
Born (No date)
Died Feb 28, 1878
She was a kind and
affectionate wife,
a fond mother and
a friend to all.
    L.L.B.

KIRBY
Farewell
Jemima Lacy Kirby
Born Dec 19, 1823
Died May 30, 1883
OUR MOTHER
"In God's own morn
her orb will rise
once more a star
of paradise".

Farewell
Henry Kirby
Born Sept 8, 1816
Died Aug 4, 1877
God gave - he took -
he will restore -
He doeth all things well.

1 Unmarked grave

DOUGLAS
BABY DOUGLAS
Born Nov 9, 1895
Died Nov 25, 1895
ANNIE DOUGLAS
Born Sept 6, 1883
Died Aug. 20, 1884
Sisters have gone to
be angels?

Madison County
(Brown's Church Cemetery p.9)

EDWARDS

DAUGHTER
Lusannah Edwards
1879 - 1887

MOTHER
Susan C. Edwards
1844-1888

FATHER
Jas F. Edwards
1848 - 1931

4 Unmarked graves

HARRIS

Jackson A. Harris
Born 1829
Died July 19, 1860
Remember friends as you
pass by As you are now,
so once was I.
As I am now, so you must
be.
Prepare for death and
follow me.

Minerva B. Harris
Born Mar 3, 1828
Died Apr 22, 1893

Thos. Harris, Sr.
Died March 26, 1852.
 Aged about 60 years.
Sleep on Father, gently
sleep within thy clay cold
bed Until the power of God
shall wake thee from the dead.

Ann E., Consort of
Thos. Harris, Sen.
Died Aug 26, 1870
 Aged 78 years.
Sleep, Mother, gently sleep
within thy clay cold bed
Until the power of God shall
wake and raise thee from the
dead.

4 Unmarked graves.

PATE

E. E. Pate
1828-1890
Nancy, His Wife
1826-1907
Leora - Daughter
1863-1918

2 Unmarked graves.

Florence Robenie, Dau.
of W.H.& Eudora Pate
Born June 11, 1875
Died June 15, 1876

Sidney T., Son of E.E.
& N. N. Pate
Born Aug 10, 1866
Died Oct 3, 1868
 Aged 2 yrs.2m.& 20 D's.

WINSLOW

Laura P., Dau. of T.H.
& S.M. Winslow
Born Sept 24, 1867
Died Sept 22, 1868
 Gone to inhabit fairer
climes.

PATE

John G. Pate' Mellie,
1855 - 1903 ' His Wife
 FATHER ' 1858-1906
 MOTHER

STEWART

Martha Louisa, Dau. of
G. W. & M. A. Stewart
Born Sept. 15, 1855
Died Sept. 28, 1857

1 Unmarked grave

NOBLES

Sacred To The Memory Of
Allen J., Son of A.D.
& M.F. Nobles
Born Dec 28, 1835
Died Apr 29, 1859

Madison County
(Brown's Church Cemetery p.10)

NOBELS
Erasmus Montgomery Nobels
Born Apr 10, 1838
Died Aug 27, 1857

NOBLES
Emily F. Nobles, Daughter
of A.D. & M. F. Nobles
Born Feb 7, 1832
Died Apr 29, 1854
The music of her voice is
hushed - Its eloquence is
risen. The star that shone
so bright on earth Shines
brighter still in Heaven.

Mary F., Wife of Doct. A.D. Nobles.
June 14, 1843
Aged 44 yrs. 4 ds.
Sleep on thou lovely mother sleep
Thy sorrows here on earth are o'er
Angels thy dusty bed shall keep
And thou shall sigh and weep no more.

BROWN
Caroline M., Wife of A. T. Brown
Born Sept 14, 1828.
(Lower part of inscription buried
(in earth).

Ann Banks, daughter of A.T.
& E. A. Brown
Born Oct 28, 1855
Died Aug 26, 1857

(Lot begins)
PEARSON
R. D. Pearson
1886 - 1925
R.D.P.

Emma Mason Rone Pearson
Born June 6, 1855
Died Sept 4, 1906
P E A R S O N

J. C. Pearson
Feb 3, 1857
Oct 17, 1919
The blessings of his quiet life
fell on us like dew.
P E A R S O N

PEARSON
Adelie L., Wife of
J. C. Pearson & dau.
of R.M. & E. A. Mason
Died Aug 15, 1884
Aged 22 years
(End of lot)

5 Unmarked graves

EDWARDS
William F., Husband
of A. F. Edwards
May 12, 1852
Jan 21, 1923
Gone but not forgotten.

Ame, Wife of
W. F. Edwards
Born Dec 23, 1854
Died July 23, 1880

1 Unmarked grave

(Lot begins)
PARISH
A. S. Parish
Born Jan 6, 1819
Died Jan 10, 1897
J. A. S. P.

3 Unmarked graves

PARRISH
Miranda C. ' John S.
1859-19 ___ ' 1855-1934
(Lot ends)

HASKINS
Cora Artie, Wife
of J. R. Haskins
July 23, 1879
June 4, 1905
At Rest

WATSON
Laura J., Wife
of W.L. Watson
Born Feb 22, 1881
Died Aug 23, 1904
Too good for earth
God called her home
W A T S O N

Madison County
(Brown's Church Cemetery p.11)

(Lot begins)
WATSON
Nancy, His wife ' J.T. Watson
Jan 3, 1850   ' Sept.17, 1844
July 8, 1916   ' Jan. 1, 1930
  MOTHER   '   FATHER

WATSON
Louie Zelma, dau.
of J.T. & N.L. Watson
Born Aug 7, 1888
Died Nov 18, 1892

Ira A., Son
of J. T. & N. L. Watson
Born Aug 13, 1877
Died April 8, 1878
(Lot ends)

BETTS
Ruth Betts
Born Sept 5, 1798
Died Apr. 7, 1883

Thomas A., Son
of E.M. & C.T. Betts
Born Nov 15, 1860
Died Aug 1, 1870

BURNSBY
S. F. Burnsby, dau.
of J. & F. Burnsby
Born July 7, 1844
Died Sept 9, 1853

BETTS
Catharine T. Betts
Born Oct 24, 1840
Died July 27, 1865

1 Unmarked grave

DORR
Henry Dorr
Born Oct 2, 1813
Died Sept 11, 1872

NANCE
Lena, Dau. of R.W.
& J. L. Nance
June 5, 1893
July 27, 1893

NANCE
One Unmarked grave

Virginia L., Wife of
Rev. R.W. Nance
Born July 10, 1867
Died Nov. 15, 1901
  Aged 34 ys. 4 ms. 5 D.
Sweetly sleeps my
precious wife
Holy Angels guard thy bed
Gently rest in Jesus,
Darling, Till he calls
thee from the dead.

BROWN
Mary S., dau. of R.F.
& Ann Brown
Aug 21, 1857
Died Sept.19th, 1857.
(This and the following
(Inscription was taken
(from brick vaults)

Sarah Ann, Wife of
R.F. Brown
Born Aug 13, 1835
Died Oct 18, 1857
"The Lord gave and the
Lord hath taken away -
Blessed be the name
of the Lord."

4 Unmarked graves
(Lot begins)
DOAK
Children of C.A. &
Georgie Doak.
Carrie
Aug 23, 1884' Lucile
Oct 30, 1884' Aug 1, 1888
        Dec. 9, 1888.
Georgia   ' Mary
Jan 30, 1890' Mar 25, 1880
June 20, 1890' Jun 23, 1880
Charles
May 23, 1881
July 21, 1881
(This is one lot & one mon-
(ument bearing all five in-
(scriptions. There are five
(small graves).

Madison County
(Brown's Church Cemetery p.12)

PARDUE
Elizabeth C., Wife of
J. J. Pardue
Born Jan 14, 1830
Died June 25, 1898
PARDUE

1 Unmarked grave

Rosa Lee, dau. of J. J.
& E. C. Pardue
Born Dec. 13, 1862
Died Sept 2, 1881

1 Unmarked grave

DAMRON
J. W., Son of W. F.
& M. E. Damron
Born March 8, 1878
Died Sept. 1, 1878

M. E., Wife of W.F. Damron
Born Sept 5, 1850
Died Mar. 17, 1875

FOGG
Mary L., Wife of Joseph Fogg
Born June 11, 1813
Died March 2, 1891

DAMRON
Christena D. Damron
Born Feb. 28, 1849
Died Jan 18, 1871
The tint of health has left
her cheek and cold is her fair
brow. Her eyes are closed, her
pulse is still.
She is an angel now.

Christina, Dau. of Wm. F. &
C. Damron
Born Jan 8, 1871
Died Aug 28, 1871

1 Unmarked grave.

(Lot begins)
KEY
Charlie Key ' Dean Mason Key
1869 - 1935 '   (No date)

MASON
Minnie E. Mason, Dau. of
R. M. & E.A. Mason
Born Mar 19, 1865
Died Apr 4, 1884

Lulu E. Mason, Daugh. of
R.M. & E. A. Mason
Born Feb 21, 1860
Died Sept 19, 1880

FATHER
MASON
Rufus M. Mason
Born July 21, 1818
Died Apr 26, 1889
  Aged 70 ys. 9 ms. 5 ds.
MOTHER
Eunice Ann, Wife of
R.M. Mason
Born July 10, 1830
Died June 25, 1880
  Aged 49 yrs. 11 ms. 15 dys.
(End of lot)

DOAK
To the Memory of
Thomas J., Son of
W. & J. Doak
Born May 5, 1825
Died Jan 8, 1860
  Aged 34 yrs. 8 m's. 3 d's.

To the Memory of
William Doak
Born June 27, 1782
Died Jan. 17, 1849
  Aged 66 yrs. 5 m's. 21 Dy's.

To the Memory of
William, Son of W. & J. Doak
Born Dec 29, 1828
Died Jan 27, 1846
  Aged 12 yrs. 28 D'ys.

Madison County
(Brown's Church Cemetery p. 13)

DOAK
To the Memory of
Gibson, Son of W. & J. Doak
Born Nov 2, 1817
Died Dec 26, 1845
   Aged 28 ys. 1 m. 24 D's.

To the Memory of
John B., Son of
W. & J. Doak
Born May 24, 1823
Died Nov 18, 1845
   Aged 22 yrs. 5 m. 24 D'ys.

To the Memory of Jane, Wife
of W. Doak
Born July 17, 1787
Died Sept 17, 1841
   Aged 54 Yrs. 1 mo.

MASON
We part to meet again
Adelia Ann, Daugh. of
R.M. & E.A. Mason
Born Aug 13, 1851
Died May 18, 1854
   Aged 2 yrs. 9 mo. 5 Dys.

3 Unmarked graves.

LOCK
In Memory of
Elizabeth Lock, wife of R.P. Lock
Born Jan 23, 1811
Died Apr 19, 1848
(This is a brick vault)

BLACKMON
M.L. Blackmon
Born July 17, 1820
Died Feb. 14, 1910
   MOTHER

Rev. James Blackmon
Born Oct 7, 1820
Died Mar 5, 1905
   Aged 84 yrs. 4 m. 26 D's.
   FATHER

1 Unmarked grave

HOWARD
Richard E., Son of
B. F. & J.F. Howard
Born Feb 23, 1862
Died Aug 16, 1871

BLACKMON
J. R.
1849 - 1933.
Mary E., his wife
1854 - 1914
Loves Last Tribute.

5 Unmarked graves.

BROWN
Nancy R., Wife of J.W. Brown
Born Aug 27, 1815
Died Aug 27, 1878

Baby Wilmur, Son of
J. D. & T.E. (Stone broken)
(No dates) (Names illegible)

EXUM
Lorena, Wife of
F. G. B. Exum
Dec 24, 1865
June 2, 1914
   MOTHER
Felix Exum
Feb 9, 1862
June 7, 1897
   Aged 35 Y. 3 M. 29 D's.
   FATHER
Infant babe of
Felix & Lorena Exum
Born & Died Apr 14, 1886
Our loved One.

Margaret C., wife of
G. W. T. Exum
July 7, 1836
Dec 12, 1882

Joesphine, wife of
G.W.T. Exum
Apr 10, 1839
June 20, 1897

Madison County
(Brown's Church Cemetery p.14)

EXUM
Asleep in Jesus
   Hope
G. W. T. Exum
Mar 27, 1827
Jan 2, 1899

WARMATH
Jennie, Wife of J.W. Warmath
Oct 24, 1860
June 27, 1906
Jennie was a true christian
and loved by all.

WARMATH
Marvin   ' Mattie
Husband   ' Wife
1880 - 1932 ' 1876 - 19____

1 Unmarked grave

RAINES
Dr. F.M. Raines
1853 - 1930

2 Unmarked graves.

THOMAS
Athamasius Thomas
Dec 28, 1832 - July 21, 1914
Truly a man of God

Elizabeth Blackmon Thomas
Nov. 1840 - (No date).

Freddie, Son of A.& L.E. Thomas
Born July 27, 1877
Died July 28, 1877

J. Willie, Son of
A.&.L.E. Thomas
Born Mar 2, 1866
Died July 31, 1872.

John P. Thomas
Born Apr 17, 1804
Died June 20, 1882

A little flower of love that
blossomed but to die
    THOMAS
Infant Son of Rev. J.J. & Mrs Thomas
Oct 13, 1893 - Oct 20, 1893.

THOMAS
Henry Clerc, Son of
James Julian & Kate Gibbs
Thomas, Born in Newbern,
Tenn. Oct 5, 1907,
& fell asleep
Oct. 6, 1908,
Safe in the arms of Jesus.

1 Unmarked grave.

LANE
Norma, Dau. of A.B.
& May Lane
1889 - 1892
   At Rest.

May, Wife of A.B. Lane
1863 - 1916
Loves last tribute.

3 Unmarked graves
BLACKMON
J. D., Son of J.W.
&N.E. Blackmon
Born Feb 11, 1884
Died Aug 11, 1884

Nannie E. Blackmon
May 19, 1853
Mar 17, 1890

James W. Blackmon
Sept 30, 1850
May 4, 1927

RONE
OUR MOTHER
Jennie L. Rone
1842 - 1907
  J. L. R.

John T. Rone
1839 - 1909
  FATHER

Kate G. Rone
1868 - 1918
  MOTHER

Willie, Son of J.T. &
Jennie L. Rone
Sept 16, 1868
Oct 16. 1870

Madison County
(Brown's Church Cemetery p.15)

RONE
Lillian Rone
1906 - 1907
(End of lot)

BLACKMON
Martha H., Wife of
Wm. Blackmon
Born Aug 13, 1819
Died Jan 15, 1898

William Blackmon
Born Nov 21, 1816
Died June 7, 1882

Infant of W.& M.H.Blackmon
(No dates)

Robert J., Son of W.
& M. H. Blackmon
Jan 16, 1858
April 1, 1859

Mary M., Dau. of W.
& M. H. Blackmon
Born Nov 29, 1845
Died Jan 25, 1858

Thomas J., Son of W.
& M. H. Blackmon
Born March 1, 1856
Died July 20, 1856

Martha R., dau. of W.
& M. H. Blackmon
Born June 16, 1854
Died Sept 15, 1855

Infant of W.E.
& M. H. Blackmon
(No dates)

Infant of W.&M.H.Blackmon
(No dates)

John C., Son of W.& M. H.Blackmon
Born Feb 21, 1839
Apr. 22, 1842.

Elizabeth Blackmon
(dates sunken in ground).

BLACKMON
William Blackmon
-- 1786
Nov 10, 1850 (Stone broken)

Infant daut's of B.
& M. E. Blackmon
Born Aug 21, 1847
Died Sep 24, 1847
Born July 30, 1854
Died Dec. 3, 1854

Eliza L., dau. of Jno.
& E. F. Blackmon
Born July 21, 1851
Died July 19, 1854

Elizabeth, daughter of
John & Amy Rollins
& wife of Fordham Blackmon
Born in 1786
Died Nov 10, 1854.

Fordham Blackmon
Born Jan 2, 1796
Died Jan 1, 1872

Margaret, Wife of
Fordham Blackmon
Born July 17, 1815
Died Sept 16, 1896
   At Rest
   --

BARKER
MOTHER
Fannie, Wife of W.R.Barker
1863 - 1886
   At Rest

PERSON
Mary E., dau. of W.A.
& E. J. Person
Born Oct 29, 1843
Died Oct 6, 1857

PERSON
W. R.
1851 - 1924
BROTHER

Madison County
(Brown's Church Cemetery p. 16)

PERSON

1 Unmarked grave

OUR FATHER & MOTHER
William A. Person
Born Sept 19, 1819
Died Nov 16, 1864

Eliza Jane, Wife of
W. A. Person
Dec 20, 1822
June 3, 1900

3 Unmarked graves.

ROLLINS
Rebecca, Wife of T.H.Rollins
Died May 16, 1866
　Aged about 30 y's.

Thomas Rollins
Born Oct 11, 1792
Died May 16, 1866

1 Unmarked grave

BOBBITT
Z. L. Bobbitt
Born Dec 16, 1816
Departed this life
Aug 28, 1875

11 Unmarked graves.

BLACKMON
　　B.T.
1887 - 1915
　　Ernest
1895 - 1908
　　Sons of
B.F. & M. T. Blackmon.

Pearce, Son of B. F.
& M. T. Blackmon
Born Nov 2, 1884
Died March 4, 1897

James D., Son of Rev. B.
& M. T. Blackmon
Died Jan 1, 1878
　Aged 2 ys. 28 d's.

BLACKMON
Ora B., dau. of B.F.
& M. T. Blackmon
1888 - 1905
She is not dead
but sleeping

BLACKMON
Rev. Benj.F. Blackmon
Oct 20, 1845
Mar 25, 1907
His many virtues form the
noblest monument to
his memory.

Eliza F., Wife of Jno.
Blackmon
Born July 10, 1819
Died Dec 7, 1869

BLACKMON
John Blackmon
Mar 6, 1819
June 7, 1901
Eliza Frances, Wife
of John Blackmon
July 10, 1819
Dec 7, 1869
Mary Anna Belle, Wife
of John Blackmon
Dec 1, 1844.
　(No date)

2 Unmarked graves

BUSH
Nancy C., Wife of
Bevly Bush
Born Jan 1, 1880
Died Feb 26, 1905

3 Unmarked graves.

CARPENTER
Little Arthur, Son of
J.W.& L.C. Carpenter
Born Dec 13, 1880
Died May 5, 1881

4 Unmarked graves

Madison County
(Brown's Church Cemetery p.17)

Mc CALLUM
Callie C., Wife of
J. F. Mc Callum
Sept 1866
Aug 20, 1912
Love never faileth

OLIVER
J. E., Son of F.C.
& T. P. Oliver
Born May 23, 1882
Died Sept 16, 1884

Jas. S. Oliver
Born Jan 13, 1804
Died Oct 9, 1882

Cordelia J. Oliver, Wife
of James Oliver
Marhh 22, 1816
March 15, 1906

OLIVER
F.C. Oliver' Tennie B.,
1871 - 1927' His wife
          1861 - 1932.
  Asleep in Jesus.

1 Unmarked grave.

RICKETTS
C. E., Wife of Wm. Ricketts
Born July 10, 1810
Died Dec 17, 1883

W. W. Rickette
(No dates)

J.F. Ricketts
(No dates)

M. J. Ricketts
(No dates)

J.P. Ricketts
(No dates)

Wm. Ricketts
(No dates

E. A. Jones
(No dates)

2 Unmarked graves.

RONE
Wyatt M.,
Died Mar 30, 1883
  Aged 30 years.

SEAMORN
Mattie A., Wife of
W.J. & Mother of
J.B. Seamorn
Born May 12, 1839
Died April 20, 1862
Her record is on high.

13 Unmarked graves.

BOBBITT
Elizabeth, Wife of
Z.L. Bobbitt
Born Dec 16, 1817
Died Feb 26, 1880

2 Unmarked graves

ROLLINS
E. Catherine, Wife
of James Rollins
Born Feb 16, 1827
Died May 23, 1888

James Rollins
Born Dec 24, 1824
Died Oct 14, 1897
  Aged 72 y. 9 m. 20 D.

PERSON
Samuel B. Person
1836 - 1909

ROLLINS
Charlie H., Son of W.F.
& Ivan Rollins
Nov 19, 1885
Feb 22, 1887

THOMPSON
Louise Thompson
Born Feb 3, 1906
Died Nov 27, 1910

ROLLINS
W.R. Rollins
1865 - 1890

Madison County
(Brown's Church Cemetery p.18)

THOMPSON
T. O. Thompson
Born Oct 28, 1875
Died Mar 22, 1910
Mattie Boren, his wife
Born Jan 22, 1878
Died Aug 31, 1808

BOREN
Dora A., dau. of
H.J. & M. J. Boren
Born June 30, 1869
Died Oct 7, 1870

BOREN
H. J. Boren ' Martha J.,
Dec 22, 1842' his wife
Aug 28, 1905' Dec 4, 1845
          Mar 30, 1923
At Rest
--

1 Unmarked grave

MAC MILLIN
W. E. Mac Millin
1838 - 1881

Corinna C. Mac Millin
1846 - 1878

John Wm. Murray Mac Millin
1875 - 1876

Nina Dora Mac Millin
1877 - 3 mo's.

2 Unmarked graves.

(Lot begins)
GOODRICH
Mary E. Goodrich
1857 - 1928

E. H. Goodrich
June 14, 1855
July 24, 1916

M.H. Goodrich
Feb 11, 1829
Jan 23, 1898

GOODRICH
Emily B., Wife of
M. H. Goodrich
Born Oct 4, 1836
Died March 26, 1888
(Lot ends)

RONE
Sarah A.M., dau. of
James & Mahulda Rone
Died Oct 28, 1867
Aged 26 yrs. 9 m's.

In Memory of
Morgan H., Son of
J. & M. Rone
Oct 25, 1833
Nov 12, 1859

In Memory of
James Rone
Born Aug 4, 1805
Died Feb 20, 1859
Aged 54 yrs.

Mahulda Rone
Born April 11, 1813
Died Aug. 23, 1888

2 Unmarked graves

Oneal
Minerva C. ' H.D.
1846 - 1916 ' 1844 -

11 Unmarked graves

(Lot begins)
ALLRIDGE
Thomas   ' Rebecca Ann
1846-1934 '   his wife
              1846 - 1919

Ernest, Son of T.
& B. R. Allridge
Born March 13, 1880
Died Oct 10, 1880

Sally C., dau. of
T. & B. R. Allridge
Born Sept 25, 1875
Died Dec 11, 1884
(Lot ends)

Madison County
(Brown's Church Cemetery p.19)

DOLLAHITE
William Edward
1888 - 1926
One of God's best men.

NELSON
Lela H.   'Arthur H.
1876 - 19___ '1874-1936
    Loves last tribute

5 Unmarked graves

(Soldier) BUMPAS
W. J. Bumpas
Jackson's Co. Tenn. Cav.
C. S. A.

RUSHING
Paul Rushing
May 14, 1905
Oct 19, 1908

2 Unmarked graves

ALLRIDGE
Tennie, Wife of
H. C. Allridge
Oct 23, 1856
July 19, 1903

6 Unmarked graves

LOWRANCE
Elisha P. Lowrance
Born Feb 20, 1797
Died July 27, 1875
    Aged 78 Y. 5 M. 7 D.

Nancy B., Wife of
E. P. Lorance
Born Nov 17, 1804
Died Jan 14, 1897
    Aged 92 Y. 2 M. 10 D.

BROWN
Adam Brown
Born August 1780
Died Nov 19, 1864

Aquilla Brown
Born Feb 22, 1785
Died Apr 3, 1860

DALLAM
Aquilla Ann
Born Aug 29, 1819
Died Sept 22, 1872

LOCK
Mary L. Lock
Born Jan 23, 1811
Died Dec (broken stone, 1876.

SMITH
Eldred H. Smith
Born Nov 2, 1812
Died Dec 19, 1891

Mrs. Matilda M.,
Wife of E. H. Smith
Born March 10, 1819
Died Oct 24, 1863.

WATSON
Thomas Emmet, Son of W.J.
& M. A. Watson
Born July 28, 1863
Died Oct 30, 1863

WATSON
FATHER   'MOTHER
W.J.Watson 'M.A.Watson
April 29,1839'Apr 19,1840
July 20, 1908'July 20,1922

WILLIAMSON
OUR MOTHER
Drucilla, Wife of
Thos. G. Williamson
Born July 9, 1815
Died Aug 22, 1886

BOREN
Fausta R. Boren
Apr 26, 1885
Aug 13, 1904
Gone but not forgotten.

In Memory of Jennie, Wife
of W. A. Boren
Jan 1, 1846
Died Apr 1, 1880

Madison County
(Brown's Church Cemetery p. 20)

BOREN
W. A. Boren
Aug 17, 1838
Feb 3, 1905
His memory is blest.

3 Unmarked graves.

FUSSELL
M. C. Fussell
Born June 11, 1828
Died Jan 11, 1889
    MOTHER
W.A. Fussell
Born Jan 8, 1830
Died Aug 24, 1878
    FATHER

Lizzie F. Fussell, Wife
of J. W. Boren
Born Sept 18, 1842
Died March 16, 1892

2 Unmarked graves.

J. F. Boren
Dec 1, 1916
June 23, 1902
    BOREN

1 Unmarked grave

JOHNSON
William   ' Cora
Sept 17, 1857 ' Wife
May 29, 1934 ' Oct 31, 1861
  FATHER   MOTHER

SMITH
Gideon T., Son of H. S.
Matilda M. Smith
Born July 19, 1846
Died March 13, 1875

John G., Son of E. H.
& M. M. Smith
June 5, 1854
Sept 17, 1888

3 Unmarked graves

(Lot begins)
HENDERSON
W. H. Henderson
Born Feb 2, 1857
Died Dec 18, 1901
They who knew him best
will bless his name
And keep his memory dear
while life shall last.

W. J. Henderson
Born March 19, 1821
Died June 1, 1900

M. E. Henderson
Born Jan 9, 1832
Died Feb 1, 1884

F. B., Son of
W. J. & M. E. Henderson
Oct 23, 1868
Oct 18, 1869

W. C., Son of
W. J. & M. E. Henderson
Oct 16, 1860
Oct 5, 1883

Serena W., Wife of
D. T. Turner
March 11, 1855
May 7, 1884 (lot ends)

One Unmarked lot

COCK
Rachel E., wife of
J. T. Cock
Born May 3, 1856
Died Apr 3, 1884

J. T. Cock
Born Feb 28, 1850
  (No date)

WALLACE
OUR MOTHER
Mary E., Wife of
M. H. Wallace
Born June 28, 1824
Died Feb 20, 1887

Madison County
(Brown's Church Cemetery p.21)

WALLACE
TO OUR FATHER
Matthew H. Wallace
Born Mar 13, 1807
Died Aug 23, 1879

CHEEK
Bettie, Dau. of J. A. &
A. J. Cheek
Born April 3, 1875
Died July 11, 1886

WALLACE
J. D., Son of J. H. &
Margaret W. Wallace
Born Jan 8, 1886
Died Aug 6, 1886

Margaret W., Wife of
J. H. Wallace
Dec 18, 1855
Jan 30, 1886

J. H. Wallace
Oct 11, 1853
Aug 5, 1893
Blessed are the dead
who die in the Lord

WALLACE
Mary E., his wife ' John R. Wallace
1874 - 1915   ' 1855 - 1912

WALLACE
Mabel E., dau. of D. J.
& I. M. Wallace
Born Oct 16, 1886
Died July 25, 1887

Idabelle
1901 - 1902

WALLACE
David J.   ' Ida M.
1862 - 1912 ' 1866 - (No date)

1 Unmarked grave

MALONE
B. J. Malone
July 16, 1849
Mar 31, 1925

MALONE
Martha A. Malone
Jan 9, 1867
May 13, 1928

WALLACE
Earnest, Son of
Mr. & Mrs. T. A. Wallace
Born Mar 28, 1907
Died May 23, 1908

Robert L. Wallace, Son
of Mr. & Mrs. T.A. Wallace
May 26, 1908
Dec 23, 1919

WALLACE
Mary J.   ' Samuel H.
1857-1903 ' 1850-1920

Infant of M. B.
& I. H. Wallace
Born & Died May 12, 1900

6 Unmarked graves

OWEN
H. T. Owen
Born in Herd Co. Ga.
Mar 8, 1847
Died July 28, 1879
A True Husband.

1 Unmarked grave

MOORE
Rev. D. G. Moore
Born Aug 2, 1821
Died Dec 29, 1876

1 Unmarked grave

MASON
Jinnie Ann, Daugh of J.A.
& A. E. Mason
Born Apr 29, 1872
Died Dec 14, 1874

MOTHER
Ann Person Mason
July 6, 1853
Feb 8, 1929

Madison County
(Brown's Church Cemetery p.22)

1 Unmarked grave

JONES
Clopton, Son of L. W.
& J. S. Jones
Born Mar 23, 1875
Died July 12, 1903

JONES

Dr. J. W. Jones
Mar 17, 1828
June 13, 1914

Jenny S., Wife
of J. W. Jones
Born in May, 1844
Died Oct. 1903

3 Unmarked graves

BLAKEMORE
Russell K., Son of T. L.
& E. C. Blakemore
Born in Front Royal, Va.
Feb 4, 1852
Died Apr. 18, 1899
To My Son

Thomas Luther Blakemore
Born in Front Royal, Va.
Jan 25, 1819
Died Aug 21, 1901
Member of Primitive Baptist Church.

Eliza Richards, Wife
of T. L. Blakemore
May 8, 1817
Died Oct 21, 1906
Having finished life's duty
She now sweetly rests.

WELSH
Archie Lee, Son of J. P.
& Eliza Welsh
Born Sept 30, 1876
Died Jan 8, 1889
  Aged 10 Y. 3 M. 9 D.

Maggie B., Daugh of J. P. & D. L. Welch
Born & died July 17, 1876
In heaven.

WELCH
D. L., Wife of J.P. Welch
Born Dec 13, 1853
Died Feb 16, 1881

WELCH
Pat Welch
Died Dec 15, 1906
  Aged 75 Years

1 Unmarked grave

PEARSON
S. W. Pearson
Mar 31, 1862
Oct 10, 1916

W. M. Pearson
Born Nov 19, 1854
Died Dec 5, 1897

Jesse I., Wife
of W.M. Pearson
Died July 22, 1894
  Aged 35 years
Also Infant
Jesse W. Pearson.

Infant, dau. of J.D.
& R. C. Pearson
Born Dec 21, 1866

R. C., Wife
of J. D. Pearson
Born Dec 30, 1833
Died July 27, 1885

J. D. Pearson
Born Jan 10, 1831
Died Apr 15, 1899

PEARSON

One Unmarked grave

(Lot)
MASON
John Rufus Mason
1884 - 1936

MASON
John M. Mason
Aug 25, 1857
Nov 1, 1924

Madison County
(Brown's Church Cemetery p.23)

MASON
Our darling
Hattie E., dau. of J.M.
& M. A. Mason
Died May 23, 1890

Infant dau. of
J. M. & M. A. Mason
Born & died Dec 9, 1894.
(Lot ends)

BLACKMON
Dr. John Ashbury Blackmon
1859 - 1925
Lula May, his wife
1861 - 19____

Walter Prentiss Blackmon
1890 - 1919
Son of Dr. John A.
& Lula M. Blackmon
The end is just beginning
The serene days here are
only a foretaste
I'll be the first to greet you.

Harry   ' Freddie ' Infant
1845-1848' 1885-1885' 1887 - -
Infant   ' Infant   ' John A., Jr.
1887   ' 1889   ' 1896-1896
    CHILDREN OF DR. JOHN A.
      & LULA M. BLACKMON

MARTIN
Nelle Blackmon
1882 - 19____
James Irwin
1882 - 1933.

WATSON
Joseph H., Son of Wm.&P.J. Watson
Born Jan 16, 1838
Died Oct 18, 1885
Gone but not forgotten.

STOUT
Isaac Hugh Roy, Son of
J. D. & Anna Stout
Oct 5, 1905
Mar 1, 1909

8 Unmarked graves.

BREWER
William Allen Brewer
Born Apr 18, 1886
Died Mar 15, 1907

4 Unmarked graves

(Lot begins)
PARISH
Charlie J. Parish
Feb 23, 1883
Mar 27, 1912
Too good for earth
God called him home.

Twin Infant sons
Died July 5, 1911
Infant dau.
Died Feb 24, 1910
  Children of Charlie
  & Ernestine Parish.
Ere sin could blight or
sorrow fade
Death turned with friendly
care
The opening bud to heaven
and bade them blossom
there.
(Lot ends)

WILLIAMS (Lot begins)
Almedia, Wife of
N. M. Williams
Born May 4, 1849
Died Dec 27, 1885
She died as she lived
trusting in God.

Newton Milton Williams
Aug 15, 1849
March 11, 1926
Loves last tribute.
                (Lot ends)

(Lot begins)
MEALS
Louise Catherine Person
Wife of W.H. Meals
Dec 20, 1848
Nov 26, 1915
Asleep in Jesus.

Madison County
(Brown's Church Cemetery p. 24)

MEALS
Infant dau. of W.H.
& L. C. Meals
Born Mar 11, 1885
When we reach the heavenly
shore, we shall meet to
part no more.
(Lot ends)

CHEEK
Ida May
Mar 29, 1902
Sept 22, 1914
She only sleeps

George Millard, Son of
J.E. & A. P. Cheek
Born Aug 21, 1894
Died Apr 6, 1904

2 Unmarked graves

HARRIS
John C., son of S.J.
& J. T. Harris
Born Oct 14, 1886
(No date)

1 Unmarked grave

(Lot begins)
MC CALLUM
Mary E. Pearson, His wife
Sept 9, 1858
Nov 10, 1932
J.R. Mc Callum
Jan 5, 1855
Mar 8, 1838
He giveth his beloved sleep.

Ernestine, dau. of
J.R. & M.E. Mc Callum
Born Sept 26, 1882
Died Nov. 14, 1884

PEARSON
N.B. Pearson   'Lizzie Reid Pearson'
1872 - 19____ ' 1872 - 1937   ?
        At Rest

TOMLINSON
(Initials on concrete
(curbing around lot)
   C-E -   B -
   S.T. -   J.R.T.

1 Unmarked grave.

TIMBERLAKE
Lizzie L., Wife of
J. W. Timberlake
Born Jan 21, 1851
Died (No date)

4 Unmarked graves.

COLE
Lonnie Cole
Born Oct 30, 1905
Died May 23, 1906

1 Unmarked grave

ROLLINS
S. G. Rollins
Oct 5, 1838
Jan 22, 1909

W.H. Rollins
Mar 22, 1845
Sept 22, 1907
  Aged 62 years 6 mos.
Darling we miss you.

MC ADOO
Bettie, his wife
1874 - 1930

J. W. Mc Adoo
1878 - 19 ____.

  - H. C -
(No dates)

CHAMBERS
Come Ye Blessed
Croatie, Wife of
W.B. Chambers
Born Sept 16, 1878
Died Apr 25, 1905

Madison County
(Brown's Church Cemetery p. 25)

COCK
Aunt Kit
Died March 14, 1922
Aged 88 years

4 Unmarked graves.

COCK
F.C. Cock ' Elenor
1858-19__ ' his wife
        ' 1861-1929
    At Rest

COCK
Orean Collins
Son of F.C. & J.E. Cock
Aug 23, 1897
July 18, 1899

Olie Lee, Infant dau.
of F.C. & J.E. Cock
Mar 17, 1887
June 13, 1887
Tis but the casket that lies here
The gem that filled it sparkles
yet.

DOAK
Charles Alfred ' Geogia Tomlinson
Mar 19, 1852 '   his wife
Sept 23, 1926 ' Jan 30, 1852
              May 29, 1934
    At Rest

(Lot begins)
DOUGLASS
Emma D. Douglass
Born Nov 13, 1900
Died Sept 6, 1908
Blessed are they that trust
in the Lord.

DOUGLASS
Mary C. Douglass ' Charlie Douglass
Born Oct 14, 1863 ' Born Oct 15, 1853
    (No dates)   ' Died Dec 2, 1901
Our sweetest hopes lie buried
here.

DOUGLASS
Infant son of W.N.
& Idella Douglass
Oct 7, 1921
Budded on earth
to bloom in heaven.

Lillian Orean, dau. of
W.N.& Idella Douglass
Sept 15, 1912
Dec. 21, 1922
Gone to a better land.
-

DOUGLASS
Idella   ' Willie N.
1893 - 19__ ' 1888-1935
 MOTHER   ' FATHER
How desolate our home
bereft of thee.
(End of lot).

LANE
Ollie Neal, Son of J.
& A. M. Lane
Born May 21, 1893
Died Mar 16, 1894

Alice Metta, Wife of
Josiah Lane
Born Mar 4, 1855
Died (illegible)

DOAK
Alford Langford, Son of
J. A. & Annie Doak
Jan 22, 1901
Apr 20, 1907

LANE
FATHER ' MOTHER ' BROTHER
W.A. Lane! SISTER ' BABY

2 Unmarked graves.

BANKS
Robt. Banks
  Co. E
 Tennessee M.T.D.
  Inf.

1 Unmarked graves

Madison County
(Brown's Church Cemetery p. 26)

CUMMINGS
M. A., Wife of
F. W. Cummings
Born Sept 9, 1848
Died July 23, 1922
Gone but not forgotten

1 Unmarked grave

CONLEY
Parilda Conley
Born Mar 26, 1872
Died Feb 9, 1900
Our darling one has
gone before To greet us
on the blissful shore.

(Lot begins)
HENDERSON
Dr. S.A.   ' Fannie May,
1862-1900 ' his wife
                    ' 1866 - 19___
--

BOONE
MOTHER   FATHER
M. E. Boone 'C. F. Boone
Feb 14,1853 'Mar 9,1851
July 10,1919'Feb 6,1914

Elizabeth L., Wife of
J. B. Boone
Born Oct 5, 1826
Died Jan 31, 1892
Sleep on dear mother and
take thy rest, God calls
away when he thinks best.
(Lot ends)

CROOM
R.C.Croom,' I.N. Croom
his wife   ' 1821-1891
1839-1912 '

MOTHER
QUILLEY
PACE
Gone but not forgotten.

PACE
FATHER
RUSHEL
PACE
1847
Sept. 27, 1911
Gone but not forgotten.

T. A. Pace
1883 - 1925
Gone but not forgotten

1 Unmarked grave.

ALDRIDGE
Dora L., Wife
of Will Aldridge
Jan 2, 1880
July 4, 1905
She died as she lived
trusting in God.

9 Unmarked graves.

(Lot begins)
TINKLE
Harvey L. Tinkle
Dec 10, 1883
Oct 10, 1918

Earl H. Tinkle
1908 - 1927

LOVE
Allen E. Love 'Agatha Nelson
Apr 22,1859   ' his wife
Oct 29,1929   'Nov 11,1868
FATHER   'Jan 5,1936
                      MOTHER
(Lot ends) ----

(Lot begins)
ALDRIDGE
Eliza Ann Aldridge
1929-1930
      Rosebud.
--

Madison County
(Brown's Church Cemetery p.27)

ALDRIDGE
CHILDREN OF A.D. &
O.D. ALDRIDGE
Infant   ' Carline
1906   ' Dec 15, 1905
           Jan 15, 1909
Budded on earth to
bloom in heaven.
(Lot ends)

DUKE
Madison M. Duke
July 16, 1877
Mar 19, 1915

(Lot begins)
PEARSON
Cecil C., son of D.H.
& M. H. Pearson
July 9, 1898
Nov 26, 1914

PEARSON
Earle E., son of D.H.
& M. H. Pearson
Oct 13, 1914
Nov 18, 1926

John D., son of D.H.
& M. H. Pearson
Oct 3, 1896
Sept 4, 1897
(Lot ends)

BUMPAS
Alexander Bumpas
Born Oct 9, 1866
Died Feb 8, 1890
Asleep in Jesus.

(Lot begins)
PEARSON
W. T. Pearson 'Emma H.,
1859-1934   'his wife
            '1856-1903
Rest Sweet Rest

Baby boy
Born Feb 1, 1901
Gone too soon.

PEARSON
Mattie, dau. of W.T.
& E.H. Pearson
Mar 13, 1891
Mar 27, 1892
Our darling one has
gone before to greet
us on that blissful
shore.
(End of lot)

EXUM
Infant of John
& Lula Exum
Born & Died
Dec 6, 1897

2 Unmarked graves

FOGG
G.N. Fogg   'T. H. Fogg
Oct 8, 1860 'Oct 8, 1860
Jan 14, 1919 'May 1, 1928
(Twin brothers).

HALTOM
Sara E., Wife of
William H. Haltom
Mar 16, 1832
Nov 30, 1916

FOGG
Mary Jane Haltom
Wife of A. B. Fogg
Sept 17, 1859
July 1, 1897

RICE
W. A. Rice
1848 - 1900

W.D.' Lela' Elizabeth Rice
1880; 1900' 1856-1927
1893;
Dewitt   ' Sarah
1893-1905' 1887-1912

Infant dau. of J.T.
& Elizabeth Rice
Dec 18, 1911.

Madison County
(Brown's Church Cemetery p.28)

CUMMINGS
James M., son of W.T.
& M. A. Cummings
Died Sept 20, 1894
  Aged 17 yrs. 23 days

3 Unmarked graves

ALLEN
Morten Allen
1893 - 1913

Jas. C. Allen
1869 - 1902
Jennie Croom, his wife
1869 - 1900

Mary Lou Allen
1895 - 1897

COCKS
Lottie Cocks
Born Dec 30, 1891
Died Jan 3, 1903

COCK
M. M., Wife of C.C. Cock
Born Sept 17, 1836
Died Feb 5, 1894

C.C. Cock
Born July 29, 1832
Died Jan. 26, 1894

HART
Delia, dau. of R. D.
& B. E. Hart
Nov 28, 1879
July 14, 1902

FATHER
Robert D. Hart
July 6, 1837
Feb 26, 1915

Elizabeth Hudson, wife of
R. D. Hart
Feb 16, 1852
Oct 12, 1891

5 Unmarked graves.

PEARSON
Sacred to the memory of
John S. Pearson
Died Nov 18, 1902
  Aged 69 years 2 mos. 11 Dys.

Martha J. Pearson
Dec 26, 1842
Oct 2, 1918
  76 yrs. 9 mos. 24 D's.
      1 Unmarked grave.

CUPPS
Emily Nelson Cupps
July 20, 1881
May 20, 1919

2 Unmarked graves

LAND
Lottie, dau. of G.M.
& E.J. Land
1897 - 1922
She died as she lived
trusting in the Lord.

2 Unmarked graves

WOOLFORK
Ruby, dau. of W.B.
& L. F. Woolfork
July 28, 1902
Oct. 13, 1906

1 Unmarked grave

TOMLINSON
James A. Tomlinson
Feb 16, 1851
Mary Tomlinson, his wife
Apr 28, 1856
Aug 29, 1931

Infant
  --------- (End)

ROGERS
Vincin B. Rogers
Apr 9, 1837
July 7, 1904
ROGERS

Madison County
(Brown's Church Cemetery p.29)

ROGERS
Cornelia, Wife of
V. A. Rogers
Sept 7, 1839
Feb.19, 1912

ROGERS

Willie B., Son of
Vincin A. & Cornelia
Rogers
Jan 29, 1879
Jan 14, 1894

Euim A. Rogers
Mar 15, 1871
Feb 22, 1906

May Rogers
May 31, 1875
Aug 6, 1908

T.C. Thompson
1847-1929
UNCLE TOM
--- (End)

M. M. SCALLIONS
M. M. Scallions
Feb 4, 1846
May 24, 1925
A. J. Scallions
Feb 25, 1847
Jan 27, 1894

SCALLIONS
Floyd Sdallions
Feb 24, 1879
Oct 6, 1902
Leon Scallions
Aug 30, 1885
Jan 8, 1903

Mrs. Lou Scallions
Wife of Mr. W.J. Scallions
Apr 14, 1873
June 19, 1897

Betty Jean, dau. of R.D.
& Lois Scallions
1935 - 1936.

COCK
J.L. Cock
Born Oct 8, 1824
Died Sept 21, 1906
Mrs. M.J. Cock, Wife of
Mr. J.L. Cock
Born Nov 24, 1832
Died May 29, 1901

PERSON
J.P. Person
Jan 20, 1833
Jan 10, 1910
Fredonia E. Person
Feb 17, 1867
Sept 8, 1920

5 Unmarked graves

SPARR
Martha A., Wife of
John Sparr
1836 - Dec 7, 1906

GREEN
Wm. G.   ' Ella
1851 - 1914 ' 1865-1918

Infant dau. of
Mr. & Mrs. W.G. Green
1897

MC CASLAND
William Harvey, Son of
J. A. & T. R. Mc Casland
Nov 5, 1896
Sept 27, 1898

Erin I. B. Mc Casland
Born Mar 11, 1910
Died Feb 14, 1911
Budded on earth
to bloom in heaven.

MC CASLAND
James A. McCasland
Born Apr 15, 1869
Died Sept 5, 1912

Madison County
(Brown's Church Cemetery p.30)

MC CASLAND
T. B., Wife of
J. A. Mc Casland
Born Mar 2, 1871
Died Dec 29, 1908

B. Mc Coy Mc Casland
Feb 18, 1889
Oct 12, 1914
Gone home to Father

6 Unmarked Graves

SPAIN
Will M. Spain
1876 - 1927
Asleep in Jesus

Emily C. Spain
1845 - 1931
SPAIN
Joseph M. Spain
1843-1917
J. Warren Spain
1867-1894
   (End)

(Lot begins)
WOOD
Mary Elizabeth, dau.
of F.B. & H.A. Wood
Born Nov 8, 1878
Died July 3, 1896

Carey Wood
Born Oct 10, 1887
Died Mar 16, 1898

J. D. Wood
Born Aug 13, 1891
Died Jan 28, 1908

WOOD
Frank D. Wood ' Hester A.,
Sept 13, 1850 ' his wife
Oct 11, 1928 ' Feb. 4, 1851
    FATHER   ' Apr. 2, 1935
                 MOTHER
(End)   -----

JONES
Susie L., Wife of
W. N. Jones
May 25, 1881
Dec 6, 1907

JONES
Mahaley J., Wife of
Jasper Jones
Born Oct 19, 1839
Died Nov 18, 1908

ALLEN
Katy Lucile, Daughter
of Luther & Leila J. Allen
Born Feb 5, 1907
Died June 29, 1908

FUSSELL
Ruth Fussell

4 Unmarked graves

WHEELER
Mattie
1858 - 1927
  MOTHER
  - -

WALKER
Ora, dau. of
J. C. & Fannie Walker
Oct 28, 1897
Nov 1, 1911

James C. Walker
Feb 3, 1857
Oct 24, 1926

Fannie, Wife of Jas. C. Walker
Mar 4, 1877
Feb 14, 1907

RUSHING
Mary C., ' Green B. ' Felix W.
his wife ' 1849-1909 ' 1886-1915
1850-1906 '   FATHER   ' BROTHER
MOTHER '   '
              - - -

1 Unmarked grave.

Madison County
(Brown's Church Cemetery p.31)

DAY
J. M. Day
1845 - 1923
Martha, his wife
1848 - 19 ___ .

RONE
J. Hermon Rone
1897 - 1934

3 Unmarked graves.

(Lot begins)
GOODRICH
Waynick

I. C. Goodrich
1852 - 1935

Fannie T. Goodrich
1866 - 1894

WAYNICK
Lilla Adell Waynick
1890 - 1925
(Lot ends)

DONNELL
Infant son of
Baxter & Birdie Donnell

1 Unmarked grave.

WOOLFOLK
Mollie B. Woolfolk
was born Wednesday
Sept 2, 1874
Departed this life
  Monday
Nov. 16, 1896

SIMPSON
Samuel R. Simpson
Mar 13, 1869
Apr 30, 1928

WOOLFOLK
John G. Woolfolk
Born June 28, 1845
Died Feb. 24, 1906

WOOLFOLK
Sue E., wife of
J. G. Woolfolk
Jan 12, 1847
Jan 8, 1917

CUMMINGS
Charley, Son of J.
& M. A. Cummings
Died June 26, 1819
  Aged 10 months
Budded on earth
to bloom in heaven.

6 Unmarked graves

KEY
Jesse Ray, Son of J.R.
& S. C. Key
Born May 17, 1884
Died July 16, 1890

GOODRICH
Jack, Son of J. W.
& Ella Lee Goodrich
Feb 17, 1909
Dec 30, 1911
Asleep in Jesus.

Infant Son of J.W.
& Ella Lee Goodrich
Born & died
Feb. 17, 1908

6 Unmarked graves

WALKER
Jesse May, dau. of A.J.
& M. P. Walker
Born July 9, 1893
Died Jan 10, 1900

Clarence, Son of A.J.
& Mollie Walker
Sept 8, 1899
Sept 22, 1900

Lessie P., dau. of
A. J. & Mollie Walker
Dec 11, 1901
Aug 30, 1903

Madison County
(Brown's Church Cemetery p.32)

WALKER
Mary P. Walker' A.J.Walker
1870 - 19___ ' 1858 - 1936
  MOTHER   '   FATHER

WALKER
Emma, Beloved wife of J.S.Walker
Born Nov 9, 1862
Died July 13, 1904

Mattie, Wife of J.S. Walker
Born Feb 26, 1875
Died June 2, 1919
Blessed are the pure in heart
for they shall see God.

MILLS
Beulah, Wife of H.V.Mills
Born Feb 14, 1888
Died Sept 5, 1914.

5 Unmarked graves.

LAWS
Emily Etta Laws, Wife of
M. R. Grant
Born July 6, 1871
Died Jan.11, 1902

Eula Bessie Laws
Mar 13, 1887
Oct 30, 1918

Josie Phine Laws
July 6, 1874
Oct 30, 1918

John Laws
Born Oct 28, 1838
Died Feb 19, 1906

Kittie, Wife of John Laws
Jan 6, 1853- June 16, 1929

GRANT
Lynn Grant
June 10, 1899
Oct 22, 1918

HOPPER
FATHER
W.M.Hopper
July 15, 1858
Dec. 6, 1911

MOTHER
R. E. Hopper
Aug 2, 1861
  There is no
  parting in heaven.

1 Unmarked grave
(Lot ends)

GOWAN
Infant Son of
E.E. & Bessie Gowan
1912

2 Unmarked graves

SIKES
Infant dau. of
V.J.Sikes & Wife
  At Rest
--

BLACKMON
Roy Blackmon
1884 - 1927
Loves last tribute.

(Lot begins)
KIMBRELL
1 Unmarked grave.

THOMPSON
James W., Jr., Son of
James W. & Leslie Thompson
Born Oct 27, 1904
Died July 30, 1906

TOMLINSON
Thomas D. Tomlinson
Jan 13, 1849
July 6, 1924

His Wife
Martha E. Person
May 15, 1845
Sept 14, 1933

Madison County
(Brown's Church Cemetery p.33)

ANDREWS
Mary E. Wife of
Dr. A. G. Andrews
Born July 9, 1840
Died July 3, 1904

Dr. A. G. Andrews
Born July 30, 1833
Died Aug 16, 1914

(Lot Begins
BLACKMON
B. F. Blackmon
Apr 9, 1857
Jan 14, 1909

Leithy M., Wife of
B. F. Blackmon
Born May 11, 1857
Died July 25, 1905

I. F. Blackmon, Son of
B. F. & L. M. Blackmon
Born Feb 5, 1883
Died Oct 10, 1889
(Lot ends)

1 Unmarked grave

FATHER
W. F. Blackmon
1873 - 1906

PARR
J. S. Parr
1873 - 1931
   At Rest

1 Unmarked grave

(Lot begins)
PLUNK
2 Unmarked graves

WATSON
Belle Young   ' Neal Watson
Nov 23, 1929 ' Sept 1, 1935

1 Unmarked grave.

HEAVNER
Clarence O. Heavner
Mar 13, 1888
Jun 25, 1914

1 Unmarked grave

HAVNER
C. L. Havner
Born Feb 16, 1866
Died Feb 13, 1909

2 Unmarked graves

THOMAS
Infant Son of Mr. & Mrs.
R. A. Thomas
Jan 16, 1909
Jan 16, 1909

KIRBY
Baby Ruth, dau. of W. L.
& L. T. Kirby
Born Dec 16, 1906
Died June 5, 1909
Budded on earth
to bloom in heaven.

Lulu T. Kirby
Born in 1868
  MOTHER
Willis London Kirby
Born 1862
Died Jan 5, 1909
  FATHER
  --

KEY
Ida Key
Oct 10, 1866
D.L. Key
Dec 25, 1859
Mar 6, 1926
 Gone but not forgotten.

(Lot begins)
  KEY
Sue F. Key ' John P. Key
Mar 12, 1861' Feb 11, 1855
Sept 15, 1917' Feb 19, 1936

Madison County
(Brown's Church Cemetery p.34)

KEY
Veola E. Key
Mar 7, 1884
Mar 6, 1909

Lula May Key
Aug 19, 1881
May 29, 1883
Buried in William Pearson
Family Burying Ground
near Claybrook, Tenn.

Mary Frances Key
1914 - 1924

Wilma Hicks Key
1892 - 1925
(Lot ends)

3 Unmarked graves.

WALLACE
Florence, Wife of
T. A. Wallace
1882-1924

Lottie
 1917
 L. W.

LOVE
Mary E., Wife of Sam Love
June 12, 1923.

Lottie Love
Born Oct 4, 1889
Died Mar 25, 1909

(Lot begins)
REID
Thomas A.,
Feb 6, 1839 - Feb 15, 1925
REID
Lena V., his wife
June 6, 1846
Apr 10, 1909

1 Unmarked grave.
(Lot ends)

BOREN
Edgar F.
Oct 25, 1871
June 27, 1910   (lot)

Little Edgar
1910 - 1915
 Our darling

Hattie Boren
1883 - 1919
MOTHER
        ---   (Lot ends)

1 Unmarked grave

HASKINS
J. R. Haskins
Nov 1, 1877
Feb 5, 1933
 At Rest

Ollie M., Wife of
J. R. Haskins
Jan 6, 1885
Apr 24, 1911
 At Rest

Baby Boy of J. R.
& O. M. Haskins
Born & Died Apr 16, 1911

PUCKETT
FATHER
Samuel Witt Puckett
1844-1907
MOTHER
Judith Howard Lowry
1846 - 1934

4 Unmarked graves

ANDERSON
Bulah C. Anderson
Oct 18, 1915
Sept 5, 1916
 Our Darling

2 Unmarked graves

Madison County
(Brown's Church Cemetery p.35)

MORGAN
DADDY
W.C. Morgan
Oct 15, 1884
Feb 13, 1933

HUDSON
Estelle Hudson
Love made us one
MOTHER

WEEKS
Will D. Weeks ' Dellia, his wife
Sept 27, 1881 ' Mar 27, 1881
Nov 4, 1918 ' Jan 11, 1920
   Sweet be thy slumbers

2 Unmarked graves

DOUGLASS
Seaborn B. Douglass
May 9, 1864
Mar 11, 1912
In life beloved,
In death lamented.

BRANCH
Jos. J. Branch   (Soldier)
     Co. F.
  7 Tenn. Cav.

1 Unmarked grave

DRUMMOND
Josephene, dau. of
W.H. & Ethel Drummond
1909 - 1909

WALKER
J. Walker
1882 - 1920
Grace, dau. of J.W.
& Hattie Walker
July 25, 1905
May 2, 1910

5 Unmarked graves.

BRANCH
Dorothy B., Dau. of Felix
& Mattie Branch
Nov 11, 1912 - Nov 18, 1914.

WEAKS
Wm. Richard, Son of W.H. & N. Weaks
Nov 8-1913 - Nov 18, 1915.

JONES
J.H. Jones   ' A. M. his wife
Oct 8, 1848 ' Mar 12, 1846
July 1, 1921' Aug 5, 1924
   Gone but not forgotten.

One Unmarked grave.

ANDERSON
MOTHER
Mary A. Anderson
1885 - 1913
Loves last tribute
   MARY

RICE
Mary Ethel, Wife of J.P. Rice
Jan 3, 1887
Nov 21, 1912
Infant dau. of
J. P. & Ethel Rice
Nov 4, 1912 - (no date).

CARL
Our Darling
Jesse Frank, Son of Rev. J.S.
& Lillie Carl
Oct 23, 1911 - Apr 3, 1912

CARL
Dau. Beuna Frances
1914 - 1916
   At Rest

CARL
Rev. J.S. Carl ' Lillie, his wife
1858-1932   ' 1873 - 1922
FATHER   ' MOTHER

1 Unmarked grave

YARBRO
Lizzie A. Yarbro
Born 1884-Died Aug 5, 1918
   At Rest

2 Unmarked graves

WEBB
Elnorah L.   ' Milner P.
Sept 17, 1854' Sep 15, 1856
Dec 17, 1930 ' Feb 3, 1916

HARVEY
W. W. Harvey
1874 - 1916
   At Rest.

Madison County
(Brown's Church Cemetery p.36)

THOMAS
Rev. James Julian Thomas
1868 - 1926
The Lord gave and the
Lord taketh away;
Blessed be the name
of the Lord.

(Lot begins)
KEY
Jesse R. Key
1858 - 1919

KEY
James David
1889 - 1937
(Lot ends)

EWELL
Elennora, Dau. of
C. F. & F.E. Ewell
Mar 28, 1915
June 28, 1915

WINSTON
Mattie   ' J.B.
his wife   ' Mar 4, 1882
Mar 14, 1880 ' July 24, 1930

CHAMBERLIN
G. W. Cgamberlin
July 13, 1850
Oct 28, 1928
Annie, his wife
Jan 10, 1860
Dec 4, 1934.

DUKE
Sarah E.,
 his wife   'N.M.Duke
July 19, 1865'Mar 25, 1865
Mar 14, 1932' (No date)
Clois Newton,'Son of
N. M. & S.E. Duke
Sept 17, 1899
July 24, 1926

WALLER
N.B. Waller
May 12, 1911
Aug 19, 1920

6 Unmarked graves.

HOOTEN
J. S. Hooten & Family
   (5 graves)
            (Lot)

BROWN
Mae Mason ' Ernest M.
1886-19___' 1882 - 1936

SHELTON
Infant Son of J.D.
& Lula M. Shelton
Mar 24, 1926

Delana Ann, dau. of
J. D. & Lula Mae Shelton
Born Nov 1, 1924
Died Nov 7, 1924

BELL
Sergt. Fred T. Bell
1894 - 1918

2 Unmarked graves.

COLE
Laura, Dau. of J.L.
& M. L. Duke,
Wife of C. A. Cole
Dec 29, 1898
Apr 2, 1919
Gone from our home
but not from our hearts.

SIKES
Alice Pauline Sikes
June 17, 1920
Oct 16, 1921

1 Unmarked grave

SIKES
B. J. Sikes
Sept 25, 1882
Nov 9, 1916
     (End of lot)

4 Unmarked graves.

ELAM
Rebecca C., Wife of
J.T. Elam
Aug 18, 1844- Oct 1, 1912.

Madison County
(Brown's Church Cemetery p.37)

ELAM
J. T. Elam
July 29, 1841
May 24, 1924

HOPPER
C.F. Hopper ' Sallie E. Hopper
Oct 3, 1858 ' 1854 - 1937
Feb 4, 1915 '
---

2 Unmarked graves

RONE
John Travis Rone
1900 - 1918

2 Unmarked graves

MC LEARY
Sarah M., dau. of R.E.
& Virginia Mc Leary
1924 - 1926

EDWARD
Margaret. dau. of E.H.
& Mamie Edwards
Oct 18, 1924
June 13, 1925

(Lot)   **MACKEY**
E.W. Mackey ' Nancy, his wife
Dec 6, 1825 ' Aged 65 Years
Sept 10, 1917 '
   Only Sleeping

MOTHER   ' FATHER
Mary J. Mackey ' E.D. Mackey
1867 - 1938 ' 1864 - 1923
               (Lot ends)

1 Unmarked grave.

MASON
Ray W. Mason
1894 - 1927

1 Unmarked grave

STOUT
Callie   ' James A. Stout
His Wife ' 1877 - 1935
1882- 19__ '
   Love made us one.

HALTOM
Joseph N. Haltom
Mar 12, 1858
Nov 4, 1927

1 Unmarked grave

SCRIBNER
Chas. Scribner
1870 - 1932

2 Unmarked graves

BIRDSONG
Sidney L.' Mattie E., his wife
1868-1928' 1873 - 1923
         --   (lot)

EDWARDS
Dan Edwards
June 10, 1875
Nov 4, 1922
 Asleep in Jesus   (lot)

CHEEK
Alice P.
1875 - 1923
   At Rest.   (lot)

MC LEARY
Sarah E.,   ' J.R.
Aug 30, 1860' Mar 15, 1859
Feb 6, 1924' Jan 31, 1933
  MOTHER   ' FATHER

REID
Will D. Reid
Oct 31, 1890
July 14, 1937

4 Unmarked graves.

Madison County
(Brown's Church Cemetery p. 38)

PEARSON
Clarence David, Son
of S. C. & Rose Pearson
Oct 23, 1905
Mar 8, 1920

Bessie Pearson
1908 - 1927

PITT
Milburn J.
Jan 4, 1904
Feb 20, 1923
Our darling one has gone.

1 Unmarked grave

DONNELL
Bluford, Son of
Mr. & Mrs. G. W. Donnell
Oct 19, 1911
Apr 8, 1924

Robert W. Donnell
Aug 5, 1871
Oct 20, 1924

HASKINS (Lot begins)
J. Frank Haskins
1883-1925
Ray, his wife
1898 - 19___

SMITH
Clarence Edward Smith
1897 - 19___
HIS WIFE
Mattie Sue
June 7, 1900
Apr 24, 1926 (End of lot)

COX
Tennie Cox 'Lynn C. Cox
1870 - 19___ '1858 - 1926
Only Sleeping

PURCELL
J. B.
Mar 29, 1886
June 21, 1930

EWELL
M. E. Ewell '
1857 - 1936 ' (Blank)
1 Unmarked grave

WINSLOW
G. G. Winslow
1854 - 1935

EXUM
Charles Clifton Exum
1890 - 1928 ' (Blank)
3 Unmarked graves

BARNES
J. B. Barnes
1871 - 1933

GUNTER
Luna A., Wife of
W. L. Gunter
June 14, 1876
Feb 20, 1908 (End of lot)

2 Unmarked graves.

OLIVE   (lot)
H. I. Olive
(No dates)

1 Unmarked grave

EUBANKS   (lot)
Mary J. Donnell, Wife
of J. D. Eubanks
Apr 13, 1848
May 24, 1924

KERR
Minnie A.   '   A.S.
his wife   ' 1857 - 1927
1862 - 1934 '
  -----
3 Unmarked graves

ROWLAND
FATHER
A. L. Rowland
May 17, 1856
June 10, 1919
    At Rest

DOUGLASS
MOTHER
W. M. Douglass

17 Unmarked graves.

-End-

MADISON COUNTY

TOMBSTONE INSCRIPTIONS
OLD SALEM CEMETERY

This Cemetery, known as "Old Salem" is located on Lexington Street, extended, otherwise known as the Cotton Grove Road. It is two miles north of Jackson, near a very small, comparatively new church which faces East (Denomination unknown)

The oldest part of the burial ground is in back, or southwest of the church. The graves are widely scattered and in dense undergrowth.

Directly south of the church and visible from the road are three recent unmarked graves, and a small wire-fenced enclosure, but without markers or sign of graves remaining.

This cemetery was at one time quite large, which is denoted by the many many sunken places in the earth; graves long vanished. The persons buried here were from prominent families in this county, which makes "Old Salem" a place of interest to residents and historians. M.W.B.
Mary E. Stovall - Mary W. Beatty, Copyists.
April 4, 1938.

GREER

James T. Greer
May 5, 1822
Feb 14, 1859
(Foot-mark)
   J.T.G.

Charles Lafayette Greer
July 30, 1834
Oct 25, 1852
  Aged 23 yrs. 2 mo. 25 days
"None knew him but to love him"
(Foot-mark)
   C.L.G.

SMITH

Miss Mary E. Smith
Jan 18, 1835
July 28, 1854
  19 Y. 6 M. 10 D.
(Inscription illegible)
(Foot-mark)
   M.E.S.

PLEASANT

Pleasant Theodore
Nov 14, 1845
  "In the 8th Year of his age.
(Foot-mark)
   P.L.

PERSON

To the Memory of Lucius, Son
of Benj. R. & Emily E. Person
May 6, 1850
June 6, 1850
(Foot-mark)
   L.

GREER

Pleasant, infant son of
Alexander & Margaret Greer's
Born Nov 3rd 1832
departed this life
July 27, 1833
 "Loving & beloved children
  Your bodies sleep together
  in the dust
  Your spirits mingle before
  his throne".
    P. G.

(Madison County
(Old Salem Cemetery p.2)

GREER

Alexander Greer
Born in Medenburg Co. N. C.
May 21, 1788
died Sept. 9, 1858
  Aged 70 yrs. 5 mo. 18 days
    A. G.

(The two following graves
are covered with concrete
slabs, which bear the
inscriptions. No headstones)

GREER

To The Memory of Margaret I. Greer
who departed this life
January 22nd 1841
in the 43rd year of her age.
    PERSON
To the Memory of
Susan H. Person, who departed this life
Oct. 27, 1842
in the 23 year of her age.

GREER

Camillus P. Greer
Aug 4, 1830
Feb 7, 1859
  C. P. G.

PERSON

Charles Lafayette, Son
of B. R. & Emily E. Person
Mar 18, 1857
May 19, 1859
  Aged 2 yrs. 2 ms. 1 day
    C. L. P.

William Marshall, Son
of B. R. & E. E. Person
June 11, 1855
Nov 21, 1859
  Aged 4 yrs. 5 ms. 10 ds.
    W. M. P.
(This stone is fallen; almost
buried in ground).

(These twelve graves mentioned
above are in one lot,
enclosed in wrought-iron fence.
These next four seem to be an
addition, also fenced in.
We discover that they mark the
resting place of one Adam
Huntsman and three wives).

HUNTSMAN

In Memory of Elizabeth, wife
of Adam Huntsman
Died 7th Jan. 1843
  Aged 33 Years.

In Memory of Sarah W., wife
of Adam Huntsman
Died Oct. 1825
  Aged 33 Years

    Nancy
Third Wife of Adam Huntsman
Born A.D. 1789
Died Dec. 4, 1858
  Aged 69 Years
    N. H.

(The following grave,
obviously the husband by
initials on foot-marker,
has the top of stone con-
taining name broken off,
leaving only dates and
inscription).

Feb 11, 1786
Died Aug 23, 1849
"Blessed are the Merciful
for they shall obtain mercy".
    A. H.

(This completes these
(fenced in lots)

Madison County
(Old Salem Cemetery p.3)

(These next six graves are
grouped together; not enclosed)

BURRUS

In Memory of Thomas Burrus
Born in Sourry County, N. C.
June 23rd, 1791
Died February 28th, 1842.
   Erected by the bereaved Wife Susan Burrus.
       T. B.

SMITH

Mary Alice, Dau. of Cynthia J.& Wm.G.Smith
Dec 16, 1849
Dec 13, 1854
    M. A. S.

WARLICK

In Memory of William Franklin, Son
of Philip & Nancy Warlick
June 22nd, 1830
Oct   5th, 1839.
      W.F.W.

    MOTHER
Nancy, Wife of Philip Warlick
Born in London Co. Va.
Oct 11, 1799
Died in Carrol Co. Tenn.
Dec 19, 1877.
      N. W.

In Memory of Philip Warlick
Born in Lincoln County, N. C.
Nov. 30th, 1791
Died February 4th
   Aged 47 Years 2 months 5 Days
      P. W.

In Memory of David Warlick
Born in Lincoln Cty.,N.C.
Jan 1st, 1800
Died May 14th,1845

(This next grave with one more
monument, appearing very old, only
the base of which is left, completes
this group).

Mc DONALD

This Stone marks the
resting place of
Little Estelle,
Daughter of Maj.J.E.
& Emma C. Mc Donald
Aug. 2, 1860
Nov. 6, 1863
  (This Monument is
   entirely up-rooted,
   leaning against a
   tree.)

JONES

In Memory of
Catherine Revels,Consort
of Timothy P. Jones,
Daughter of Richard
& Sarah Fenner
Born in Franklin County,
N.C. January 6th, 1821
Died April 17th, 1843.
  Member of the
  Episcopal Church.
(This grave and the
next are also covered
with slabs, which were
partly buried and
entirely over-grown.
They are obviously the
only ones left of many
in this group; signs of
a brick wall and sunken
earth show that there
were other graves).

Sacred to the Memory of
    Atlas Jones
January 18th, 1782
November 17th, 1841
  A Native of
  Massachusetts.

(Madison County
(Old Salem Cemetery p.4)

GARRETT

Thomas H. Garrett
1827 - 1900
 and Wife Susan R. Garrett
1835 - 1903
   FATHER
(Next to this large stone lie
two small (about 4' slabs,
joined without writing).
These three graves are in a family
lot about 15' by 20'. It is badly
over-grown but with low wall still
intact).

Sacred to the Memory of Martha J.,
Consort of T. H. Garrett, a daughter of Robert & S. L. Brown
Feb. 12, 1831
June 9, 1858
   Aged 27 years, 3 mos. 16ds.
"Farewell vain world I am going home
 My Savior smiles and bids me come."

Here lies 2 infants of Thomas H.
& M. J. Garrett
"Suffer little children
 to come unto me and forbid them not."

CALDWELL

James Caldwell
Feb. 25, 1776
Mar. 10, 1841

ANDERSON

Gabriel Anderson
Born in Newberry District, S.C.
Feb. 15, 1774
Jan. 19, 1850

HOLT.

Jordan C. Holt
Born in Bedford Co. Tenn.
Dec. 25, 1822
Died in Madison Co. Tenn.
Oct. 8, 1851.

WORD

Elizabeth Word
Born A.D. 1782
Died Apr. 6, 1860
   Aged 78 Years

LOCKARDD

C. V. Lockard
July 1, 1852
Nov. 28, 1852

BROWN

Mary A. Brown, Dau. of
Robert & Susan L. Brown
Sept. 8, 1836
Mar. 13, 1853
"It was an angel that
visited the green earth
and took a flower away"

RAINEY

Martha O. (or D), wife
of W.B. Rainey
May 10, 1814
Mar 29, 1840

PAVATT

Margreth Pavatt
Died Aug 27, 1841
   Aged 57 years

BETTS

Elmina L. Betts
Dec. 9, 1832
Oct 5, A.D. 1835
   Aged 2 Y. 9 M. & 26 D.

ROGERS

In Memory of H. Rogers
Born - 16, 1778 and
Died - 10, 1842
(This stone is almost
(entirely gone; broken in
(half).

(Madison County
(Old Salem Cemetery p.5)

BROWN

Infant dau. of
Robert & Susan L. Brown
Born dead Oct. 13, 1841.
"Budded on earth to bloom in heaven"

George Washington Brown, Son
of Robert & Susan L. Brown
May 14, 1848
July 7, 1848
"Sleep on, sweet babe, and
take thy rest, God called
thee home. He thought it best.
 (They are side by side)

HENDERSON

M. E. Henderson
July 19, 1844
Oct 18, 1920

Markers:
 Mother
 Father
 Brother
 Brother.

(This is a low walled-
in lot, with graves
caved in and overgrown
with trees.
There is a large, modern
monument at one end of
the lot, bearing above
inscription.
Lot about 12' by 20'.

MADISON COUNTY

TOMBSTONE INSCRIPTIONS
TAYLOR'S CEMETERY

Taylor's Cemetery is located about two and one-half miles north of
Jackson, Tennessee, on the Old Medina Road. Some of the most prominent families in Madison County are represented here. Unmarked Graves 15.
Mary E. Stovall - Mary W. Beatty.
May 26, 1938.

CHERRY
Cherry Ann, Wife of D.B.Cherry
Born Oct. 8, 1835
Died July 1, 1884
Farewell, dear Mother
a long farewell, your sorrows
and suffering are o'er - May each
of us live that we'll join you at
last, on the beautiful heavenly
shore.

HICKS
Annie C., dau. of W.A.& M.P.Hicks
Born April 18, 1890
Died April 29, 1895

Infant Son of W.A.& M.P. Hicks
Feb. 4, 1897

William A. Hicks
May 25, 1866
Feb 18, 1911
Blessed are the pure in heart
For they shall see God.

Maggie C.
May 13, 1870
Nov 17, 1927
  - MOTHER -

Marguerite Hicks Lifsey
1907 - 1934

Mark Franklin, Son of J.W.&
N.A.S. Hicks
Born Oct 22, 1871
Died Oct 25, 1885
Weep not Father and Mother for me
For I am waiting in Glory for thee.

HICKS
Jas. W. Hicks
June 28, 1834
June 16, 1916

Annie S., his wife
Jan 5, 1841
Aug 11, 1911

(Enclosed lot begins)

HICKS
James Edgar Hicks
1869 - 1915

James Thomas, Infant Son of
J.E. & Eunie Hicks
Born Oct 17, 1902
Died Nov 28, 1902

In loving remembrance of
Lulu J., Wife of
R.B. Hicks
Died Oct 1, 1888
  Aged 24 yrs.2 mo.14 D's.
A precious one from us has
gone. A voice we love is
stilled. A place is vacant
in our home, that never
can be filled.

God in His wisdom has recalled the boon his love had
given - And though the body
slumbers here, the soul is
safe in heaven.

Madison County
(Taylor's Cemetery p.2)

HICKS
Jimmie B.., Son of R. B.
& Lulu J. Hicks
Born July 29, 1888
Died May 16, 1891

Fannie Jones Hicks, Wife of
Robert B. Hicks
Born Nov 13, 1866
Died Oct 24, 1898

Adelle Hicks
Sept 1, 1898
May 18, 1899

Baby Hicks
Nov 2, 1909

(End of lot)

(Enclosed lot begins)

VANTRESSE
V. C. Vantresse
June 27, 1851
April 15, 1935

Virginia T., his wife
Oct 25, 1852
July 9, 1937

Anna, Wife of
Joseph Longmire
Born Jan 6, 1817
Died Dec 27, 1899

B. R. Smith
Born Sept 29, 1855
Died   (No date)

Alice Longmire, wife of
B. R. Smith
Dec 22, 1856
Nov 22, 1897.

(End of lot)

WYATT
Nelia A., Wife of
J. W. Wyatt
Born Oct 25, 1861
Died Feb 28, 1883

TRICE
Jane Trice
Born April 7, 1826
Died Oct 16, 1888

Edward J. Trice
Born Aug 7, 1817
Died Jan 19, 1885

Nancy J., Dau. of E.J.
& M. J. Trice
Jan 19, 1857
Apr 7, 1877

Mary E., Daughter of
E.J. & M.J. Trice
Born Mar 8, 1855
Died Mar 10, 1875

Laura Virginia, Daughter
of E.J. & M.J. Trice
Born May 7, 1852
Died Nov 20, 1872

Martha Jane, Wife of
E. J. Trice
Born April 7, 1826
Died Oct 13, 1868
Blessed are the dead
which die in the Lord.

Thomas G. Trice
Born Feb 11, 1865
Died Sept 21, 1889
Slowly fading, lingering,
dying, His young life passed
away Heeding not our tears
of anguish Heaven has claim-
ed its own today.

JOHNSTON
Emma Allen Johnston
Died Sept 7, 1882
  5 yrs. 9 mos. 26 D's.

Madison County
(Taylor's Cemetery p.3)

Enclosed lot (begins)

TAYLOR
Hollie Wilson Taylor
1882 - 1912

Nancy A., Wife of Mark Taylor
Born in N. C. July, 1815
Died Feb 28, 1876

Mark Taylor
Born in N. C. Jan 17, 1785
Died July 3, 1862

Richard H. Taylor
Born May 11, 1856
Died May 8, 1877

William Anderson Taylor
1868 - 1914

Tennessee V., Wife of
Wyatt A. Taylor
Born May 8, 1838
  Married July 29, 1858
Died July 27, 1872

Little Ella, Dau. of
W. A. & T. V. Taylor
Born Aug 5, 1862
Died May 18, 1863

Matilda Anderson, Dau. of
W.A. & T. V. Taylor
Born May 15, 1859
Died July 23, 1860
  Aged 1 yr. 2 mo. 7 D's.

Elvira, Wife of W. A. Taylor
Born Dec 12, 1841
Died July 27, 1877

Cliff W., Son of W.A.&E.E.Taylor
Died Mar 13, 1879
  Aged 2 yrs. 7 mo. 26 D's.

Wyatt Adam Taylor ' Mary Emma Taylor
Nov 18, 1834   ' Mar 4, 1846
Nov 20, 1905   ' June 18, 1918.

TAYLOR
J. H. Taylor   ' Fannie, His Wife
1850-19____   ' 1853 - 1909
Though lost to sight
To memory dear.

(End lot)

OUTLAN
John N., Son of J. F.
& W. E. Outlan
Born Dec 10, 1883
Died June 25, 1884

(Begin lot) One Unmarked grave.

YANDELL
Maud H., Wife of
G. T. Yandell
Born Oct 9, 1859
Died Apr 5, 1898

Rebecca H. Taylor, Wife of
J. W. Price
Born Jan 25, 1838
Died June 16, 1877

Maud H. Price, Wife of
Geo. T. Yandell
Born Oct 9, 1859
Died Apr 5, 1898.

Mary E. Price
Born Apr 26, 1855
Died June 4, 1874

Josie R. Price, Wife
of W. R. Myers
Born Apr 10, 1857
Died Nov 19, 1880
  (End of lot)

MOORE
Wm. M. Moore
1868 - 1934

Mattie T., Wife
of W. M. Moore
1866 - 1919

Madison County
(Taylor's Cemetery p.4)

MOORE
Infant dau. of
W. & M. T. Moore
Born & Died July 26, 1893.

Rebecca, his wife
1842 - 1870

S. P. Moore
1840 - 1919

(End of lot)

PAYNE
Lulu Trice Payne
Jan. 27, 1862
Mar 16, 1910
The Lord is my Shepard
I shall not want.

HICKS
John R. Hicks
1830 - 1900

1 Unmarked grave.

James Thomas, Son of
J. R. & E. E. Hicks
Born Mar 3, 1856
Died Sept 14, 1868

Elizabeth E., Wife of
John R. Hicks
Born Mar 18, 1836
Died Feb 28, 1860

HENDERSON
Hugh C. Henderson 'Mary S. Henderson
Born 1800   'Born June 1824
Died Dec 15, 1862 'Died Jan. 15, 1910
    God gave, He took,
    He will restore
    He doeth all things well.

Edgar (Henderson)
1868 - 1869

Catherine Henderson
1847 - 1872
    MOTHER

HENDERSON
W. T. Henderson '   Ida
1844 - 1919 ' 1860-1898
    FATHER   '   MOTHER
        OUR LOVED ONES.

Clyde - Infant
____ (No dates)_____

James W., Husband of
Annie Sue Henderson
Aug 4, 1848
Apr 12, 1917

1 Unmarked grave.

E. L. Wood, Son of J.N.
& T. J. Henderson
Born June 23, 1884
Died Nov 16, 1892.

1 Unmarked grave

LAWRENCE
Swanie Burrus Lawrence
1843 - 1920

Eugenia W., Wife of
S. B. Lawrence
Born June 13, 1852
Died May 27, 1888

Claud H., Son of S. B.
& E.W. Lawrence
Born Nov 30, 1877
Died Mar 6, 1878

Zilphy L., Wife
of S. B. Lawrence
Born Jan 6, 1846
Died June 10, 1871
Adieu to this beautiful earth
It is filled with transient
pleasure. But the good book
tells us that here we can have
no lasting treasure.
I bid adieu to earthly joys
and close my dying eyes, Hoping
that loved ones here will meet
me in paradise.   Z.L.L.

Madison County
(Taylor's Cemetery P.5)

TAYLOR
Josephine H., dau. of
M & N. Taylor
Born Jan 27, 1843
Died Apr 19, 1855

1 Unmarked grave

Elizabeth, Wife of
Henry Taylor
Born in N. C.
  Aged about 62 years.

CLEMENT
C.R. Clement
Born Sept 12, 1812
Died Nov 5, 1883

NEWTON
Mrs. Martha J. Newton
Born Oct 29, 1821
Died Jan 31, 1886

CATHEY
Rebecca A., Wife of
Robt. A. Cathey
Born Mar 29, 1826
  Married Nov 12, 1856.
Died May 16, 1883.

Robert A. Cathey
Born Feb. 26, 1832
Died Mar 21, 1874

Mary B. Cathey
Born Dec 7, 1807
Died Mar 11, 1871

WOOTEN
Annie D., dau. of
W.S. & M. A. Wooten
Born May 23, 1879
Died Jan 19, 1880

CAMPBELL
Mamie H., dau. of R.B.
& E. J. Campbell
Born Jan 22, 1870
Died Sept 5, 1873

One unmarked grave.

HENDERSON
T. J. Henderson
1855 – 1930
FATHER

Mary E., His Wife
1864 – 1932
MOTHER

HOLLAND
Mary, Wife of G. Holland
Born Mar 5, 1812
Died July 27, 1880

Theodosia, dau. of
G. & M. Holland
Born Feb 15, 1857
Died July 7, 1880

ROWLETT
Cora Holland Rowlett
Jan 4, 1878
Oct 8, 1894

PIERCY
Infant Son of W.S.
& M. L. Piercy
Oct 30, 1896
May 30, 1897

Jimmie F., Son of W.S.
& M. L. Piercy
Born Feb 2, 1889
Died Sept 28, 1892
Budded on earth
to bloom in heaven

Lula May, dau. of
W.S. & M.L. Piercy
Born Feb 15, 1887
Died Apr 8, 1888
Too pure for earth
God called her home

Evert G. Pearcy
Soldier Mexican War
Born in Chalam Co. N.C.
Feb 27, 1819
Died Apr 30, 1897
One we loved has passed
away But leaves a hope
behind That he is not
dead but only sleeps And
in heaven we him can find.

Madison County
(Taylor's Cemetery p.6)

Mc KNIGHT
Sallie Ann Mc Knight
Born 1859
Died 1911

LAMB
Ann Eliza Lamb
Born 1874
Died 1911

Clifford Lamb
Born Oct 4, 1902
Died May 5, 1907
A little time on earth he spent
Till God for him his Angels sent.

One unmarked grave.

HENDERSON
Lynn Henderson
Feb 6, 1872
June 15, 1915

BOYKIN
C.M. Boykin
1843 - 1927
   At Rest.

PIERCEY
Robert Lee
Sept 4, 1885
Feb. 18, 1920

Arthur Piercey
Apr 19, 1881
Feb 16, 1909

2 unmarked graves.

ROWLETT
Infant dau. of J. H.
& Lennie Rowlett
Born & died May 10, 1903.

Freeda Alline, dau. of
J.H. & Lennie Rowlett
Born Nov. 20, 1901
Died Jan. 14, 1904.

ROWLETT
Trula Orine, Dau. of J.H.
& Lennie Rowlett
Born Jan 12, 1906
Died July 4, 1906
Gone to be an Angel.

(Lot begins)
ADCOCK
M.T.J. Adcock
Oct 16, 1936
   Aged 74 yrs. 4 m. 10 dys.

Mrs. T.J. Adcock
Sept 12, 1935
   Aged 62 years

Chester Adcock
   American Legion Insignia
(Lot ends)

HOLLAND
Paralee, Wife of
S. L. Holland
Born Mar 6, 1861

S. L., Husband of
Paralee Holland
Born Dec 2, 1854
Died May 6, 1924

HOLLAND
M.L. Holland   ' Mary D.
1843-1917   ' His Wife
             ' 1859-1915
May they rest in peace.

Bruce Holland
1894 - 1910

BAKER
Virginia T., dau. of
H.T. & S.C. Baker
Born Mar 22, 1885
Died Oct 27, 1918
Angels called her away.

Mrs. Sarah Baker
      (No stone)

Madison County
(Taylor's Cemetery p. 7)

BAKER
H. T. Baker
Born Mrc. 27, 1845
Died Dec 19, 1907
A loving husband
Father Dear
A faithful friend
lies buried here.

Infant Son of J. F.
& L. M. Baker
Born & Died Oct 19, 1803.

(Lot begins)
VANDIVER
Ezzell Vandiver
1907 - 1924

Vandiver
John   ' De Etta
1874-1912 ' 1874-1934.
They are gone from our home
but nôt from our hearts.

J. A. Vandiver
1839 - 1923

Martha, His Wife
1840 - 1919

1 unmarked grave.
(End of lot)

GILBERT
MOTHER
Mattie Gilbert, Wife of
W. T. Henderson
1871 - 1936

3 unmarked graves

ROWLETT
Infant Son of W.O.
& E. F. Rowlett
Born & died Oct 17,1909
Gone to be an Angel.

CASE
W. M. Case
1849 - 1927
FATHER

Mary Ellen, his wife
1857 - 1927
MOTHER
 Love's last tribute

Rufus M. Case
Born Oct 19, 1886
Died June 18,1905
    Case.

2 unmarked graves.

John Case
1861 - 1936.

LAMB
Wm. Thomas Lamb
Jan 7, 1878
Jan 8, 1912

Newman Lamb
Born June 24, 1905
Died Sept 26, 1907

HOLLAND
Mary Ellen, Wife of
L. L. Holland
Born Sept 30, 1849
Died Oct. 3, 1902

Mollie J. Holland
Jan 4, 1880
Oct 27,1913

3 unmarked graves

CAMPBELL
E.J. Campbell
Born Feb 8, 1882
Died June 9,1912

Benj.R. Campbell
Born Apr 29, 1918
Died June 13,1903.

Madison County
(Taylor's Cemetery p.8)

HENDERSON
Ruby Katheryn Henderson
Apr 14, 1911
Oct 13, 1929

YONDELL
Edgar Lawrence
Machinist's Mate
2nd Class Co. 93
U.S. Navy
Aug 3, 1894
Jan 18, 1918

MC CONN
William T. Moore,
Son of W. A.
& Zula Z. McConn
Dec 28, 1902
Jan 11, 1903

ADAMSON, Benj. G. (Dr.), 49
ADAMSON, Elizabeth Larkin, 49
ADAMSON, Frederick Wm., 49
ADAMSON, Greenberry, 49
ADAMSON, Susan E., 49
ADAMSON, T. W., 49
ADCOCK, Chester, 118
ADCOCK, M. T. J., 118
ADCOCK, T. J. (Mrs.), 118
AKIN, Buna, 57
AKIN, J. M., 57
ALDERSON, Annie J., 36
ALDERSON, Ida, 36
ALDERSON, Mary A., 36
ALDERSON, T. B., 36
ALDERSON, Wm. C., 36
ALDRIDGE, A. D., 96
ALDRIDGE, Carline, 96
ALDRIDGE, Dora L., 95
ALDRIDGE, Eliza Ann, 95
ALDRIDGE, O. D., 96
ALDRIDGE, Will, 95
ALDRIDGE, infant, 96
ALEXANDER, Annie Kell, 9
ALEXANDER, Carris (f), 9
ALEXANDER, E., 42
ALEXANDER, E. F., 11
ALEXANDER, Edwin F., 11
ALEXANDER, Elizabeth, 42
ALEXANDER, J. F., 11
ALEXANDER, J. P., 9
ALEXANDER, L. J., 42
ALEXANDER, Mary Hughes, 42
ALEXANDER, Nannie, 9
ALEXANDER, Thos. N., 11
ALEXANDER, W. F., 42
ALEXANDER, W. F. jr., 42
ALEXANDER, W. H., 42
ALEXANDER, W. M. (Capt.), 42
ALLEN, Annie Dixon, 64
ALLEN, Bessie, 1
ALLEN, George, 1
ALLEN, Hamner, 1
ALLEN, Jas. C., 97
ALLEN, Jennie Croom, 97
ALLEN, Katy Lucile, 99
ALLEN, Leila J., 99
ALLEN, Luther, 99
ALLEN, Mary Lou, 97
ALLEN, Morten, 97
ALLEN, Robert B., 18
ALLEN, Robert Jackson, 1
ALLISON, R. A., 35
ALLRIDGE, B. R., 87
ALLRIDGE, Ernest, 87
ALLRIDGE, H. C. (m), 88
ALLRIDGE, Rebecca Ann, 87
ALLRIDGE, Sally C., 87
ALLRIDGE, T., 87
ALLRIDGE, Tennie, 88
ALLRIDGE, Thomas, 87
ALSTON, John R., 55
ALSTON, Ross Belle, 55
AMIS, J. T., 6

AMIS, J. T. (m), 6
AMIS, Sue Noel, 6
ANDERSON, Benjamin Letcher, 14
ANDERSON, Bulah C., 103
ANDERSON, Charlie, 73
ANDERSON, Cora Belle, 21
ANDERSON, Ella Dunaway, 14
ANDERSON, Ellen, 15
ANDERSON, Ellen Bond, 15
ANDERSON, Ellen D., 14
ANDERSON, Elmer B., 73
ANDERSON, Emma Burdette, 58
ANDERSON, F. C., 73
ANDERSON, Flora C., 73
ANDERSON, Gabriel, 111
ANDERSON, Gilbert Christian, C.S.A., 18
ANDERSON, H. I.?, 73
ANDERSON, Hu C., 15
ANDERSON, Hugh, 58
ANDERSON, Hugh C., 58
ANDERSON, Ida, 74
ANDERSON, Isabella Christian, 18
ANDERSON, J. J. (m), 72
ANDERSON, J. W. (m), 73
ANDERSON, James E., 75
ANDERSON, James R., 75
ANDERSON, James W., 14
ANDERSON, Jane T., 72
ANDERSON, Jas. W., 14
ANDERSON, Lena B., 73
ANDERSON, Lena M., 58
ANDERSON, Lillie M., 72
ANDERSON, Lizzie, 73
ANDERSON, Lucy A., 71
ANDERSON, M. F., 76
ANDERSON, Mahola Wisdom, 14
ANDERSON, Martha, 18
ANDERSON, Mary A., 104
ANDERSON, Mary Walstrum, 50
ANDERSON, Matilda W., 72
ANDERSON, Minnie C., 22
ANDERSON, Minnie Maud, 73
ANDERSON, N., 75
ANDERSON, Nancy, 59
ANDERSON, R. D. (m), 50
ANDERSON, Ralph Burgan, 30
ANDERSON, Robert, 73
ANDERSON, Robert Henry, 18
ANDERSON, Rogelia E., 14
ANDERSON, S. C., 76
ANDERSON, S. G., 75
ANDERSON, S. H., 72
ANDERSON, S. H., 73
ANDERSON, T.? H., 72
ANDERSON, V. H. (f), 75
ANDERSON, Virgie L., 75
ANDERSON, Virginia H., 75
ANDERSON, W. T. (m), 71
ANDERSON, Wm. L., 59
ANDERSON, Wm. T., 14
ANDERSON, infant (f), 76

ANDERSON?, Little Lena, 58
ANDERSON?, twins, 73
ANDREWS, A. G. (Dr.), 102
ANDREWS, Mary E., 102
ANDREWS, Thos. A., 3
ANGEL, Geo., 44
ARRINGTON, John, DDS, 50
ARRINGTON, Sallie H., 50
BAILEY, L. B., 39
BAINHILL, Caroline, 9
BAINHILL, W. A. (m), 9
BAIRD, Louanna M., 3
BAIRD, R. L., 3
BAKER, Caroline, 47
BAKER, Caroline, 47
BAKER, Chris, 47
BAKER, Chris Lawrence, 47
BAKER, Ellen, 18
BAKER, Fannie, 47
BAKER, H. T., 118
BAKER, H. T., 119
BAKER, J. F., 119
BAKER, Jacob, 47
BAKER, John (Col.), 62
BAKER, L. M., 119
BAKER, Louis, 18
BAKER, Martha, 62
BAKER, S. C., 118
BAKER, Sarah (Mrs.), 118
BAKER, Virginia T., 118
BALCH, Annie, 14
BALCH, Annie, 15
BALCH, Annie Fay, 14
BALCH, David L., 4
BALCH, Eliza P., 4
BALCH, J. P. (m), 14
BALCH, J. P. (m), 15
BALCH, John P., 47
BALCH, Richard L., 4
BALCH, Terrell Bond, 15
BALLEW, Joseph, 47
BALLEW, Martha, 47
BALLEW, Paralee, 47
BANKS, Ann, 79
BANKS, Robt., 94
BARBER, John Taylor jr., 10
BARKER, Fannie, 84
BARKER, Frank, 77
BARKER, Susan, 77
BARKER, W. R. (m), 84
BARNES, Annie A. Martin, 26
BARNES, J. B., 107
BARNES, Laurel, 77
BARNES, T. J. (m), 77
BARNES, W. H. (m), 26
BARNETT, S. D., 50
BARR, Father, 31
BARR, Mother, 31
BATES, Charles Tappen, 32
BATES, Pattie L., 32
BATES, Sister, 32
BAXTER, J. T., 12
BAXTER, M., 12
BAXTER, Sammie, 12
BEAL, Bessie, 32
BEAL, Walter, 32
BEAL, Walter Henry, 32

BEARD, Susan, 66
BEARD, Thomas, 66
BEATTY, Lee, 47
BEATTY, Lucy, 47
BEATTY, Rachel, 47
BEATTY, Sophie G., 11
BECK, Clara, 40
BECK, John J., 40
BECK, Wilhelmine, 40
BELL, Delia M., 13
BELL, Fred T. (Sgt.), 105
BELL, James C., 33
BELL, Mattie D., 33
BENTON, Isaac O., 42
BENTON, Willie B., 42
BENZ, Chas. C., 30
BENZ, E., 30
BENZ, Edward, 30
BENZ, I., 30
BENZ, Isabella, 30
BESSENBURG, D. F. (Mrs.), 62
BESSENBURG, Lottis (f), 62
BESSENBURG, Mary Stoddard, 62
BESSENBURG, Thomas E., 62
BEST, Mabel Ella, 31
BEST, Myron Ira, 30
BEST, Myrtle Irene, 31
BETTS, C. T., 80
BETTS, Catharine T., 80
BETTS, E. M., 80
BETTS, Elmina L., 111
BETTS, Ruth, 80
BETTS, Thomas A., 80
BEVERIDGE, Amanda, 25
BEVERIDGE, Ann W., 25
BEVERIDGE, J. T. (m), 25
BEVERIDGE, Thos., 25
BIGLOW, Elijah L., 69
BIGLOW, Maria A., 69
BIRDSONG, Mattie E., 106
BIRDSONG, Sidney L. (m), 106
BISHOP, Polk, 52
BIVENS, Nathaniel N., 39
BLACK, Bessie, 45
BLACK, Lewis, 45
BLACK, Mary Janice, 45
BLACKARD, Lella Wade Utly, 13
BLACKARD, W. T. (m), 13
BLACKARD, Warner McCoy, 23
BLACKARD, Willie P., 14
BLACKARD, Wm. Thomas, 13
BLACKMON, B., 70
BLACKMON, B., 84
BLACKMON, B. (Rev.), 85
BLACKMON, B. F., 85
BLACKMON, B. F. (m), 102
BLACKMON, B. T., 85
BLACKMON, Benj. F. (Rev.), 85
BLACKMON, Burrell, 70
BLACKMON, Charlie B., 71
BLACKMON, E. F. (f), 84
BLACKMON, Eliza F., 85
BLACKMON, Eliza F., 85

Index to Madison Co. Tennessee Tombstones

BLACKMON, Eliza Frances, 85
BLACKMON, Eliza L., 84
BLACKMON, Elizabeth, 84
BLACKMON, Elizabeth, 84
BLACKMON, Ernest, 85
BLACKMON, Fannie, 71
BLACKMON, Fordham, 84
BLACKMON, Freddie, 92
BLACKMON, Harry, 92
BLACKMON, I. F., 102
BLACKMON, J. D. (m), 83
BLACKMON, J. R., 82
BLACKMON, J. W., 83
BLACKMON, James (Rev.), 82
BLACKMON, James T., 85
BLACKMON, James W., 83
BLACKMON, Jno., 84
BLACKMON, Jno., 85
BLACKMON, John, 85
BLACKMON, John A. jr., 92
BLACKMON, John Ashbury (Dr.), 92
BLACKMON, John C., 84
BLACKMON, John J., 74
BLACKMON, Leithy M., 102
BLACKMON, Lenna V., 71
BLACKMON, Lula May, 92
BLACKMON, M. E., 84
BLACKMON, M. L., 82
BLACKMON, M. T., 85
BLACKMON, Margaret, 84
BLACKMON, Margarete, 75
BLACKMON, Martha Frances, 74
BLACKMON, Martha H., 84
BLACKMON, Martha R., 84
BLACKMON, Mary Anna Belle, 85
BLACKMON, Mary E., 70
BLACKMON, Mary M., 84
BLACKMON, N. E., 83
BLACKMON, Nannie E., 83
BLACKMON, Nelle, 92
BLACKMON, Ora B., 85
BLACKMON, Ora Cleveland, 74
BLACKMON, Pearce, 85
BLACKMON, Robert J., 84
BLACKMON, Roy, 101
BLACKMON, Thomas J., 84
BLACKMON, W. F. (m), 102
BLACKMON, Walter Prentiss, 92
BLACKMON, Wm., 84
BLACKMON, Wm., 84
BLACKMON, infant, 84
BLACKMON, infant, 84
BLACKMON, infant, 84
BLACKMON, infant (f), 84
BLACKMON, three infants, 92
BLAIR, John B., 11
BLAIR, Mary J., 10
BLAKE, N. O. (Rev.), 56
BLAKEMORE, E. C., 91
BLAKEMORE, Eliza Richards, 91
BLAKEMORE, Russell K., 91

BLAKEMORE, T. L., 91
BLAKEMORE, Thomas Luther, 91
BLEDSOE, Elizabeth H., 63
BLEDSOE, George, 46
BLEDSOE, H. M., 46
BLEDSOE, Horace, 63
BLEDSOE, Horace G., 63
BLEDSOE, Jeff D., 1
BLEDSOE, Lelia May, 1
BLEDSOE, M. M., 1
BLEDSOE, Minna L., 1
BLEDSOE, S. E. (f), 46
BLEDSOE, Susan, 46
BLOUNT, Richard, 36
BLOUNT?, John Jacob, 36
BLOUNT?, Mary Louisa, 36
BOBBITT, Elizabeth, 86
BOBBITT, Z. L., 85
BOBBITT, Z. L. (m), 86
BOGUE, Catherine R., 41
BOND, B. F., 47
BOND, C. G., 16
BOND, Chas. A., 24
BOND, Chester G., 16
BOND, Ellen, 15
BOND, Etta, 28
BOND, F. E., 28
BOND, Infant (m), 16
BOND, Jas. P., 4
BOND, John D., 24
BOND, K. J., 16
BOND, Katherine J. Royster, 16
BOND, Mary Cartmell, 24
BOND, Mary Jane, 16
BOND, Nannie Jane, 49
BOND, Nell B., 16
BOND, R. H., 16
BOND, R. W., 47
BOND, Sampson Royster, 16
BOND, Sarah, 47
BOND, Sidney S., 49
BOND, Theo., 4
BOND, ____, 49
BONNER, Michael F., 9
BOON, Elisa Ann, 17
BOON, J. W., 60
BOON, Maggie Louise, 60
BOON, Mary E., 60
BOON, Mary Lou, 60
BOON, Robert Reese, 60
BOON, Sion W., 60
BOONE, C. F. (m), 95
BOONE, Elizabeth L., 95
BOONE, J. B. (m), 95
BOONE, M. E. (f), 95
BOREN, Dora A., 87
BOREN, Edgar F., 103
BOREN, Fausta R., 88
BOREN, H. J. (m), 87
BOREN, Hattie, 103
BOREN, J. F., 89
BOREN, J. W. (m), 89
BOREN, Jennie, 88
BOREN, M. J., 87
BOREN, Martha J., 87
BOREN, W. A., 89

BOREN, W. A. (m), 88
BOREN, little Edgar, 103
BOSTICK, Phie Chester (f), 32
BOSTICK, Richard H., 32
BOTTS, John T., 7
BOTTS, Lyda T., 7
BOWEN, Menard Kennerly, 53
BOYCE, Jennie, 13
BOYCE, Joshua, 59
BOYCE, Martha, 59
BOYCE, Mary, 13
BOYD, C. A., 41
BOYD, J. W., 41
BOYD, Lew Morgan (f), 41
BOYD, Milton B., 26
BOYKIN, C. M., 118
BRADBERRY, Elise Mary, 6
BRADBERRY, Mary, 6
BRADBERRY, W. D. (m), 6
BRADFORD, Dorthala, 36
BRADLY, Kate, 20
BRADLY, W. M. (m), 20
BRADY, R.?, 71
BRANCH, Dorothy B., 104
BRANCH, Felix, 104
BRANCH, Jos. J., 104
BRANCH, Mattie, 104
BRANNER, Rachael, 9
BRAY, W. C., 55
BREWER, Wm. Allen, 92
BRIGGS, E. E., 9
BRIGGS, I. H., 32
BRIGGS, J. W., 32
BRIGGS, R. A., 32
BRIGGS, Sarah Bell, 55
BRIGHAM, Tabitha, 6
BRIGHT, James Eaton, 54
BRIGHT, Josephine Saunders, 54
BRITTLE, James M., 44
BRITTLE, Minnie C., 44
BROAD, George, 2
BROAD, Mary Jane, 2
BROOKS, Addie, 54
BROOKS, Charles G., 60
BROOKS, J. J. (Gen.), 7
BROOKS, Jno. (Rev.), 54
BROOKS, Julian Marcus, 40
BROOKS, Laura, 55
BROOKS, Loretta W., 7
BROOKS, Louis J., 55
BROOKS, Lucinda, 66
BROOKS, Mary Louise, 55
BROOKS, Sarah Acton, 54
BROOKS, W. A., 40
BROOKS, infant (f), 40
BROSIUS, G. N., 57
BROWN, A. T., 79
BROWN, A. T. (m), 79
BROWN, Adam, 88
BROWN, Alex I., 61
BROWN, Ann, 80
BROWN, Ann Banks, 79
BROWN, Aquilla, 88
BROWN, Benjamin H., 17
BROWN, Caroline M., 79
BROWN, E. A., 79

BROWN, Elisha H. G., 58
BROWN, Elisha W., 58
BROWN, Elizabeth, 48
BROWN, Ernest M., 105
BROWN, Geo. Washington, 112
BROWN, Hays, 23
BROWN, Hervy, 61
BROWN, J. W. (m), 82
BROWN, James, 35
BROWN, Jas. M., 17
BROWN, Laura Ann, 17
BROWN, Little Fannie, 61
BROWN, Locke, 44
BROWN, M. W. (f), 17
BROWN, Mae Mason, 105
BROWN, Martha J., 111
BROWN, Martha Lenora, 61
BROWN, Mary A., 111
BROWN, Mary S., 58
BROWN, Mary S., 80
BROWN, Mary W., 17
BROWN, Matilda, 24
BROWN, Milton, 61
BROWN, Milton, 61
BROWN, Milton I., 61
BROWN, Nancy R., 82
BROWN, Ora L., 48
BROWN, R. C., 48
BROWN, R. F. (m), 80
BROWN, Robert, 111
BROWN, Robert, 111
BROWN, Robert, 112
BROWN, Robert, 58
BROWN, Robert, 58
BROWN, Robert F., 48
BROWN, S. L., 111
BROWN, Samuel E., 24
BROWN, Sarah Ann, 80
BROWN, Sarah E., 61
BROWN, Sarah F., 61
BROWN, Sarah R., 48
BROWN, Susan L., 111
BROWN, Susan L., 112
BROWN, Susan L., 58
BROWN, Susana, 58
BROWN, Wm. Stoddert, 61
BROWN, ____ (f), 35
BROWN, infant (f), 112
BROWN?, J. T.?, 82
BROWN?, T. E., 82
BROWN?, Wilmur (baby), 82
BUCHANAN, James Wilson, 70
BUDDKE, I. W. (Dr.), 65
BUDDKE, Janie Porter, 65
BUFORD, John W. sr. (CSA), 31
BUMPAS, Alexander, 96
BUMPAS, W. J. (CSA), 88
BUNTIN, Mary Holm, 13
BUNTIN, Will, 13
BURGE, J. T., 45
BURGESS, Martha Elizabeth, 35
BURKETT, J. W. N., 14
BURKETT, John Robbins, 14
BURNSBY, F., 80
BURNSBY, J., 80
BURNSBY, S. F. (f), 80
BURRUS, S. (f), 76

BURRUS, S. (m), 76
BURRUS, Susan, 110
BURRUS, Thomas, 110
BURRUS, Thomas, 76
BUSH, Bevly? (m), 85
BUSH, Emma, 2
BUSH, Nancy C., 85
BUTLER, Armeta Paralee, 69a
BUTLER, Eugenia B., 29
BUTLER, Mary B., 69a
BUTLER, Thos., 29
BUTLER, Wm. E. jr. (Capt. CSA), 20
BUTLER, Wm. H., 44
BUTLER, Wm. Henry, 69a
BUTLER, Wm. Ormond, 69
CALDWELL, Dan G., 11
CALDWELL, Fannie M., 52
CALDWELL, Fannie Taylor, 53
CALDWELL, James, 111
CALDWELL, Lella R., 11
CALDWELL, M. W., 42
CALDWELL, R. D., 52
CALDWELL, Richie Donnell (Mrs.), 52
CALDWELL, Robert Samuel, 52
CALDWELL, S. C. (Rev.), 53
CALDWELL, Thos. Lyndon, 52
CALDWELL, W. A., 52
CALDWELL, Wm. Addison, 52
CALLAHAN, Catherine P., 18
CALLAHAN, Franklin G., 67
CALLAHAN, Jessie B., 67
CALLAHAN, P. C. (m), 18
CALLAWAY, E. M. (f), 60
CALLAWAY, James Hubbard, 60
CALLAWAY, John, 60
CALLAWAY, Mattie, 60
CALLAWAY, Wm. S., 60
CAMERON, Don, 26
CAMERON, Margaret, 26
CAMERSON, Emma, 31
CAMPBELL, A. D., 35
CAMPBELL, A. M., 35
CAMPBELL, A. W., 35
CAMPBELL, A. W. (Gen.), 64
CAMPBELL, A. W. jr., 64
CAMPBELL, Alex W., 64
CAMPBELL, Alexander, 35
CAMPBELL, Allen, 16
CAMPBELL, Allen jr., 16
CAMPBELL, Ann D., 66
CAMPBELL, Anne Delesseline, 66
CAMPBELL, Annie Allen, 35
CAMPBELL, Annie D., 34
CAMPBELL, Annie Dixon, 64
CAMPBELL, Benj. R., 119
CAMPBELL, C. D. N., 29
CAMPBELL, E. J., 117
CAMPBELL, E. J., 119
CAMPBELL, E. S. (Dr.), 66
CAMPBELL, Eliza L. Theus, 66
CAMPBELL, Eliza Lenud, 66
CAMPBELL, Elizabeth, 44
CAMPBELL, Emma A., 35

CAMPBELL, Frances Watkins, 20
CAMPBELL, Jane Eliza, 35
CAMPBELL, Jeanette, 20
CAMPBELL, Jennie E., 2
CAMPBELL, John W., 34
CAMPBELL, John W., 35
CAMPBELL, Katherine, 35
CAMPBELL, Louisa A., 64
CAMPBELL, Maj. William, 65
CAMPBELL, Mamie H., 117
CAMPBELL, Maria Womack, 20
CAMPBELL, Mary Eunice, 29
CAMPBELL, R. B., 117
CAMPBELL, T. T., 29
CAMPBELL, W. F., 43
CAMPBELL, W. S., 34
CAMPBELL, W. T. (m), 44
CAMPBELL, infant (m), 34
CARL, Beuna Frances, 104
CARL, J. S. (Rev.), 104
CARL, Jesse Frank, 104
CARL, Lillie, 104
CARMACK, John M., 60
CARPENTER, Annie Laura, 61
CARPENTER, Cora P., 69
CARPENTER, J. J. sr., 61
CARPENTER, J. W., 85
CARPENTER, John Collins, 61
CARPENTER, L. C., 85
CARPENTER, Lewis, 61
CARPENTER, Little Arthur, 85
CARPENTER, Maria Taylor, 61
CARPENTER, Sarah Rebecca, 61
CARPENTER, Virginia Louise, 61
CARTER, C. L., 17
CARTER, Elissa May, 5
CARTER, Emma W., 5
CARTER, FAnnie May, 17
CARTER, Floyd S., 5
CARTER, Iona C., 45
CARTER, J. G. (m), 5
CARTER, Lenora L., 45
CARTER, M. G., 5
CARTER, M. N., 17
CARTER, Margarette, 5
CARTER, Mary A., 6
CARTER, Sallie E., 3
CARTER, T. J., 45
CARTMELL, Fannie Augusta, 52
CARTMELL, J. M., 52
CARTMELL, Jemima, 34
CARTMELL, Jemima A. Sharp, 34
CARTMELL, Lizzie, 34
CARTMELL, M. J., 34
CARTMELL, M. J., 34
CARTMELL, Margaret, 34
CARTMELL, Margaret Helen, 34
CARTMELL, Martin, 34
CARTMELL, Martin, 34
CARTMELL, Mary, 24

CARTMELL, Mary Jane, 34
CARTMELL, Mary Lou, 52
CARTMELL, R. H., 34
CARTMELL, Robert H., 34
CARTMELL, Sarah Dean, 34
CARTMELL, Sophia R., 52
CARTMELL, Wm. E., 34
CARTMELL, infant (m), 34
CARTMELL, infant (m), 34
CARTMELL, infant (m), 34
CARUTHERS, Ella Brown, 61
CARUTHERS, Frances A., 64
CARUTHERS, Frances Alice, 63
CARUTHERS, Frances E., 63
CARUTHERS, Frances Eliza McCorry, 63
CARUTHERS, J. A. (m), 63
CARUTHERS, James, 63
CARUTHERS, James, 64
CARUTHERS, James jr., 65
CARUTHERS, Laura E., 63
CARUTHERS, M. J., 63
CARUTHERS, Penelope Marie, 64
CARUTHERS, Sallie Parker, 66
CARUTHERS, Stoddert, 61
CARUTHERS, Susan M., 64
CARUTHERS, Susan Medora, 65
CARUTHERS, T. J., 63
CARUTHERS, Thomas, 63
CARUTHERS, Thomas, 63
CARUTHERS, Virginia, 63
CARUTHERS, Wm., 63
CARUTHERS, Wm., 65
CASE, John, 119
CASE, Mary Ellen, 119
CASE, Rufus M., 119
CASE, W. M., 119
CASON, Joe (Dr.), 16
CASON, Nell Spencer, 16
CASON, Thos. D., 23
CATES, SAllie B., 42
CATHEY, Addie L., 46
CATHEY, Ella D., 58
CATHEY, Mary B., 117
CATHEY, Rebecca A., 117
CATHEY, Robt. A., 117
CAVINESS, John T., 9
CEMETERY, Riverside, 1
CHAMBERLIN, Annie, 105
CHAMBERLIN, G. W. (m), 105
CHAMBERS, Croatie, 93
CHAMBERS, W. B. (m), 93
CHANDLER, Belle, 49
CHANDLER, C. A., 49
CHANDLER, Clara, 49
CHANDLER, Edgar, 49
CHANDLER, Edgar, 49
CHAPPEL, Martha, 23
CHAPPELL, A., 23
CHAPPELL, Bettie, 23
CHAPPELL, J. G., 23
CHAPPELL, Joel R., 22
CHAPPELL, Mary Frances, 16
CHAPPELL, Wm. Henry, 16
CHEEK, A. J., 90

CHEEK, A. P., 93
CHEEK, Alice P., 106
CHEEK, Bettie, 90
CHEEK, George Millard, 93
CHEEK, Ida May, 93
CHEEK, J. A., 90
CHEEK, J. E., 93
CHERRY, Cherry Ann, 113
CHERRY, D. B. (m), 113
CHESTER, 3 infants of Dr. John, 32
CHESTER, Ella Ragland, 35
CHESTER, James W., 54
CHESTER, Jessie L., 17
CHESTER, John (Dr.), 32
CHESTER, Laura Oconnor, 41
CHESTER, Margaret H., 16
CHESTER, Mary J. Long, 16
CHESTER, Mary R., 54
CHESTER, Nora, 42
CHESTER, R. H., 16
CHESTER, Richard, 35
CHESTER, Rob I., 41
CHESTER, Robert I., 17
CHESTER, Robert I. jr., 32
CHESTER, S. H. (Dr.), 35
CHESTER, Sally, 16
CHESTER, W. B. (m), 42
CHESTER, W. L. (M.D.), 16
CHESTER, Wm. A., 35
CHESTER, Wm. Butler (Capt.), 41
CHESTER, infant (f), 42
CHESTER?, J. P. (surname abbreviated), 41
CHILDRESS, John B., 72
CHILDS, Amoziah, Esq., 69
CHILDS, J. G., 53
CHILDS, Mary Ann, 69
CHILDS, Sallie, 53
CHILDS, Virgie, 53
CHRISTIAN, Ellen M. (Mrs.), 18
CHRISTIAN, G. L., 19
CHRISTIAN, G. L. (m), 18
CISCO, Bertie, 38
CISCO, Georgie Pursley, 38
CISCO, J. G., 38
CLARK, Annie Land, 73
CLARK, Calvin, 37
CLARK, Charles, 36
CLARK, E. A. (Maj.), 72
CLARK, E. A. (m), 72
CLARK, Edward P., 37
CLARK, Elizabeth Patterson, 37
CLARK, Frances B., 37
CLARK, John F., 73
CLARK, John H., 36
CLARK, John Harvey, 73
CLARK, Laura, 59
CLARK, Martha Ann, 72
CLARK, Mary E., 73
CLARK, Mary J., 73
CLARK, Sallie, 36
CLARK, Stephen Gray, 41
CLARK, Thomas H., 38
CLARK, Thos., 37

Index to Madison Co. Tennessee Tombstones

CLARK, Thos., 37
CLARK, Thos. P., 37
CLARK?, Will C., 36
CLAYTON, B. T. (m), 30
CLAYTON, H. M., 17
CLAYTON, H. M. (m), 17
CLAYTON, Hamilton M., 17
CLAYTON, Lloyd M., 17
CLAYTON, M. L., 17
CLAYTON, Mary Janes, 30
CLAYTON, Mary L., 17
CLAYTON, R. S., 30
CLAYTON, Rebecca S., 30
CLEMENT, C. R., 117
COBB, Annie T., 69
COBB, J. B., 62
COBB, Lou Emma, 69
COBB, Mabelle, 64
COBB, Mary A. (Mrs.), 62
COBB, R. E. (m), 64
COBB, Robert Edgar jr., 64
COBB, S. J., 69
COBB, W. K. (m), 69
COBB, Wm. K., 64
COBB?, Jo Henry, 64
COBB?, Sallie P., 64
COBB?, Stoddert, 64
COCHRAN, D. (Rev.), 19
COCHRAN, David (Rev.), 19
COCHRAN, John Clark, 40
COCHRAN, John T., 19
COCHRAN, Martha M. (Mrs.), 19
COCK, C. C. (m), 97
COCK, Elenor, 94
COCK, F. C., 94
COCK, F. C., 94
COCK, J. E., 94
COCK, J. L. (m), 98
COCK, J. T. (m), 89
COCK, Kit (f), 94
COCK, M. J. (Mrs.), 98
COCK, M. M. (f), 97
COCK, Orean Collins (m), 94
COCK, Rachel E., 89
COCKRILL, Susan, 40
COCKS, Lottie, 97
COLE, C. A. (m), 105
COLE, J. F. (Dr.), 6
COLE, Laura, 105
COLE, Lonnie, 93
COLE, Nanie D., 24
COLE, Sallie E., 6
COLE, W. R. (Dr.), 5
COLLETT, Mary E., 32
COLLINS, Amelia, 32
COLLINS, Callie Mae, 75
COLLINS, Charles (Capt.), 11
COLLINS, Daisy, 25
COLLINS, Dr. J. W. (wife of), 48
COLLINS, Eliza Ann, 41
COLLINS, Elizabeth Thompson, 48
COLLINS, Fannie L., 75
COLLINS, Fannie Whitfield, 32
COLLINS, J. P., 32

COLLINS, J. W. (Dr.), 48
COLLINS, James A., 11
COLLINS, John E., 75
COLLINS, John J., 75
COLLINS, Judith Ann, 47
COLLINS, Julia A., 75
COLLINS, Landon A., 43
COLLINS, Mary L., 75
COLLINS, Mattie, 43
COLLINS, Oscar F., 48
COLLINS, Samuel, 43
COLLINS, Samuel L., 41
COLLINS, Viola McCabe, 41
COLLINS, Wm. N., 48
CONCORD, Louisa W., 40
CONGER, A., 53
CONGER, Annie C., 53
CONGER, B. J., 53
CONGER, Carrie Lucile, 15
CONGER, Cora C., 53
CONGER, Horace W., 15
CONGER, J. B., 15
CONGER, J. W., 15
CONGER, P. D. W., 53
CONGER, Rowena, 15
CONGER, S. R., 53
CONGER, Virginia S., 15
CONKLIN, Vir. Alexander, 51
CONKLIN, Wm. P., 51
CONLEY, Parilda, 95
CONNALLY, Fanny, 34
CONNALLY, Thomas D., 34
CONNER, Betty, 18
CONNER, Chas. H., 17
CONNER, W. H., 4
COOK, P. D., 12
COOKE, Elizabeth T., 21
COOKSEY, Elizabeth, 68
COOKSEY, J. R., 68
COOKSEY, James, 68
COOPER, J. B., 18
COOPER, Lucille, 18
COOPER, Sarah, 18
COPELAND, Thos., 2
CORRIN, Matilda, 4
COX, Lynn C., 107
COX, Tennie, 107
COZART, Irene, 24
CRABTREE, Mary, 4
CRABTREE, Robert, 4
CRABTREE, Willie Corrin, 4
CRAWFORD, Jennie L., 46
CREEVY, Samuel James, 45
CREGO, Fred Warren, 9
CROOM, I. N., 95
CROOM, Jennie, 97
CROOM, R. C., 95
CROSNOE, Addie, 71
CROSNOE, J. W. (m), 71
CROSNOE, Malinda, 71
CRUTCHER, Percy, 28
CULLEN, J. E., 12
CUMMINGS, Charley, 100
CUMMINGS, F. W. (m), 95
CUMMINGS, J., 100
CUMMINGS, James M., 97
CUMMINGS, M. A., 100

CUMMINGS, M. A., 97
CUMMINGS, M. A. (f), 95
CUMMINGS, W. T., 97
CUNDIFF, G. W., 27
CUNDIFF, Geo. Lea, 27
CUNDIFF, Little Mazie, 27
CUNDIFF, S. A., 27
CUNNINGHAM, May Talbot, 1
CUPPS, Emily Nelson, 97
CURTIS, Charles S., 22
CURTIS, H. H. (m), 22
CURTIS, Horace Horatio, 22
CURTIS, Mary Sybert, 22
DADO, John, 50
DADO, Josephine, 50
DADO, Mary, 50
DALLAM, Aquilla Ann, 88
DALTON, David A., 26
DALTON, Mary W., 45
DALTON, Wm. G., 45
DAMRON, C., 81
DAMRON, Christena D., 81
DAMRON, J. W. (m), 81
DAMRON, M. E., 81
DAMRON, W. F., 81
DAMRON, Wm. F., 81
DANCY, Clifton, 61
DANCY, Sarah Brown, 61
DANNATT, Elizabeth, 48
DANNATT, Henry, 48
DANNATT, Mark, 48
DARR, A. G., 56
DARR, J. M., 56
DARR, Leslie E., 56
DARR, Wm. Hale, 56
DASHIEL, A. T., 34
DASHIEL, Annie Ridgley, 34
DASHIEL, Eliza Jane, 34
DASHIEL, R. R., 34
DASHIEL, Richard Henry, 34
DASHIEL, Richard Ridgly, 34
DAVIDSON, Benjamin, 52
DAVIDSON, Elisabeth, 52
DAVIDSON, S. B., 67
DAVIS, Blanche C., 49
DAVIS, Edie R., 69
DAVIS, Genl. W., 69
DAVIS, L. D., 55
DAVIS, Nathaniel G., 17
DAVIS, Wiley W., 7
DAWSON, Effie M., 12
DAWSON, Eugene R., 12
DAWSON, Margaretta, 12
DAWSON, Mary E., 12
DAWSON, Robert L., 12
DAY, A. D., 35
DAY, Emma, 35
DAY, J. D., 35
DAY, J. M., 100
DAY, Martha Elizabeth Burgess, 35
DAY, Mayme, 1
DAY, Virginia, 21
DEBERRY, Allen, 53
DEBERRY, Ann, 53
DEBERRY, Annie Tarver, 53
DEBERRY, Matthias, 53

DEBERRY, Mattie, 53
DECOURCEY, Frank, 30
DEER, George H., 46
DEGOURGY, Gertrude, 28
DEJARRATT, M. A., 49
DELEISSELINE, Ann, 66
DEMPSTER, Alice, 30
DEMPSTER, G., 30
DEMPSTER, Gilbert, 30
DEMPSTER, James, 30
DEMPSTER, Robert K., 30
DEMPSTER, Robert Kerr, 30
DEVINEYARD, Carl, 33
DICKSON, Milly, 41
DIFFEE, J. L. (m), 4
DIFFEE, Jennie Vieve L., 4
DIXON, Elizabeth, 37
DOAK, Alford Langford, 94
DOAK, Annie, 94
DOAK, C. A. (m), 80
DOAK, Charles, 80
DOAK, Charles Alfred, 94
DOAK, Georgia, 80
DOAK, Georgia Tomlinson, 94
DOAK, Georgie, 80
DOAK, Gibson, 82
DOAK, J., 81
DOAK, J., 82
DOAK, J. A. (m), 94
DOAK, Jane, 82
DOAK, John B., 82
DOAK, Lucile, 80
DOAK, Mary, 80
DOAK, Thomas J., 81
DOAK, W., 81
DOAK, W. (m), 82
DOAK, Wm., 81
DODD, Mary Ann, 59
DODDS, J. Laura, 56
DODDS, Lewis, 56
DODDS, Sarah J., 56
DOLLAHITE, Wm. Edward, 88
DONNELL, Baxter, 100
DONNELL, Birdie, 100
DONNELL, Bluford, 107
DONNELL, G. W. (Mr.), 107
DONNELL, G. W. (Mrs.), 107
DONNELL, Mary J., 107
DONNELL, Robert W., 107
DONNELL, infant (m), 100
DORR, Henry, 80
DOUGLAS, Annie, 77
DOUGLAS, baby, 77
DOUGLASS, Charlie, 94
DOUGLASS, Emma D., 94
DOUGLASS, Idella, 94
DOUGLASS, Lillian Orean, 94
DOUGLASS, Mary C., 94
DOUGLASS, Seaborn B., 104
DOUGLASS, W. M. (f?), 107
DOUGLASS, W. N. (m), 94
DOUGLASS, Willie N., 94
DOUGLASS, infant (m), 94
DRAKE, John Miller, 60
DRAKE, Louisa M., 60
DRAKE, Thomas H., 60
DRUMMOND, Ethel, 104

DRUMMOND, Josephine, 104
DRUMMOND, W. H. (m), 104
DUDLY, A. F., 35
DUGAN, A. S., 45
DUGAN, Ada Shinkle, 45
DUGAN, G. M., 45
DUGAN, George Martin, 45
DUGAN, James M., 45
DUGAN, James Montgomery, 45
DUGAN, Reese Hill, 45
DUGGER, Wm. Arthur, 16
DUKE, Clois Newton, 105
DUKE, J. L., 105
DUKE, John H., 58
DUKE, Laura, 105
DUKE, M. L., 105
DUKE, Madison M., 96
DUKE, N. M., 105
DUKE, Sarah E., 105
DUKE, Susan W., 58
DUNAWAY, Lula, 14
DUNAWAY, Mahuldah, 5
DUNAWAY, R. P. (m), 5
DUNAWAY, Sarah E., 5
DUNAWAY, Wm. E., 14
DUNAWAY, Wm. M. (Rev.), 14
DUNCAN, C. A. (m), 49
DUNCAN, C. C. (m), 49
DUNCAN, Crawford A., 49
DUNCAN, Elizabeth, 49
DUNCAN, Johnie, 68
DUNCAN, L. L., 68
DUNCAN, N. M., 60
DUNCAN, W. R., 68
DUNCAN, son, 68
DUNN, Ateliah, 5
DUNN, Benjamin C., 5
DUNN, Doma P., 6
DUNN, Elmore, 5
DUNN, Lucius C., 5
DUNN, S. M. (m), 6
DUPREE, E. B., 2
DUPREE, Emma Bush, 2
DUPREE, Mamie, 66
DUPREE, T. J. jr., 66
DUPREE, W. D. (Capt.), 2
EAD, John, 33
EARLY, Word (Rev.), 32
EDENTON, Pansy Harris, 37
EDENTON, Vernon, 37
EDRINGTON, Theresa, 23
EDWARDS, A. F. (f), 79
EDWARDS, Ame, 79
EDWARDS, Dan, 106
EDWARDS, E. H. (m), 106
EDWARDS, Eliza, 56
EDWARDS, Jack, 56
EDWARDS, Jas. F., 78
EDWARDS, John D., 56
EDWARDS, Lusannah, 78
EDWARDS, Mamie, 106
EDWARDS, Margaret, 106
EDWARDS, Pope, 56
EDWARDS, S. W., 56
EDWARDS, Sarah, 56
EDWARDS, Susan C., 78
EDWARDS, Wm. F., 79

EDWARDS?, E. E., 56
EDWARDS?, E. F., 56
EDWIN, Charlie, 21
ELAM, J. T. (m), 105
ELAM, J. T. (m), 106
ELAM, Rebecca C., 105
ELDER, Amanda Caroline, 33
ELDER, Benj., 33
ELDER, Eliza A., 33
ELGIN, Albert Joel, 46
ELGIN, Carl, 46
ELGIN, Dorie Oneida, 46
ELGIN, Earl, 46
ELGIN, Emma Laura, 46
ELGIN, Jesse Wells, 46
ELGIN, Joel, 46
ELGIN, Pinckney, 46
ELLINGTON, A. H., 56
ELLINGTON, Nannie P., 56
ELLIS, Edna May, 66
ELLIS, F. E., 66
ELLIS, J. H., 66
ELROD, Brother, 31
ELROD, Brother James, 31
ELROD, Dollie, 29
ELROD, James, 64
ELROD, James L., 29
ELROD, Jas., 29
EMMONS, A. A. (Mrs.), 6
EMMONS, Fannie, 6
EMMONS, John Fenner, 6
EMMONS, T. G., 6
EMMONS, T. J. (m), 6
ENLOE, F. M., 42
EPPERSON, Bettie S., 41
EPPERSON, Elizabeth, 56
EPPERSON, T. N. E. (m), 41
EPPERSON, Thos. N., 41
EPPERSON, Unie, 55
EPPINGER, Joseph H., 53
EPPINGER, Louis, 53
EPPINGER, Rosa Barbara, 53
ESTES, Frances Henry, 13
ESTES, Wm. G., 21
EUBANKS, J. D. (m), 107
EUBANKS, Mary J. Donnell, 107
EVANS, J. H. (Rev.), 65
EVANS, Joseph Dashiel, 65
EVANS, Joseph H., D. D., 3
EVANS, V. M. (f), 65
EWELL, C. F., 105
EWELL, Elennora, 105
EWELL, F. E., 105
EWELL, M. E., 107
EXUM, Charles Clifton, 107
EXUM, F. G. B. (m), 82
EXUM, Felix, 82
EXUM, G. W. T., 83
EXUM, G. W. T. (m), 82
EXUM, John, 96
EXUM, Josephine, 82
EXUM, Lorena, 82
EXUM, Lula, 96
EXUM, Margaret C., 82
EXUM, infant, 82
EXUM, infant, 96

FAIL, Mattie, 30
FAIL, T. A. (m), 30
FAIL, W. T. (m), 30
FARIS, M. B. (Rev.), 9
FARISS, A. (m), 5
FARISS, Bettie A., 5
FARISS, Betty A., 5
FARISS, Daisy Dean, 5
FARISS, T. Thorp, 5
FARISS, Wm. H., 5
FEATHERSTON, T. J., 17
FEATHERSTON, Vida L., 17
FENNER, Catherine Revels, 110
FENNER, Jno. S., 21
FENNER, Martha Day, 21
FENNER, Richard, 110
FENNER, Sarah, 110
FENNER, Virginia Day, 21
FLEMING, Dr., 22
FLEMING, Emma Williams, 28
FLEMING, Fannie E., 22
FLEMING, R. W. (Mrs.), 22
FOGG, G. N. (m), 96
FOGG, Joseph, 81
FOGG, Mary Jane Haltom, 96
FOGG, Mary L., 81
FOGG, T. H. (m), 96
FORD, Robt. Haskins, 25
FOSTER, J. W., 19
FOSTER, M. A., 19
FOSTER, Mary L., 19
FOSTER, Thos. A., 19
FRANCIS, J. E., 67
FRANCIS, T. H., 67
FRANCIS, daughter, 67
FRANKLIN, A. F. (m), 43
FRANKLIN, Phoebe J. Miller, 43
FREEMAN, James, 63
FREEMAN, Jas., 32
FREEMAN, Joseph B., 63
FREEMAN, John W., 60
FREEMAN, Susan A., 32
FREEMAN, Virginia, 63
FRENCH, Albert, 68
FRIAR, Margot, 19
FRILEY, Rebecca, 17
FRYER, Barney M., 19
FULLERTON, M. O., 33
FULMER, Jagoe, 57
FULMER, Maria, 57
FULMER, dau. of Jagoe 2 yrs., 57
FUSSELL, Jas., 72
FUSSELL, Lizzie F., 89
FUSSELL, M. C., 89
FUSSELL, Matilda W., 72
FUSSELL, Nancy, 72
FUSSELL, Ruth, 99
FUSSELL, W. A., 89
GAFFNEY, Nicholis Arthur, 12
GAFFNEY, P. J., 12
GAFFNEY, S. M., 12
GAITHER, H. E., 1
GAITHER, J. T., 65
GAITHER, J. W., 1
GAITHER, Little Billie, 1
GAITHER, Mary E., 69

GALBAUGH, John C., 67
GAMEWELL, Meville F., 32
GAMEWELL, Thos. W., 32
GANNAWAY, Hattie, 28
GARRETT, A. T. (m), 6
GARRETT, Fannie, 71
GARRETT, M. J., 111
GARRETT, Martha J., 111
GARRETT, Nannie, 6
GARRETT, Oma, 71
GARRETT, Robert S., 6
GARRETT, Susan R., 111
GARRETT, Thomas H., 111
GARRETT, Wm. T., 71
GARRETT, infant (m), 71
GARRISON, Elzira, 67
GARRISON, Lavinia, 67
GARRISON, Susan, 67
GARSIDES, Margaret, 62
GARY, John H., 28
GASTON, Alice, 57
GASTON, T. C., 57
GATES, Ann M., 32
GATES, B. F. (m), 21
GATES, Bell, 24
GATES, Benjamin F., 21
GATES, Caledonia Jane Jester, 21
GATES, Callie P., 21
GATES, Carolyn P., 27
GATES, Carrie P., 60
GATES, Edgar A., 21
GATES, Elizabeth J. Roper, 21
GATES, Elizabeth R., 21
GATES, Emma H., 21
GATES, Emma Neill, 3
GATES, Georgia B., 60
GATES, Hewitt P., 27
GATES, Hunter, 3
GATES, James, 21
GATES, John W., 60
GATES, Laura M., 43
GATES, Mary, 27
GATES, Mary C., 21
GATES, Narcisa Newsum, 21
GATES, Norman, 21
GATES, Robert, 21
GATES, Susanah, 27
GATES, Thomas M., 43
GATES, Thos. E., 2
GATES, W. W., 32
GATES, Wm. W., 60
GATES, Wm. Word, 27
GAULDING, C. S., 68
GAUSMAN, Mausoleum?, 9
GAUSMAN, Wagner, 9
GETTY, Daniel Warren, 54
GIBBS, Kate, 83
GIFFEE, Wm. E., 13
GILBERT, J. H., 8
GILBERT, Mattie, 119
GILKINS, Maria, 57
GILL, Samuel H., 14
GILL, Sarah W., 14
GILMORE, Elizabeth Jane, 60
GILMORE, Henry Brown, 60
GILMORE, J. T., 61

GILMORE, John Taylor, 61
GILMORE, John Taylor (Dr.), 60
GILMORE, L. J., 61
GILMORE, Mary, 61
GILMORE, Milton Brown, 60
GLASS, Jack, 58
GLASS, Mother, 34
GLASS, Sadie B., 58
GOFF, John G., 34
GOFORTH, Alsia, 38
GOFORTH, Lee, 38
GOODE, H. C., 3
GOODE, Mina Belle, 4
GOODE, R. F. (m), 3
GOODELL, Fannie A., 59
GOODELL, Laura Clark, 59
GOODELL, Lorenzo, 59
GOODELL, Oren, 59
GOODELL?, infant (f), 59
GOODELL?, infant (m), 59
GOODRICH, E. H., 87
GOODRICH, Ella Lee, 100
GOODRICH, Emily B., 87
GOODRICH, Fannie T., 100
GOODRICH, Harriet Wilson, 76
GOODRICH, I. C., 100
GOODRICH, J. P., 74
GOODRICH, J. W., 100
GOODRICH, Jack, 100
GOODRICH, M. H. (m), 87
GOODRICH, M. M. (Mrs.), 74
GOODRICH, Martha Frances, 74
GOODRICH, Mary E., 87
GOODRICH, Samuel, 9
GOODRICH, Waynick, 100
GOODRICH, infant (m), 100
GOODWIN, Sarah, 68
GORDON, Fannie C., 65
GORDON, Sarah L., 65
GORHAM, Dent, 47
GORHAM, Docia, 47
GORHAM, George, 47
GORHAM, Harry, 47
GOWAN, Bessie, 101
GOWAN, E. E. (m), 101
GOWAN, infant (m), 101
GRAHAM, Belle G., 58
GRAHAM, W. A., 2
GRAHAM, W. A. (m), 58
GRAIL, C. C., 67
GRANT, Emily Etta, 101
GRANT, Lynn, 101
GRANT, M. R., 101
GRAVETTE, Mary Lou, 77
GRAY, Jno. W., 67
GREEN, Ella, 98
GREEN, Lucy M., 37
GREEN, W. E. (m), 37
GREEN, W. G. (Mrs.), 98
GREEN, Wm. G., 98
GREEN, infant (f), 98
GREER, Alexander, 108
GREER, Alexander, 109
GREER, Alice M. Ingram, 31
GREER, Camillus P., 109

GREER, Charles Lafayette, 108
GREER, James T., 108
GREER, John A., 31
GREER, John A., 53
GREER, John A., 53
GREER, Joseph H., 67
GREER, Louisa Ingram, 53
GREER, Margaret, 108
GREER, Margaret I., 109
GREER, Pleasant, 108
GRIPP, Anna B., 42
GRIPP, P. M., 42
GRIZZARD, Charles O., 52
GROVES, Lewis, 66
GUNN, J. S. (m), 8
GUNN, Lou Ellen, 8
GUNTER, Luna A., 107
GUNTER, W. L. (m), 107
GUTHRIE, Andrew, 62
GUTHRIE, Mary A., 62
GUTHRIE, Wm. Henry, 62
HABAWAY, Isabella, 39
HABAWAY, Jas. F., 39
HACKNEY, J. D., 50
HACLITZ, G., 66
HADEWAY, Alice, 59
HADEWAY, John A., 59
HAGGARD, J. W., 36
HAGGARD, M. O., 36
HAGGARD, Mary Lou, 36
HALE, Harriet A., 65
HALE, Harriet A., 65
HALE, Thomas, 65
HALE, Wiley Pope, 65
HALL, A. J. (Rev.), 62
HALL, Frances, 36
HALL, Isaac Taylor, 62
HALL, Martha C., 17
HALL, R. W., 16
HALL, Susan Taylor, 62
HALL, Willie Ewen, 17
HALTOM, Joseph N., 106
HALTOM, Mary Jane, 96
HALTOM, Sara E., 96
HALTOM, Wm. H., 96
HAMILTON, Cora H., 48
HAMILTON, D. H. (f), 15
HAMILTON, Deneta H., 15
HAMILTON, Ethel, 48
HAMILTON, F. B. (Dr.), 15
HAMILTON, F. H. (Dr.), 15
HAMILTON, Frank B. jr., 3
HAMILTON, Frank B. sr., 3
HAMILTON, Geo. D., 3
HAMILTON, Little Florence, 15
HAMILTON, Robert T., 48
HAMILTON, Wm. W., 3
HAMLINE, Charles William, 59
HAMMERLY, Ada F., 16
HAMMERLY, Henry, 16
HAMMERLY, Joseph, 16
HAMMERLY, Virginia B., 16
HAMMOND, L. C., 20
HAMMOND, M. M. (m), 20
HAMMOND, Margaret, 20
HAMMOND?, Dora, 20
HAMMOND?, Josie, 20

HAMMOND?, Wade, 20
HAMNER?, Sarah California, 41
HAMPTON, David, 33
HAMPTON, Harriet H., 33
HAMPTON, Mary A., 61
HANEBUTH, Bena, 57
HANEBUTH, Charles, 57
HANEBUTH, Chas., 57
HANEBUTH, Nina, 57
HANEBUTH, Nina Collins, 57
HANEBUTH, infant (m), 57
HARPER, Fannie, 39
HARPER, Jesse H., 33
HARPER, Josephine, 33
HARPER, Kate, 33
HARPER, Robert P., 33
HARPER, Sarah E., 33
HARRINGTON, Joseph, 32
HARRINGTON, Mary Margaret, 32
HARRINGTON, Mattie, 32
HARRIS, Ann E., 78
HARRIS, B. R. (m), 15
HARRIS, Benjamin R., M.D., 15
HARRIS, C. N. (m), 44
HARRIS, Charlie, 44
HARRIS, Eliza Ann, 38
HARRIS, Ellen Anderson, 15
HARRIS, Fannie S., 44
HARRIS, G. N., 38
HARRIS, Georgie Belle, 44
HARRIS, Gideon Blackburn, 10
HARRIS, I. F. (Mrs.), 68
HARRIS, J. T., 93
HARRIS, Jackson A., 78
HARRIS, John C., 93
HARRIS, Kate Chester, 16
HARRIS, Louanna, 54
HARRIS, Mary, 40
HARRIS, Minerva B., 78
HARRIS, Ophelia, 15
HARRIS, Pansy, 37
HARRIS, S. J., 93
HARRIS, Thos., 40
HARRIS, Thos. sr., 78
HARRIS, W. N., 40
HART, B. E., 97
HART, Delia, 97
HART, Elizabeth Hudson, 97
HART, R. D., 97
HART, R. D. (m), 97
HART, Robert D., 97
HARVEY, W. W., 104
HASKELL, Wm. T. (Gen.), 33
HASKINS, Cora Artie, 79
HASKINS, J. Frank, 107
HASKINS, J. R. (m), 103
HASKINS, J. R. (m), 79
HASKINS, Ollie M., 103
HASKINS, infant (m), 103
HAVNER, C. L., 102
HAWKINS, Allene, 47
HAWKINS, Ariadne Fay, 47
HAWKINS, Giles, 28
HAWKINS, Giles, 29
HAWKINS, Sarah, 28
HAWKINS, W. B., 28

HAWKINS, W. H. (m), 47
HAWKS, David B., 45
HAWKS, Elizabeth, 45
HAWTHORNE, B. J., 25
HAWTHORNE, E., 25
HAYES, Benj. A. (Rev.), 49
HAYES, John Taylor, 49
HAYES, Tennessee, 49
HAYLEY, James T., 63
HAYLEY, N. E. (Mrs.), 63
HAYLEY, Ora, 63
HAYLY, Martha A., 25
HAYNES, Robert W., 14
HAYS, Angie, 2
HAYS, Elinor Virginia, 66
HAYS, G. S., 68
HAYS, Middleton, 63
HAYS, Middleton (Capt.), 66
HAYS, Richard Hartwell, 68
HAYS, Richard Jackson, 68
HAYS, S. P., 63
HAYS, Sallie Parker Caruthers, 66
HAYS, Sarah Ballou, 68
HAYS, Stokeley Donelson, 68
HEARD, Annie, 61
HEARD, James A., 61
HEARD, infant (f), 61
HEAVNER, Clarence O., 102
HEAVNER, Susan Elvira, 46
HEAVNER, U. P. (m), 46
HELD, Fannie Augusta, 52
HENDERSON, Anna Eliza, 28
HENDERSON, Annie Sue, 116
HENDERSON, Arleen P., 23
HENDERSON, Calvin, 38
HENDERSON, Catherine, 116
HENDERSON, Corinna A., 64
HENDERSON, E. L. Wood, 116
HENDERSON, Edgar, 116
HENDERSON, Eliza, 38
HENDERSON, F. B., 89
HENDERSON, Fannie May, 95
HENDERSON, Hugh C., 116
HENDERSON, Ida, 116
HENDERSON, Isabella, 21
HENDERSON, J. N., 116
HENDERSON, James W., 116
HENDERSON, Lynn, 118
HENDERSON, M. E., 112
HENDERSON, M. E., 89
HENDERSON, Marian, 37
HENDERSON, Mary E., 117
HENDERSON, Mary Ormond, 20
HENDERSON, Mary S., 116
HENDERSON, Mattie Gilbert, 119
HENDERSON, Richard, 37
HENDERSON, Robert, 21
HENDERSON, Ruby Katheryn, 120
HENDERSON, S. A. (Dr.), 95
HENDERSON, T. J., 116
HENDERSON, T. J., 117
HENDERSON, Thomas, 28
HENDERSON, Thomas, 37

Index to Madison Co. Tennessee Tombstones

HENDERSON, Thomas Clark, 37
HENDERSON, Thos., 20
HENDERSON, Thos. A., 37
HENDERSON, W. C. (m), 89
HENDERSON, W. H. (m), 89
HENDERSON, W. J., 89
HENDERSON, W. T. (m), 116
HENDERSON, W. T. (m), 119
HENRY, Arney (m), 8
HENRY, Edith Knight, 8
HENRY, Fenner, 8
HENRY, Frank, 8
HENRY, Mary K., 51
HERRON, Ida May, 22
HERRON, J. T. (Dr.), 22
HEWITT, Carolyn D., 29
HICKS, Adelle, 114
HICKS, Anna Bell, 8
HICKS, Annie C., 113
HICKS, Annie S., 113
HICKS, Arrington B., 39
HICKS, E. E., 116
HICKS, Elizabeth E., 116
HICKS, Eunie, 113
HICKS, Fannie Jones, 114
HICKS, Fannie K., 51
HICKS, Florence, 75
HICKS, J. E., 113
HICKS, J. L. (m), 75
HICKS, J. R., 116
HICKS, J. R., 39
HICKS, J. W., 113
HICKS, James Edgar, 113
HICKS, James Thomas, 113
HICKS, James Thomas, 116
HICKS, Jas. W., 113
HICKS, Jimmie B., 114
HICKS, John R., 116
HICKS, John R., 116
HICKS, John R., 51
HICKS, John T., 27
HICKS, Joseph Benjamin, 19
HICKS, Jule Gideon, 74
HICKS, Jule L., 74
HICKS, Jule L., 75
HICKS, Lee, 75
HICKS, Lulu J., 113
HICKS, Lulu J., 114
HICKS, M. P., 113
HICKS, Maggie, 74
HICKS, Maggie, 75
HICKS, Maggie C., 113
HICKS, Margarete, 75
HICKS, Mark Franklin, 113
HICKS, N. A. S., 113
HICKS, R. B. (m), 113
HICKS, R. B. (m), 114
HICKS, Robert B., 114
HICKS, Robert O., 47
HICKS, W. A., 113
HICKS, Willie A., 113
HICKS, baby, 114
HICKS, infant (m), 113
HIGGASON, Addie L., 5
HIGGASON, J. T. (m), 5
HILL, A. H. (m), 55

HILL, Lena May, 1
HILL, Mary A., 55
HILL, Minnie H., 55
HILL, Mollie T., 55
HILL, Robert, 1
HILL, W. H., 18
HILLMAN, Charlie, 51
HILLMAN, Della, 51
HILLMAN, W. A., 51
HILLMAN, W. A. (m), 51
HILLMAN, Wm. Augusta, 51
HINTON, Artif B.T.A., 43
HIRSCH, Ada Byron, 51
HIRSCH, J. H., 51
HIRSCH, Jacob Henry, 51
HIRSCH, May, 51
HODGE, Elizabeth Woods, 26
HODGE, Jas., D. D., 26
HOFELL, Rudolph, 9
HOFFMAN, C. P., 52
HOFFMAN, Carroll Peirce, 52
HOFFMAN, Mary Lou, 52
HOGSETT, Chas. Todd jr., 39
HOGSETT, James Todd sr., 39
HOGSETT, Jemima S., 39
HOGSETT, Jno. Arnold, 39
HOGSETT, June, 39
HOGSETT, Mary Ann, 39
HOLLAND, Bruce, 118
HOLLAND, G., 117
HOLLAND, Harriet E., 59
HOLLAND, Hattie B., 59
HOLLAND, L. L. (m), 119
HOLLAND, M., 117
HOLLAND, M. L. (m), 118
HOLLAND, Mary, 117
HOLLAND, Mary D., 118
HOLLAND, Mary Ellen, 119
HOLLAND, Mollie J., 119
HOLLAND, Paralee, 118
HOLLAND, S. L. (m), 118
HOLLAND, Theodosia, 117
HOLLAND, W., 59
HOLLOWAY, Johnnie, 40
HOLLOWAY, ____, 50
HOLT, Jordan C., 111
HOOSER, Kate Hammerly, 16
HOOTEN, J. S., 105
HOOTEN, family, 105
HOPPER, C. F., 106
HOPPER, Daniel, 76
HOPPER, Daniel, 76
HOPPER, Daniel B., 76
HOPPER, Dolphus L., 76
HOPPER, F. S., 9
HOPPER, Fannie, 9
HOPPER, Lucinda, 76
HOPPER, Lucinda, 76
HOPPER, Mary A., 76
HOPPER, Mary Lou, 76
HOPPER, R. E., 76
HOPPER, R. E., 9
HOPPER, R. E. (f), 101
HOPPER, Sallie E., 106
HOPPER, W. M., 76
HOPPER, W. M. (m), 101
HOPPER, Wilson Barzilla, 76

HOSFORD, Erie S., 61
HOSFORD, Erie S. jr., 61
HOSFORD, Lucile E., 61
HOSFORD, Willie W., 61
HOTCHKISS, C. R., 54
HOUSTON, J. M., 33
HOUSTON, M. L., 33
HOUSTON, son, 33
HOWARD, B. B., 26
HOWARD, B. F., 82
HOWARD, B. J. jr., 57
HOWARD, Ben J., 57
HOWARD, E. A., 20
HOWARD, Elizabeth A., 20
HOWARD, Elizabeth H., 56
HOWARD, J. F., 82
HOWARD, John W., 57
HOWARD, Katie A., 20
HOWARD, Lizzie A., 20
HOWARD, Mary K., 20
HOWARD, Nina E., 57
HOWARD, R. E., 26
HOWARD, Richard E., 82
HOWARD, Richard Leroy, 26
HOWARD, W. P., 26
HOWARD, Wm. F., 20
HOWARD, Wm. P., 20
HOWARD, Wm. R., 20
HOWLETT, Ann Eliza, 39
HOWLETT, W. R. (m), 39
HOWLETT, Wm. L., 39
HUBBARD, B. H. (Rev.), 59
HUDSON, Estelle, 104
HUGHES, B. O., 58
HUGHES, D. W., 8
HUGHES, George G., 56
HUGHES, James, 58
HUGHES, Jeanette, 8
HUGHES, Martha W., 58
HUGHES, Sarah H., 56
HUGHES, T. L., 58
HUGHES, Thomas jr., 56
HUGHES?, Nellie, 58
HULIHAN, Louisa J., 75
HUNT, Bennie R. (m), 51
HUNT, Bettie, 23
HUNT, Howell A., 24
HUNT, J. B. (m), 23
HUNT, J. D., 51
HUNT, June, 51
HUNT, Lillian Pearl, 33
HUNT, Mollie James, 51
HUNT, Nannie, 33
HUNT, Thos. J., 51
HUNT, W. J. (m), 33
HUNT?, Baby Laurange, 51
HUNTER, J. H., 54
HUNTER, J. H. jr., 54
HUNTSMAN, Adam, 109
HUNTSMAN, Elizabeth, 109
HUNTSMAN, Nancy, 109
HUNTSMAN, Sarah W., 109
HURT, Absolem DeBerry, 62
HURT, Annie Meriwether, 51
HURT, Eliza Allen, 51
HURT, Elte May, 51
HURT, Fannie Guthrie, 62

HURT, J. R., 23
HURT, James Meriwether, 51
HURT, John D., 59
HURT, M. B., 51
HURT, Milton B., 51
HURT, Nannie E., 23
HURT, Rebecca, 51
HURT, T. E., 23
HUTCHERSON, Elizabeth P., 20
HUTCHERSON, F. M., 74
HUTCHERSON, L. W., 74
HUTCHERSON, Samuel Elmore, 74
HUTCHERSON, infant (f), 74
HUTCHINGS, Christopher, 65
HUTCHINGS, Frances, 65
HUTCHINGS, Louise, 65
HUTCHINGS, Wm. Edward, 65
ILLLINGWORTH, David, 50
ILLLINGWORTH, Harry Martin, 50
ILLLINGWORTH, Mary, 50
INGERSOLL, Duane Henry, 10
INGERSOLL, Edward Ross, 10
INGRAM, Alice M., 31
INGRAM, Ann, 53
INGRAM, John (Dr.), 53
INGRAM, Louisa, 53
INGRAM, Lydia, 53
INGRAM, Mary J., 24
INGRAM, Wm. Ashley, 24
IRBY, Elizabeth, 2
IRBY, H. C., 2
IRVINE, Annie Myrtle, 1
IRVINE, J. M., 1
IRVINE, M. M., 1
IRWIN, James, 92
JACKSON, A. (Dr.), 66
JACKSON, Alexander (Dr.), 65
JACKSON, Harriet Wilson, 76
JACKSON, J. B., 55
JACKSON, John Z., 76
JACKSON, Maggie M., 57
JACKSON, Mary, 55
JACKSON, Mary W., 66
JACKSON, Philip, 55
JACKSON, Sarah E., 76
JACKSON, Susan A., 32
JACKSON, W. H. (m), 76
JACOB, John, 36
JAMES, Anna Bell Hicks, 8
JAMES, Blance, 27
JAMES, E. L., 31
JAMES, E. L., 8
JAMES, Elnora, 51
JAMES, Elte May, 51
JAMES, G. B. (m), 45
JAMES, Jessie (f), 45
JAMES, K. S., 31
JAMES, Lizzie S., 45
JAMES, Robert Emmet, 51
JAMES, Ted, 31
JAMES, Walter P., 51
JARMAN, Everett, 8
JARMAN, Maggie L., 8
JARMAN, Willie Street, 8
JARVOS, Charles, 66

JAYNES, Harmon Estelle (f), 68
JAYNES, L. M., 68
JAYNES, L. T., 68
JESTER, Caledonia Jane, 21
JESTER, Ella Spence, 12
JESTER, J. G., 43
JESTER, R. H. Stringer (f), 43
JETER, D. E. (m), 44
JETER, Lizzie, 44
JETER, Robert John, 66
JOBE, A. (m), 66
JOBE, Andrew, 66
JOBE, Annie M., 5
JOBE, Lucinda, 66
JOBE, Lucy, 5
JOHNSON, C. E. (m), 36
JOHNSON, Cora, 89
JOHNSON, E. C., 11
JOHNSON, Henry Clay (Rev.), 77
JOHNSON, J. D., 13
JOHNSON, J. S., 62
JOHNSON, J. S. (m), 62
JOHNSON, Julius (Dr.), 62
JOHNSON, Julius Adams, 62
JOHNSON, M. C., 11
JOHNSON, Maggie, 56
JOHNSON, Maggie H., 15
JOHNSON, Marie Deleisseline, 11
JOHNSON, Mary Elizabeth, 11
JOHNSON, Mary Howson, 62
JOHNSON, Maud, 62
JOHNSON, Nancy, 59
JOHNSON, Pearl Nourse, 36
JOHNSON, Walter Fenner, 62
JOHNSON, Wm., 89
JOHNSTON, Annie I., 12
JOHNSTON, Emma Allen, 114
JOHNSTON, Ingram, 53
JOHNSTON, J. R., 12
JOHNSTON, James A., 53
JOHNSTON, John I., 53
JOHNSTON, Lydia, 53
JOHNSTON, Mary E., 12
JONES, A. B.?, 29
JONES, A. D. Cartmell, 52
JONES, A. M. (f), 104
JONES, A. W. (Rev.), 29
JONES, A. W. (m), 29
JONES, Amanda C., 29
JONES, Amanda C., 29
JONES, Amos W., 29
JONES, Atlas, 110
JONES, Catherine Revels, 110
JONES, Clopton, 91
JONES, E. A., 86
JONES, E. B., 61
JONES, Eddie C., 29
JONES, Edith, 9
JONES, G. C., 29
JONES, Gates M. (Dr.), 24
JONES, Henry, 40
JONES, Ida B., 29
JONES, Ira B., 29
JONES, J. H. (m), 104
JONES, J. S., 91

JONES, J. W. (Dr.), 91
JONES, Jas. B., 9
JONES, Jas. T. (Dr.), 24
JONES, Jasper, 99
JONES, Jenny S., 91
JONES, John E., 29
JONES, John W., 75
JONES, Josephine, 40
JONES, L. L., 29
JONES, L. W., 91
JONES, Laura, 75
JONES, Little Alfred, 9
JONES, M. Frances, 39
JONES, Mahaley J., 99
JONES, Mary E., 29
JONES, S. A., 72
JONES, Susie L., 99
JONES, Timothy P., 110
JONES, W. F., 72
JONES, W. N. (m), 99
JONES, W. T., 40
JONES, Wm. T., 72
JONES?, J. A., 26
JORDON, E. (m), 20
JORDON, Mary E., 20
JOYCE, Hanna, 41
JOYCE, Mary Ann, 41
JOYCE, Patrick, 41
JOYCE, Sarah, 41
JOYNER, F. E., 34
JOYNER, Mary Elizabeth, 34
KEITH, Charles S., 8
KEITH, John, 8
KEITH, Thos. W., 8
KELL, Annie, 9
KELLY, Catherine, 39
KELLY, Ella W., 51
KELLY, Ellen, 39
KELLY, George F., 51
KELLY, Peter, 39
KELLY, ____, 49
KENDRICK, Theophilies Lacy, 37
KERR, A. S. (m), 107
KERR, Minnie A., 107
KERSHAW, Adey, 52
KERSHAW, Mary E., 68
KERSHAW, Sarah A., 9
KERSHAW, T. B. (m), 68
KERSHAW, Thomas B., 68
KEY, Charlie, 81
KEY, D. L., 102
KEY, Dean Mason, 81
KEY, Ida, 102
KEY, J. R., 100
KEY, James David, 105
KEY, Jesse R., 105
KEY, Jesse Ray, 100
KEY, John P., 102
KEY, Lee Blackmon, 70
KEY, Lula May, 103
KEY, Mary Frances, 103
KEY, S. C., 100
KEY, Sarah C., 24
KEY, Sue F., 102
KEY, Veola E., 103
KEY, Wilma Hicks, 103

KIEROLE, Jennie E., 2
KIEROLE, W. D. (m), 2
KIMBRELL, ____ (unmarked), 101
KIMBROUGH, Amos B., 46
KIMBROUGH, Annie D., 46
KIMBROUGH, D. L., 46
KIMBROUGH, Daisy V., 46
KIMBROUGH, Lemia, 46
KIMBROUGH, R. A. (m), 46
KIMBROUGH, R. G. (m), 46
KIMBROUGH, Sarah P., 46
KINCAID, M. A. (m), 43
KINCAID, Mrs. M. A., 43
KINCAID, Willie Scott, 43
KING, D. H., 24
KING, D. Hamner, 69
KING, George Thomas, 24
KING, J. S. (m), 50
KING, James Rivers, 50
KING, Lena, 50
KING, Sarah C., 24
KIRBY, Henry, 77
KIRBY, Jemima Lacy, 77
KIRBY, L. T., 102
KIRBY, Lulu T., 102
KIRBY, Ruth, 102
KIRBY, W. L., 102
KIRBY, Willis London, 102
KISBER, Chas. E., 9
KNIGHT, Edith, 8
KUNZ, Charles, 43
KUNZ, Christian, 47
KUNZ, Elizabeth, 43
LACKEY, Annie, 7
LACKEY, B. Ann, 6
LACY, D., 45
LAIRD, Alice Talbot, 1
LAMB, Ann Eliza, 118
LAMB, Clifford, 118
LAMB, Newman, 119
LAMB, Wm. Thomas, 119
LANCASTER, Anna, 28
LANCASTER, Anna Eliza, 28
LANCASTER, Anna Terrell, 28
LANCASTER, Anne T., 28
LANCASTER, Anselum Lynch, 28
LANCASTER, Christine, 28
LANCASTER, Eleanor, 28
LANCASTER, George L., 28
LANCASTER, Henrietta Snider, 28
LANCASTER, Janie, 28
LANCASTER, John L., 28
LANCASTER, John Lynch, 28
LANCASTER, Nat E., 28
LANCASTER, Parthenia Frances, 45
LANCASTER, Peter, 13
LANCASTER, Robert Henry, 45
LANCASTER, Samuel, 28
LANCASTER, Samuel, 28
LANCASTER, infant (m), 28
LAND, Annie, 73
LAND, E. J., 97
LAND, G. M., 97

LAND, H. M., 72
LAND, Lottie, 97
LAND, Pattie E., 72
LAND, S. P., 72
LANDIS, Chas. W., 55
LANDIS, James K., 55
LANDIS, Martha D., 55
LANE, A. B. (m), 83
LANE, A. M., 94
LANE, Alice Metta, 94
LANE, Bishop, 13
LANE, Frances, 13
LANE, Isaac, 13
LANE, J., 94
LANE, Josiah, 94
LANE, Martha, 13
LANE, Mary E., 13
LANE, May, 83
LANE, Norma, 83
LANE, Ollie Neal, 94
LANE, P. W. (Rev.), 13
LANE, W. A., 94
LANE, W. H. (Dr.), 13
LANGFORD, A. B., 53
LANGFORD, Cora C., 53
LANGLEY, L. D., 45
LANGLEY, Maud May, 45
LANGLEY, S. E., 45
LANGLEY, Sarah Elizabeth, 45
LASIER, Joseph Earl, 31
LAW, Dreb, 59
LAWLER, Merle, 30
LAWRENCE, Claud H., 116
LAWRENCE, E., 75
LAWRENCE, Edgar (US Navy), 120
LAWRENCE, Eugenia W., 116
LAWRENCE, Fanny, 75
LAWRENCE, Herbert, 75
LAWRENCE, L. D., 75
LAWRENCE, S. B. (m), 116
LAWRENCE, Swanie Burrus, 116
LAWRENCE, Zilphy L., 116
LAWS, Emily Etta, 101
LAWS, Eula Bessie, 101
LAWS, John, 101
LAWS, Josie Phine, 101
LAWS, Kittie, 101
LEE, Alice, 44
LEE, Elizabeth, 21
LEE, Ira, 44
LEE, James, 36
LEE, Jos. S., 1
LEE, Lena P., 44
LEE, Lizzie, 21
LEE, R. A., 44
LEE, Robert E., 44
LEE, ____, 44
LELAND, Georgie Belle, 44
LELAND, R. G. (m), 44
LEMON, June Hogsett, 39
LEONARD, J. W. (Dr.), 7
LEWIS, Charles Edward, 59
LEWIS, Isham, 17
LEWIS, Tella, 17
LIFSEY, Marguerite Hicks, 113

LIFT, C. E. McClanahan (f), 40
LIFT, Jas. M., 40
LIGON, B. H. (Dr.), 66
LIGON, Eliza Ann, 66
LINDSEY, baby, 31
LIVELY, Martha J., 41
LOCK, Elizabeth, 82
LOCK, Mary L., 88
LOCK, R. P. (m), 82
LOCKARD, C. V., 111
LOCKARD, J. P., 6
LOCKARD, M. J., 6
LOCKARD, Willie G., 6
LOCKE, David Rhodes, 31
LOCKE, Leah Rhodes, 31
LONG, Addie Brooks, 54
LONG, Anna McGee, 59
LONG, Clay Virginia, 54
LONG, Dollie Vernon, 29
LONG, E. L. (m), 46
LONG, Elizabeth, 29
LONG, Elizabeth J., 29
LONG, Ida K., 10
LONG, J. B. (m), 59
LONG, J. H., 54
LONG, James H., 54
LONG, Jennie W., 59
LONG, Jonnie (f), 46
LONG, L. (m), 46
LONG, Lizzie Leighton, 54
LONG, Mary J., 16
LONG, Thos. C., 30
LONG, Wm., 29
LONG, Wm. H., 10
LONG, Wm. Harrison, 29
LONG, Zillah Ann, 46
LONGMIRE, Alice, 114
LONGMIRE, Anna, 114
LONGMIRE, Joseph, 114
LORENZ, John, 69
LOSIER, Joseph Cameron, 31
LOSIER, Joseph J., 31
LOSIER, Joseph Johanas, 31
LOSIER, Joseph L., 31
LOSIER, Vina May Rose, 31
LOUISE, Ruby, 9
LOVE, Agatha Nelson, 95
LOVE, Allen E., 95
LOVE, Lottie, 103
LOVE, Mary E., 103
LOVE, Sam, 103
LOVETT, Anna Mae, 69
LOVETT, M. D., 69
LOVETT, S. I., 69
LOWRANCE, E. P. (m), 88
LOWRANCE, Elisha P., 88
LOWRANCE, Nancy B., 88
LOWRY, Judith Howard, 103
LUCKEY, H. P., 14
LUCKEY, Samuel, 14
LUKER, V. Bettie, 18
LUKER, W. E. V., 18
LUKER, Walter E., 18
LUKER, Wm. V., 18
LUNSFORD, Little Etta, 42
LYALLS, Mary Ada, 4
LYERLA, Arthur C., 48

LYERLA, Bonnie, 48
LYERLA, D. A., 48
LYERLA, Lena, 48
LYERLA, M. A., 48
LYNCH, Anna, 28
LYNCH, Anna Terrell, 28
LYNCH, John, 28
LYON, Eliza, 38
LYON, M. D. (Mrs.), 38
LYON, Mary Reid, 2
LYON, Samuel W., 38
LYON, Wade W., 2
LYON, Wade W., 2
MACKEY, E. D. (m), 106
MACKEY, E. W. (m), 106
MACKEY, E. W. (m), Nancy
MACKEY, Mary J., 106
MACKIE, H. C., 9
MACKIE, Harry, 9
MACKIE, Lottie, 9
MACKIE?, Minnie, 9
MACMILLIN, Corinna C., 87
MACMILLIN, John Wm. Murray, 87
MACMILLIN, Nina Dora, 87
MACMILLIN, W. E., 87
MACON, G. E., 67
MAGRANE, John, 39
MALLORY, Callie Parker, 10
MALLORY, Edmund Skinner, 10
MALLORY, Jennie Parker, 10
MALLORY, Martha A., 10
MALLORY, Martha Skinner, 10
MALONE, B. J., 90
MALONE, Martha A., 90
MALONE, R. G. (Mrs.), 56
MALONE, Willis B., 56
MALONE?, Little Fannie, 56
MANLY, C. A. (Dr.), 18
MANLY, Horace B., 18
MANLY, Sarah F., 18
MANN, Harriett A., 29
MANN, John, 29
MANN, Robt., 22
MANOR, John H., 18
MANOR, John McCoy, 59
MARCH, Emma, 9
MARKS, Frances Hall, 36
MARKS, Sue Clark, 37
MARKS, W. A. (m), 36
MARSHALL, W. B., 39
MARTIN, Annie A., 26
MARTIN, I. W., 10
MARTIN, James Irwin, 92
MARTIN, Joseph E. (Priest & Dr.), 62
MARTIN, Mary Jane, 59
MARTIN, Mary Jane, 59
MARTIN, Mary Samuel, 10
MARTIN, Mary Walstrum, 50
MARTIN, Millie B., 25
MARTIN?, Nelle Blackmon, 92
MASON, A. E., 90
MASON, Adelia Ann, 82
MASON, Adelie L., 79
MASON, Ann Person, 90

MASON, E. A., 79
MASON, E. A., 81
MASON, E. A., 82
MASON, Elvira A., 55
MASON, Eunice Ann, 81
MASON, Hattie E., 92
MASON, Henry, 26
MASON, J. A., 90
MASON, J. H., 57
MASON, J. M., 92
MASON, Jinnie Ann, 90
MASON, John M., 91
MASON, John Rufus, 91
MASON, Lulu E., 81
MASON, M. A., 92
MASON, Minnie E., 81
MASON, R. M., 79
MASON, R. M., 81
MASON, R. M., 82
MASON, Ray W., 106
MASON, Rufus M., 81
MASON, T. T. (m), 55
MASON, infant (f), 92
MASON?, George, 55
MASON?, Mary, 55
MATHESON, L. E., 67
MATTHEWS, Clara Chandler, 49
MATTHEWS, Malinda R., 38
MAXWELL, Georgia, 61
MAXWELL, J. A., 61
MAXWELL, J. A. jr., 61
MAY, Laura Dimond, 31
MAY, W. M. (m), 31
MAYO, Charlie H., 20
MAYO, Margaret M., 20
MAYO, Nannie Jane, 49
MAYO, Wm. H., 19
MCADOO, Bettie, 93
MCADOO, J. W. (m), 93
MCALEXANDER, Alice, 59
MCBRIDE, Henry H., 11
MCBRIDE, Robert A., 11
MCBUCKNER, Lunda, 42
MCCABE, Alleane?, 12
MCCABE, Charles B., 12
MCCABE, E. R., 12
MCCABE, Elizabeth R., 12
MCCABE, J. G., 12
MCCABE, Jas. G., 12
MCCABE, Nora B., 12
MCCABE, Viola, 41
MCCABE, Wm. G., 12
MCCALL, Jeanette Hughes, 8
MCCALLUM, Callie C., 86
MCCALLUM, Ernestine, 93
MCCALLUM, J. F., 86
MCCALLUM, J. R. (m), 93
MCCALLUM, Mary E. Pearson, 93
MCCARLEY, L. B., 40
MCCARLEY, Sarah McCabe, 40
MCCASLAND, B. McCoy, 99
MCCASLAND, Erin I. B., 98
MCCASLAND, J. A., 98
MCCASLAND, J. A. (m), 99
MCCASLAND, James A., 98

MCCASLAND, T. B. (f), 99
MCCASLAND, T. R., 98
MCCASLAND, Wm. Harvey, 98
MCCLANAHAN, C. E. (f), 40
MCCLANAHAN, J. A., 40
MCCLANAHAN, Laura, 40
MCCLANAHAN, Lou (f), 8
MCCLANAHAN, M. A., 40
MCCLANAHAN, Nannie Louisa, 40
MCCLANAHAN, Nelson, 40
MCCLANAHAN, Norma? Jeanette, 40
MCCLANAHAN, Samuel, 40
MCCLANAHAN, Willie D. H., 40
MCCLARAN, Annette Walsh, 15
MCCLARAN, Robert S., 15
MCCLATHERY, George M., 38
MCCLATHERY, J. M., 38
MCCLATHERY, Joseph L., 38
MCCLELLAN, Isabella G., 63
MCCLELLAN, J. D. jr., 63
MCCLELLAN, James D., 63
MCCLINTOCK, D. Fletcher, 33
MCCLINTOCK, Daisy, 33
MCCLOHN, Geo., 4
MCCLOHN, Little George, 4
MCCLOHN, Little Pron, 4
MCCLOHN, Minnie, 4
MCCOLPIN, E. H., 23
MCCOLPIN, Rebecca Cason, 23
MCCONN, W. A., 120
MCCONN, Wm. T. Moore, 120
MCCONN, Zula Z., 120
MCCORD, A. N., 66
MCCORD, Frank, 66
MCCORD, N. L., 66
MCCORRY, Corina A., 63
MCCORRY, Corinna A. Henderson, 64
MCCORRY, Corinna Ann, 64
MCCORRY, Elinor, 64
MCCORRY, Frances Eliza, 63
MCCORRY, H. W. (m), 63
MCCORRY, Henry (CSA), 63
MCCORRY, Henry Wood, 64
MCCORRY, Masidora Clark, 64
MCCORRY, Sallie I., 64
MCCORRY, Sallie Jones Parker, 64
MCCORRY, Thomas, 64
MCCORRY, Thomas, 64
MCCORRY, Wm., 63
MCCOWAT, Fannie, 21
MCCOWAT, Frances Jane, 21
MCCOWAT, P. C., 21
MCCOWAT, T. R. (m), 22
MCCOY, Irene, 12
MCCUTCHEN, Anna, 29
MCCUTCHEN, Annie T., 49
MCCUTCHEN, Eunice E., 29
MCCUTCHEN, Fannie B., 29
MCCUTCHEN, H. C., 29
MCCUTCHEN, J. T. (Capt.), 49
MCCUTCHEN, Mary E., 29

MCCUTCHEN, W. T., 29
MCCUTCHEON, Anne Bess, 58
MCCUTCHEON, David McAlpin, 61
MCCUTCHEON, J. M. (m), 58
MCCUTCHEON, Minnie, 58
MCCUTCHEON, W. M., 19
MCCUTCHEON?, Fred (infant), 58
MCDONALD, Emma C., 110
MCDONALD, Emma G., 10
MCDONALD, Estelle, 110
MCDONALD, J. E. (Maj.), 110
MCDONALD, Joseph W., M.D., 10
MCDONALD, Samuel D., 10
MCGEEHEE, Wm. Abner, 31
MCGILL, Hattie F., 33
MCGILL, J. M. (m), 33
MCGILL, John Annie, 33
MCGRAW, D. E., 29
MCGRAW, Sophia F., 29
MCINTOSH, Annie A., 64
MCINTOSH, Annie Allen, 35
MCINTOSH, Campbell Allen, 35
MCINTOSH, Caro? Madoline, 64
MCINTOSH, Katharine Preston, 64
MCINTOSH, Louise, 64
MCINTOSH, Wiley R., 64
MCINTOSH, Wiley Robert, 35
MCKINNEY, Collin (Rev.), 26
MCKINNEY, J. A., 15
MCKINNEY, J. F., 15
MCKINNEY, Matilda Plumer Shepard, 26
MCKINNEY, Wm. Plumer, 26
MCKINNIE, John R., 5
MCKINNIE, Kate A., 5
MCKINNIE, Vanden?, 5
MCKNIGHT, Sallie Ann, 118
MCLEAN, J., 36
MCLEAN, John, 36
MCLEAN, Lizzie, 36
MCLEAN, Margaret, 36
MCLEAN, Margaret A., 37
MCLEAN, Margaret Digan, 37
MCLEAN, Michael J., 37
MCLEAN, Thomas J., 36
MCLEAN, Wm. A., 36
MCLEARY, J. R. (m), 106
MCLEARY, R. E. (m), 106
MCLEARY, Sarah E., 106
MCLEARY, Sarah M., 106
MCLEARY, Virginia, 106
MCMARKS, J. A., 20
MCMILLAN, Armeta Paralee, 69a
MCMILLAN, J. H. (m), 4
MCMILLAN, John H., 69a
MCMILLAN, John Harrison, 4
MCMILLAN, Mary, 69a
MCMILLAN, Mary Spah, 69a
MCMILLAN, Wm. Henry, 69a

MCMILLIN, Andrew Murray, 43
MCNATT, G., 5
MCNATT, M. J., 5
MCNATT, Mary E., 5
MCNEIL, E. B. (Rev.), 55
MCNEIL, Earl Taylor, 55
MCNEIL, Eaton K. (Dr.), 55
MCNEIL, Edw. Benton (Rev.), 55
MCNEIL, Jessie, 55
MCNEIL, Jessie A. K., 55
MCNEIL, Mattie, 55
MCNEIL, Percy R., 55
MCREE, Ernest, 13
MCREE, Jas. M., 2
MCREE, Olivia (f), 2
MCREE, Parrie W. (f), 13
MCREE, R. S., 2
MCREE, Wm. H., 13
MCREE, Wm. H., 13
MEALS, L. C. (f), 93
MEALS, Louise Catherine Person, 92
MEALS, W. H. (m), 92
MEANS, Ernest H., 2
MENZIES, A. E., 30
MENZIES, Alice Gibson, 30
MENZIES, Rosalie, 30
MENZIES, W. B., 30
MERCER, Garnett W., 17
MERCER, Harry, 17
MERCER, J. W. (m), 17
MERCER, Rebecca Friley, 17
MERIWETHER, Annie, 51
MERIWETHER, David, 54
MERIWETHER, E. A. (Mrs.), 51
MERIWETHER, Fannie Etta, 47
MERIWETHER, James, 51
MERIWETHER, Lydia A., 54
MERIWETHER, M. D., 54
MERIWETHER, Mamie, 54
MERIWETHER, Mary, 47
MERIWETHER, Thomas, 51
MERIWETHER, Wm., 47
MERONEY, Ivo C., 48
MICHIE, Charlie O., 54
MICHIE, Horace H., 54
MICHIE, J. B. (m), 54
MICHIE, Little Jodie, 54
MICHIE, M. J. (f), 54
MILLENDER, Annie E., 5
MILLENDER, D. H. (m), 5
MILLER, Alice, 60
MILLER, Eula S., 11
MILLER, John Horace, 60
MILLER, John S., 60
MILLER, Mary Louisa, 41
MILLER, Phoebe J., 43
MILLER, Pitser, 60
MILLER, Sallie Phipps, 60
MILLER, Sarah, 60
MILLER, W. P., 60
MILLS, Alex, 69
MILLS, Beulah, 101
MILLS, Birdie, 69

MILLS, H. V. (m), 101
MITCHELL, Bernard, 60
MOFFAT, Eva May, 46
MOFFAT, Keith sr., 46
MOFFAT, Nettie, 46
MOODY, Dolopes, 64
MOODY, Evelyn, 64
MOODY, J. B., 67
MOODY, John M., 67
MOODY, S. A., 67
MOODY, Van Ellis, 64
MOORE, Anderson J., 65
MOORE, D. G. (Rev.), 90
MOORE, Fannie C., 65
MOORE, Frances Lee, 43
MOORE, Gilliam J., 65
MOORE, Harriet, 65
MOORE, M. T., 116
MOORE, Malissa E., 62
MOORE, Mattie T., 115
MOORE, Minerva, 13
MOORE, Rebecca, 116
MOORE, Robt. C., 62
MOORE, S. P., 116
MOORE, Sarah L., 65
MOORE, W., 116
MOORE, W. J., 65
MOORE, Willis, 65
MOORE, Wm. M., 115
MOORE, Wm. Stuart, 53
MOORE, Wm. Stuart jr., 53
MOORE, infant (f), 116
MORENAS, B. R. (Capt.), 58
MORENAS, James R., 58
MORGAN, James D., 40
MORGAN, W. C. (m), 104
MORRILL, J. M. Donald, 58
MOSS, A. C., 50
MOSS, Little Ladell (f), 50
MOSS, Little Mabelle, 50
MOSS, W. B., 50
MULVOY, Lizzie McLean, 36
MULVOY, Michael, 36
MUNFORD, Emma, 3
MURDOCH, Minnie Neely, 8
MURPHY, Dennis (soldier), 18
MURPHY, W. J., 60
MURRAY, Cornelius M., 2
MURRAY, Eloise MacPherson, 2
MURRAY, Ernest McPherson, 2
MURRAY, Jeter? James, 2
MURRAY, Little, 43
MURRELL, E. D. (f), 63
MURRELL, Emily Perkins, 63
MURRELL, George, 19
MURRELL, Henry Still, 19
MURRELL, James, 63
MURRELL, Leila, 19
MURRELL, Lendepum DeWest, 19
MURRELL, R. L., 19
MURRELL, Sallie, 19
MUSE, Albert, 23
MUSE, Elizabeth, 23
MUSE, L. E., 12
MUSE, Nora, 23
MUSE, Theresa Edrington, 23

MUSE, Thos. G., 23
MUSE, Wm. C., 23
MUSE, Wm. Collier, 23
MYERS, Gene, 71
MYERS, Josie R., 115
MYERS, W. R. (m), 115
MYLER, W. W., 55
NAGLE, Elizabeth, 10
NAGLE, Thos., 10
NALL, Jas. Hodge (Rev.), 26
NALL, Robt. (Rev., D.D.), 26
NANCE, J. L., 80
NANCE, Lena, 80
NANCE, Ludes (m), 9
NANCE, Martha Anderson, 3
NANCE, Mollie River, 9
NANCE, R. W., 80
NANCE, R. W. (Rev.), 80
NANCE, Virginia L., 80
NANCE, Walter C., 32
NANCE, Walter C. jr., 32
NAYLOR, A. N., 31
NEDORFER, J. G., 65
NEDORFER, Myron W., 65
NEDORFER, Nannie D., 65
NEELY, Lou McClanahan, 8
NEELY, M. S. (Dr.), 8
NEELY, M. S. (m), 8
NEELY, Mrs. Rosamond, 26
NEELY, Samuel, 26
NEFF, Charles David, 8
NEFF, David, 23
NEFF, Ella, 8
NEFF, Jas. D., 23
NEFF, John Amos, 8
NEFF, Liddie Maud, 23
NEFF, Lila May, 8
NEFF, M. A., 23
NEFF, M. D., 23
NEFF, M. I., 23
NEFF, S. C., 7
NEFF, S. H., 7
NEFF, S. H., 8
NEFF, Sallie, 7
NEFF, Samuel H., 7
NEFF, Sarah Elizabeth, 8
NEFF, Wm., 23
NEIL, G. F., 3
NELSON, Agatha, 95
NELSON, Arthur H., 88
NELSON, Charles, 23
NELSON, Lela H., 88
NELSON, Martha Chappel, 23
NELSON, Mattie, 53
NELSON, R. B. (Dr.), 62
NELSON, W. T., 53
NELSON, W. T. (Mrs.), 53
NELSON, W. T. (m), 53
NEUDORFER, J. G., 43
NEWBY, Nannie B., 51
NEWSOM, John F., 22
NEWSOM, Newt (Dr.), 49
NEWSOM, Susan M., 22
NEWSOM, Tennessee, 49
NEWTON, Eunice, 25
NEWTON, Eunice T., 26
NEWTON, J. D., 26

NEWTON, J. D. (m), 25
NEWTON, J. P. jr., 25
NEWTON, Martha J., 117
NEWTON, Thos. W., 25
NICHOL, E. M., 41
NICLEY, A. R., 8
NICLEY, J. J., 8
NICLEY, John D., 8
NOBLES, A. D., 78
NOBLES, A. D., 79
NOBLES, A. D. (Dr.), 79
NOBLES, Allen J., 78
NOBLES, Emily F., 79
NOBLES, Erasmus Montgomery, 79
NOBLES, M. F., 79
NOBLES, M. T.?, 78
NOBLES, Mary F., 79
NOEL, B. F., 19
NORTON, Irene, 13
NORVELL, J. B. (m), 33
NORVELL, John, 34
NORVELL, John G., 33
NORVELL, Sarah, 33
NORVELL, Susan D., 33
NORVELL, Thos. G., 33
NORWOOD, Arthur G., 47
NORWOOD, Mary A., 47
NOURSE, Georgia Lee, 36
NOURSE, Pearl, 36
NOURSE, Sallie Clark, 36
NOURSE, W. H. (m), 36
OATES, David Austin, 64
OATES, John T., 64
OATES, Mary, 64
OATES, Mary E., 64
OCONNOR, Anne, 22
OCONNOR, Annie, 22
OCONNOR, C. E., 22
OCONNOR, Fannie E., 22
OCONNOR, Ida, 22
OCONNOR, Ida May, 22
OCONNOR, Irene, 22
OCONNOR, James, 22
OCONNOR, James, 22
OCONNOR, Little Horace, 22
OCONNOR, May, 22
OCONNOR, W. J. (m), 22
ODDIE?, Hattie, 2
ODDIE?, Little, 2
OGLESBY, Mary, 36
OLIVE, H. I., 107
OLIVER, Cordelia J., 86
OLIVER, F. C., 86
OLIVER, F. C., 86
OLIVER, J. E., 86
OLIVER, James, 86
OLIVER, Jas. S., 86
OLIVER, T. P., 86
OLIVER, Tennie B., 86
ONEAL, Annie E., 72
ONEAL, F. M. (m), 72
ONEAL, Minerva C., 87
OUTERBRIDGE, Martha, 38
OUTLAN, J. F., 115
OUTLAN, John N., 115
OUTLAN, W. E., 115

OWEN, Bettie, 7
OWEN, Charles, 7
OWEN, Edward, 7
OWEN, Eliza K., 7
OWEN, H. T. (m), 90
OWENS, John B., 61
OZMENT, Edna D., 50
OZMENT, J. C. (m), 50
PACE, Quilley, 95
PACE, Rushel, 95
PARDUE, Elizabeth C., 81
PARDUE, J. J. (m), 81
PARDUE, Rosa Lee, 81
PARHAM, Ernest R., 28
PARHAM, Martha W., 58
PARISH, A. S., 79
PARISH, Charlie J., 92
PARISH, E. G., 48
PARISH, Edna, 48
PARISH, Elizabeth, 70
PARISH, Ernestine, 92
PARISH, F. W. (m), 70
PARISH, John S., 79
PARISH, Lou Lee, 48
PARISH, Lucile, 48
PARISH, Miranda C., 79
PARKER, Abie Dew (f), 32
PARKER, Anna M., 10
PARKER, C. K., 32
PARKER, Callie King, 10
PARKER, Cally, 32
PARKER, Elinor, 64
PARKER, F. C., 32
PARKER, Fannie C. (Mrs.), 10
PARKER, J. M., 10
PARKER, J. M., 32
PARKER, Jennie, 10
PARKER, Louisa Ann, 32
PARKER, M., 32
PARKER, Phoeba T., 42
PARKMAN, Elizabeth Helena, 17
PARR, J. S., 102
PARSONS, Alberta M., 54
PARSONS, H. C., 54
PATE, E. E., 78
PATE, E. E. (m), 78
PATE, Eudora, 78
PATE, Florence Robenie, 78
PATE, John G., 78
PATE, Leora, 78
PATE, Mellie (f), 78
PATE, N. N., 78
PATE, Nancy, 78
PATE, Sidney T., 78
PATE, W. H., 78
PATTERSON, Allen L., 38
PATTERSON, Dogia S., 35
PATTERSON, Drucilla J., 38
PATTERSON, James, 38
PATTERSON, John Kemp, 38
PATTERSON, Morton, 35
PATTON, Robert, 21
PAVATT, Margreth, 111
PAYNE, Lulu Trice, 116
PAYNE, Sallie R., 62

PAYNE, Wm. P., 6
PEARCY, Lottie D., 52
PEARCY, Lula F., 52
PEARCY, Wm. H., 52
PEARSON, Adelie L., 79
PEARSON, Annie E., 20
PEARSON, Bessie, 107
PEARSON, Cecil C., 96
PEARSON, Clarence David, 107
PEARSON, D. H., 96
PEARSON, Earle E., 96
PEARSON, Emma H., 96
PEARSON, Emma Mason Rone, 79
PEARSON, J. C. (m), 79
PEARSON, J. D. (m), 91
PEARSON, J. L. (m), 20
PEARSON, Jesse I. (f), 91
PEARSON, Jesse W. (infant), 91
PEARSON, John D., 96
PEARSON, John L., 20
PEARSON, John S., 97
PEARSON, Lizzie Reid, 93
PEARSON, M. H., 96
PEARSON, Martha J., 97
PEARSON, Mary E., 93
PEARSON, Mattie, 96
PEARSON, N. B., 93
PEARSON, R. C. (f), 91
PEARSON, R. D., 79
PEARSON, Rose, 107
PEARSON, S. C. (m), 107
PEARSON, S. W., 91
PEARSON, Thos. D., 20
PEARSON, W. M. (m), 91
PEARSON, W. T., 96
PEARSON, Wm., 103
PEARSON, infant (f), 91
PEARSON?, baby boy, 96
PEGUES, A. T., 60
PEGUES, H. H., 29
PEGUES, J. T., 29
PEGUES, Mary A., 29
PERKINS, Emily, 63
PERRY, D. J., 47
PERRY, David J., 47
PERRY, J. A., 47
PERRY, L. A., 47
PERRY, Lucy A., 47
PERRY, Nancy McDonald, 47
PERRY, Wm. Thomas, 47
PERSON, Alexander, 3
PERSON, B. A., 3
PERSON, B. F. (m), 109
PERSON, B. R., 109
PERSON, B. R., 3
PERSON, Ben M., 3
PERSON, Benj. R., 108
PERSON, Charles Lafayette, 109
PERSON, E. E., 109
PERSON, E. J., 84
PERSON, Eliza Jane, 85
PERSON, Elnora S., 3
PERSON, Emily E., 108
PERSON, Emily E., 109
PERSON, Emily Greer, 3

PERSON, Fannie Clark, 37
PERSON, Fredonia E., 98
PERSON, J. P., 98
PERSON, John Ford, 43
PERSON, Louise Catherine, 92
PERSON, Lucius, 108
PERSON, Martha E., 101
PERSON, Mary E., 84
PERSON, Mother, 43
PERSON, Rush, 43
PERSON, Samuel B., 86
PERSON, Susan H., 109
PERSON, W. A., 84
PERSON, W. R., 84
PERSON, Walter, 10
PERSON, Wm. A., 85
PERSON, Wm. Marshall, 109
PERSON, _____ (unmarked), 85
PHILLIPS, Ella I., 70
PHILLIPS, Jas. T., 15
PHILLIPS, T. L. (m), 70
PHILLIPS, Thomas L., 71
PHIPPS, Sarah, 60
PIERCEY, Arthur, 118
PIERCEY, Robert Lee, 118
PIERCY, Evert G., 117
PIERCY, Jimmie F., 117
PIERCY, Lula May, 117
PIERCY, M. L., 117
PIERCY, W. S., 117
PIERCY, infant (m), 117
PITT, Milburn J., 107
PLEASANT, Theodore, 108
PLUNK, _____ (2 unmarked), 102
POLK, J. J., 33
POLK, Willie Rogers, 33
POLL, Charlie W., 50
POLL, Pattie, 50
POLL, W. W. (m), 50
POOLE, Alfred S., 67
POOLE, Sarah Annetta, 67
POPE, D. T. jr., 18
POPE, David T., 18
POPE, Eliza, 6
POPE, Haniah, 6
POPE, James E., 57
POPE, Joseph L., 10
POPE, Mary Annie, 7
POPE, Sallie, 10
POPE, T. W. (m), 57
POPE, Willis, 6
POPE, Wm. B., 57
POTTS, Martha L., 12
POTTS, W. W. (m), 12
POWERS, E. C., 43
PREWETT, Annie T., 69
PREWITT, Dicie Ann, 64
PREWITT, R. E. (m), 64
PRICE, J. W. (m), 115
PRICE, Jas. H., 17
PRICE, Josie R., 115
PRICE, Mary E., 115
PRICE, Maud H., 115
PRICE, Rebecca H. Taylor, 115
PRINGLE, Charlie, 1

PRINGLE, J. A., 1
PRINGLE, John A., 1
PRINGLE, M. A. (f), 1
PROTHY, Bryan B., 67
PRYOR, Eliza Jane, 30
PRYOR, John P., 30
PUCKETT, Samuel Witt, 103
PURCELL, J. B., 107
PURSLEY, Georgie (f), 38
PYBAS, A. M., 37
PYBAS, J. G., 37
PYBAS, Thos. Clark, 37
PYLES, A., 19
PYLES, Addison, 19
PYLES, Laura C., 19
PYLES, Martha, 19
PYLES, Mary, 19
PYLES, Wallace C., 19
PYLES, Willie C., 19
QUINN, Mary, 37
RACHELLE, Alice, 35
RACHELLE, W. F. (Dr.), 35
RAGLAND, Ella, 35
RAINES, F. M. (Dr.), 83
RAINEY, Martha O.?, 111
RAINEY, W. B., 111
RAMSEY, Emma G., 55
RAMSEY, Emma L., 55
RAMSEY, G. H. (m), 55
RAMSEY, Greenville H., 55
RAMSEY, M. L. (Mrs.), 55
RAMSEY, W. W. jr., 14
RAMSEY, Wm. Walter, 14
RANSOM, A. W., 49
RANSOM, Emma B., 49
RAWLINGS, C. I., 39
RAY, J. O., 14
READ, John, 24
READ, John J. D., 24
READ, Mary, 24
REAVIS, Albert, 35
REAVIS, Alice, 57
REAVIS, Alice A., 35
REAVIS, Amelia, 50
REAVIS, Elizabeth, 56
REAVIS, Fannie, 56
REAVIS, Fannie, 57
REAVIS, Fannie E., 57
REAVIS, Frank F., 50
REAVIS, J. H. (infant), 57
REAVIS, J. M., 57
REAVIS, J. M. (Mrs.), 57
REAVIS, Maggie M., 57
REAVIS, R. A., 56
REAVIS, R. A., 57
REAVIS, Robert, 57
REAVIS, Robert A., 57
REAVIS, S. E., 57
REAVIS, Samuel E., 19
REAVIS, Thos. C., 35
REAVIS, Thos. G., 19
REID, Anna, 7
REID, C. J., 7
REID, G., 11
REID, George, 7
REID, George R., 55
REID, Lena V., 103
REID, Mary, 2
REID, Sophie Beatty, 11
REID, Thomas A., 103
REID, W. A., 75
REID, Will D., 106
RENSHAW, Anderson C., 74
RENSHAW, Easter, 73
RENSHAW, Elizabeth, 74
RENSHAW, J. S., 73
RENSHAW, J. S., 74
RENSHAW, John (Rev.), 73
RENSHAW, Luna May, 73
RENSHAW, S. E., 73
RENSHAW, S. E., 74
RHODES, Lucy H., 31
RHODES, May L., 31
RHOES, Lucy A., 31
RICE, Annie C., 4
RICE, Elizabeth, 96
RICE, J. J., 4
RICE, J. J. (Capt.), 4
RICE, J. P. (m), 104
RICE, J. T. (m), 96
RICE, Lela Elizabeth, 96
RICE, Mary Ethel, 104
RICE, Sarah A., 4
RICE, W. A., 96
RICE, W. D., 96
RICE, infant (f), 104
RICHARDSON, A. S. (m), 40
RICHARDSON, Francis S., 40
RICHARDSON, Maude, 40
RICHARDSON, Ora L., 48
RICKETTS, C. E. (f), 86
RICKETTS, J. F., 86
RICKETTS, J. P., 86
RICKETTS, M. J., 86
RICKETTS, W. W., 86
RICKETTS, Wm., 86
RICKETTS, Wm., 86
RITCH, Mary A., 6
RIVER, Mollie, 9
ROACH, Lilbern Ray, 67
ROBB, Margaretta, 64
ROBBINS, Bettie, 67
ROBBINS, Florence Ione, 67
ROBBINS, James M., 7
ROBBINS, Tracy (m), 67
ROBERTS, Mildred A., 3
ROBERTSON, Charlie, 27
ROBERTSON, J. A., 27
ROBERTSON, Louanna Harris, 54
ROBERTSON, M. A., 27
ROBERTSON, Mamie, 54
ROBERTSON, Nell, 57
ROBERTSON, W. P. (m), 54
ROBINS, Sarah C., 14
ROBINSON, A. (m), 5
ROBINSON, Ham, 11
ROBINSON, Ham jr., 12
ROBINSON, Hattie B., 5
ROBINSON, Horace, 11
ROBINSON, Malinda, 35
ROBINSON, Ruth, 11
ROGERS, Alice, 5
ROGERS, C. A., 71
ROGERS, Cornelia, 98
ROGERS, Euin? A., 98
ROGERS, H., 111
ROGERS, Iva Rollins, 37
ROGERS, J. P. (m), 37
ROGERS, J. Walter, 5
ROGERS, Kate J., 5
ROGERS, Lucy A., 71
ROGERS, May, 98
ROGERS, V. A., 71
ROGERS, V. A. (m), 98
ROGERS, Vincin A., 98
ROGERS, Vincin B., 97
ROGERS, W. T. (m), 5
ROGERS, W. Whitlow, 5
ROGERS, Willie B., 98
ROLLINS, Amy, 84
ROLLINS, Charlie H., 86
ROLLINS, E. Catherine, 86
ROLLINS, Elizabeth, 84
ROLLINS, Iva (Mrs.), 37
ROLLINS, Ivan, 86
ROLLINS, James, 86
ROLLINS, John, 84
ROLLINS, Rebecca, 85
ROLLINS, S. G., 85
ROLLINS, T. R.? (m), 85
ROLLINS, Thomas, 85
ROLLINS, W. F. (f), 86
ROLLINS, W. H., 93
ROLLINS, W. R., 86
RONE, J. Hermon, 100
RONE, J. T. (m), 83
RONE, James, 87
RONE, Jennie L., 83
RONE, Jennie L., 83
RONE, John T., 83
RONE, John Travis, 106
RONE, Kate G., 83
RONE, Lillian, 84
RONE, Mahulda, 87
RONE, Morgan H., 87
RONE, Sarah A. M., 87
RONE, Willie, 83
RONE, Wyatt M., 86
ROOK, Walter T. sr., 17
ROOKS, Ada A., 45
ROOKS, P. A. (m), 45
ROPER, Elizabeth J., 21
ROPER, Mildred A. (Aunt Millie), 21
ROSAMOND, Mrs., 26
ROSE, Ben, 45
ROSS, James Walker, 46
ROWE, Benjamin, 31
ROWE, C., 31
ROWE, E., 31
ROWE, George, 31
ROWE, Peter, 31
ROWLAND, A. L. (m), 107
ROWLAND, D. W. (Rev.), 8
ROWLAND, Edward D., 8
ROWLAND, H. B., 50
ROWLAND, J., 8
ROWLAND, Mary, 50
ROWLAND, T. D., 50
ROWLAND, infant, 50
ROWLETT, Cora Holland, 117
ROWLETT, E. F., 119
ROWLETT, Freeda Alline, 118
ROWLETT, J. H., 118
ROWLETT, J. H. (m), 118
ROWLETT, Lennie, 118
ROWLETT, Lennie, 118
ROWLETT, Trula Orine, 118
ROWLETT, W. O., 119
ROWLETT, infant (f), 118
ROWLETT, infant (m), 119
ROYSTER, Katherine J., 16
ROZELL, B. L. (Dr.), 38
ROZELL, Lizzie G., 38
RUFFIN, Malissa A., 54
RUFFIN, Robert James, 54
RUFFIN, Thomas David, 54
RUSH, August W., 3
RUSH, J. A., 9
RUSH, J. W., 3
RUSH, John Thomas, 55
RUSH, M. E., 9
RUSH, M. O., 9
RUSH, Mary A., 3
RUSH, Sarah A. Kershaw, 9
RUSH, Susan C., 3
RUSH, W. H., 9
RUSH, W. H. (m), 9
RUSHING, A. M., 3
RUSHING, Felix W., 99
RUSHING, Green B., 99
RUSHING, Mary C., 99
RUSHING, Paul, 88
RUSSELL, A. S., 59
RUSSELL, Annie, 49
RUSSELL, Bessie, 49
RUSSELL, Caroline A., 49
RUSSELL, D. G., 49
RUSSELL, David jr., 49
RUSSELL, Edna Louise, 59
RUSSELL, Elijah P., 1
RUSSELL, Irene Claiborne, 25
RUSSELL, J. jr., 25
RUSSELL, Jess, 24
RUSSELL, Layton A., 25
RUSSELL, Martha J., 25
RUSSELL, Nettie, 22
RUSSELL, Pearl McCann, 25
RUSSELL, Robert R., 24
RUSSELL, Sarah H., 24
RUSSELL?, Abbie Lillian, 49
RUSSELL?, Carrie A., 49
RUSSELL?, Willie D., 49
RYLEY, J. E., 28
SANDERS, Wm. A., 53
SCALLIONS, A. J., 98
SCALLIONS, Betty Jean, 98
SCALLIONS, Floyd, 98
SCALLIONS, Leon, 98
SCALLIONS, Lois, 98
SCALLIONS, Lou (Mrs.), 98
SCALLIONS, M. M., 98
SCALLIONS, R. D., 98
SCALLIONS, W. J. (Mr.), 98
SCHARMAHORN, J. B. (m), 62
SCHARMAHORN, Laura G., 62
SCHEFOLD, Eva Neal, 6

Index to Madison Co. Tennessee Tombstones

SCOTLAND, Sterling, 59
SCOTT, J. E., 69
SCOTT, Jane E., 35
SCOTT, Mary Lee, 12
SCOTT, Preston B., 35
SCOTT, infant (f), 35
SCRIBNER, Chas., 106
SCRUGGS, Cora Weatherly, 53
SCRUGGS, W. T., 53
SEABORN, Addie Euphemia, 46
SEABORN, J. H., 46
SEABORN, L. J., 46
SEALE, Jessie Newton, 68
SEALE, Sophia Spratt, 68
SEAMORN, J. B., 86
SEAMORN, Mattie A., 86
SEAMORN, W. J. (m), 86
SEAROY, Albert, 39
SEWARD, J. W. (m), 13
SEWARD, M. E. (f), 13
SEWELL, Joseph H., 61
SEWELL, Mary A., 61
SEYMOUR, Edwin M., 50
SHARP, J. G. (m), 39
SHARP, Jemima A., 34
SHARP, Martha, 39
SHARP, Wm. Eugene, 39
SHELTON, Henry W., 35
SHELTON, J. D. (m), 105
SHELTON, L. B., 4
SHELTON, L. B., 4
SHELTON, L. B., 4
SHELTON, Lula M., 105
SHELTON, Neff, 49
SHELTON, S., 4
SHELTON, S. Sanford, 49
SHELTON, Sarah Willie, 4
SHELTON, infant (m), 105
SHEPARD, Matilda Plumer, 26
SHOFFNER, R. M., 15
SHOFFNER, Rowena Conger, 15
SHORTT, Walter M., 8
SIKES, Alice Pauline, 105
SIKES, B. J., 105
SIKES, V. J., 101
SIKES, infant (f), 101
SIKES, wife, 101
SILER, J. L., 29
SILER, Ruth, 29
SILER, infant (m), 29
SIMMONS, Mary C. (Mrs.), 4
SIMPSON, E. L. (f), 74
SIMPSON, Nelly Bly, 45
SIMPSON, S. C. (m), 74
SIMPSON, Samuel R., 100
SKILLERN, J. A., 55
SLATER, E. G. (Dr.), 32
SLATER, Mary, 32
SLATER, Word Early (Rev.), 32
SMALLEY, John S , 31
SMALLEY, Rose S., 31
SMALLEY, _____, 31
SMITH, A. J., 68
SMITH, Alice Longmire, 114
SMITH, B. J., 42
SMITH, B. R., 114

SMITH, Blanche, 42
SMITH, Catherine, 72
SMITH, Clarence Edward, 107
SMITH, Cynthia J., 110
SMITH, Dan H., 14
SMITH, Della, 51
SMITH, E. H., 88
SMITH, E. H., 89
SMITH, Eldred H., 88
SMITH, Emaline, 32
SMITH, Emma, 44
SMITH, Gideon T., 89
SMITH, H. F., 47
SMITH, H. S.? (m), 89
SMITH, Henry G., 42
SMITH, J. C. sr., 44
SMITH, John G., 89
SMITH, Joseph, 68
SMITH, Katie DeMay, 44
SMITH, M. M., 89
SMITH, Margaret Bell, 47
SMITH, Marie D., 56
SMITH, Mary Alice, 110
SMITH, Mary E., 108
SMITH, Matilda M., 88
SMITH, Matilda M., 89
SMITH, Mattie Sue, 107
SMITH, Mildred Bertie, 42
SMITH, R. B., 42
SMITH, S. J., 32
SMITH, T. H., 72
SMITH, W. D., 42
SMITH, Wm. M., 110
SMITH, Wm. R., 56
SNEED, B. F., 22
SNEED, B. J., 22
SNEED, Helen, 22
SNIDELL, D. J., 63
SNIDELL, Louis I., 63
SNIDER, B. D., 30
SNIDER, B. O. (m), 30
SNIDER, Baby Eleanor, 30
SNIDER, J. F., 10
SNIDER, Kate, 28
SNIDER, Louise (Mrs.), 52
SNIDER, Mary Roxie, 30
SNIDER, R. M., 30
SNIDER, Roxie M., 30
SNIPES, Edwin, 48
SNOW, Fletcher J., 16
SNOW, J. J. (m), 40
SNOW, Nellie Robinson, 15
SNOW, Polly B., 16
SNOW, Sarah McCabe, 40
SPAH, F., 4
SPAH, Lora, 4
SPAH, Mary, 4
SPAH, Mary, 69a
SPAIN, Emily C., 99
SPAIN, J. Warren, 99
SPAIN, Joseph M., 99
SPAIN, Will M., 99
SPARKS, Samuel Lawrence, 7
SPARR, John, 98
SPARR, Martha A., 98
SPENCE, Katie Bell, 44
SPENCE, W. W. (m), 44

SPENCE, Walter G., 12
SPENCER, George B., 16
SPENCER, M. B., 16
SPENCER, Mark B., 16
SPENCER, Nancy Ann, 16
SPENCER, Nell, 16
SPENCER, Will Branson, 16
SPIVEY, Calvin J., 14
SPIVEY, M. A. E. (f), 14
SPIVEY, P. S., 14
SPIVEY, R. B., 14
SPRAGINS, Bertha, 58
SPRAGINS, Clarence, 58
SPRAGINS, Mary S., 58
SPRAGINS, Thomas J., 58
SPRAGUE, Josie Dado, 50
SPRATT, Etta Josephine, 68
SPRATT, Henry Bishop, 68
SPRATT, Louise Parker, 68
SPRATT, Sophia, 68
STALEY, D. R., 52
STALEY, Maud Celeste, 20
STALEY, O. R. (m), 20
STANDEFER, Valena M., 3
STARK, Emmaline, 65
STARK, Robert, 65
STEDMAN, Dorothy L., 12
STEELMAN, Charles Byrd, 7
STEELMAN, Chas. W., 7
STEELMAN, Maggie E., 7
STEELMAN, Myrtle Bessie, 7
STEGALL, R. G., 40
STEGALL, Susan Cockrill, 40
STEIGER, Catharina, 45
STEIGER, D., 45
STEIGER, M., 45
STEMM, Dewitt, 77
STEMM, Susan Rebekah, 77
STEMM, Wm. D., 76
STEMM, Wm. Duncan, 77
STEPHENS, Annie Louise, 41
STEPHENS, J. K., 41
STEPHENS, James Kemp, 41
STEPHENS, Julia L., 2
STEPHENS, M. L., 41
STEPHENS, Mary Louisa Miller, 41
STEPHENS, Sarah Eliza, 41
STERLING, Janie Porter, 65
STERLING, P. P., 65
STERLING, Robert (Col.), 65
STETZEL, Baby, 42
STETZEL, F., 42
STETZEL, Fred, 42
STETZEL, Katherine Allois, 42
STETZEL, M. E., 42
STEWART, G. W., 78
STEWART, J. M., 76
STEWART, M. A., 78
STEWART, Martha Louisa, 78
STEWART, Mary A., 76
STILL, Fannie Harper, 39
STILL, James F., 39
STILL, Stanford A. (Dr.), 39
STOCKTON, Helen Haysels, 44
STOCKTON, Margaret O., 44
STODDERT, Wm., 64

STOUT, Anna, 92
STOUT, Callie, 106
STOUT, Isaac Hugh Roy, 92
STOUT, J. D. (m), 92
STOUT, James A., 106
STOUT, Richard A., 68
STRIBLING, Fay (Mrs.), 47
STRINGER, R. H. (f), 43
STRINGFELLOW, C. F. (m), 17
STRINGFELLOW, T. S., 17
STRINGFELLOW, Virgie E. (f), 17
STRINGFELLOW, Will, 17
STROTHERS, Margaret McConicke, 7
STUTTS, F. C., 36
SULLIVAN, John Bolton O'Neal, 53
SUTTON, R. P. (Rev.), 8
SWAN, Louisa Dorothea, 59
SWAYNE, J. S. (m), 56
SWAYNE, Luella, 56
SWAYNE, Maggie, 56
SWAYNE, Merritt, 56
SWAYNE, Mildred Medora, 56
SYBERT, Mary, 22
SYMONS, Annie Neilson, 20
SYMONS, Charles Randolph, 20
TALBOT, Almedia Ann, 67
TALBOT, Joseph H., Esq., 67
TALBOT, L. E. (CSA), 52
TARKINGTON, E. G. (m), 39
TARKINGTON, Martha S., 39
TARVER, Annie, 53
TATE, Alice L., 57
TATE, Green B., 67
TATE, Mat Lacy, 55
TATE, S. E. (f), 67
TATE, Thomas, 57
TAYLOR, Cliff W., 115
TAYLOR, Elizabeth, 117
TAYLOR, Ella, 115
TAYLOR, Elvira, 115
TAYLOR, Fannie, 115
TAYLOR, Fannie, 53
TAYLOR, George W., 62
TAYLOR, Henry, 117
TAYLOR, Hollie Wilson, 115
TAYLOR, J. Frank, 42
TAYLOR, J. H. (m), 115
TAYLOR, J. I. (Dr.), 53
TAYLOR, J. R., 62
TAYLOR, James R., 62
TAYLOR, John T., 52
TAYLOR, Josephine H., 117
TAYLOR, Laura Clapp, 53
TAYLOR, Laura G., 62
TAYLOR, M., 117
TAYLOR, Mark, 115
TAYLOR, Mary E., 52
TAYLOR, Mary Emma, 115
TAYLOR, Matilda Anderson, 115
TAYLOR, Mildred, 43
TAYLOR, N., 117
TAYLOR, Nancy A., 115
TAYLOR, Rebecca H., 115

TAYLOR, Richard H., 115
TAYLOR, Robert, 65
TAYLOR, Sallie, 62
TAYLOR, Sarah McClanahan, 62
TAYLOR, Tennessee V., 115
TAYLOR, Thos., 43
TAYLOR, Tommie, 52
TAYLOR, Walter H., 52
TAYLOR, Wiley H., 65
TAYLOR, Wm., 43
TAYLOR, Wm. Anderson, 115
TAYLOR, Wyatt A., 115
TAYLOR, Wyatt Adam, 115
TEMPLE, Hattie, 48
TEMPLE, Lillie, 48
TEMPLE, T. H., 48
TEMPLE, Thomas H., 48
TEMPLE, son of T. H. & Lillie, 48
TENAIN, Addie V., 6
TENAIN, J. J., 6
TENAIN, John J., 6
TENAIN, S. J., 6
THEUS, Edward Croft, 66
THEUS, Eliza L., 66
THEUS, Eliza Love, 66
THEUS, F. D., 65
THEUS, F. D., 66
THEUS, Fannie, 65
THEUS, Henry L. (Dr.), 66
THEUS, Howard Croft, 66
THEUS, J. Maxey, 66
THEUS, Jno., 15
THEUS, Jno. Womack, 15
THEUS, L. A., 65
THEUS, L. A., 66
THEUS, Lenud, 65
THEUS, Lucy A., 66
THEUS, Lucy A., 66
THEUS, Mamie, 66
THEUS, Mattie, 10
THEUS, Ophelia, 15
THEUS, Wm. R., 10
THEUS, Wm. R., 66
THOMAS, A., 83
THOMAS, Athamasius, 83
THOMAS, Elizabeth Blackmon, 83
THOMAS, Freddie, 83
THOMAS, Henry Clerc, 83
THOMAS, J. Willie, 83
THOMAS, James Julian, 83
THOMAS, James Julian (Rev.), 105
THOMAS, John P., 83
THOMAS, Kate Gibbs, 83
THOMAS, L. E., 83
THOMAS, R. A. (Mr.), 102
THOMAS, R. A. (Mrs.), 102
THOMAS, infant (m), 102
THOMAS, infant (m), 83
THOMPSON, Annie Ruth, 15
THOMPSON, Atwell, 2
THOMPSON, Edna Louise, 47
THOMPSON, Elizabeth, 77
THOMPSON, Ellen Sneed, 77

THOMPSON, Emma V., 48
THOMPSON, Evalyn Dorothy, 15
THOMPSON, J. A., 15
THOMPSON, James W., 101
THOMPSON, James W. jr., 101
THOMPSON, John Edgar, 77
THOMPSON, John T., 48
THOMPSON, L. I., 15
THOMPSON, L. S., 15
THOMPSON, Leslie, 101
THOMPSON, Leula, 15
THOMPSON, Lillie D., 49
THOMPSON, Louise, 86
THOMPSON, Mattie Boren, 87
THOMPSON, T. C., 98
THOMPSON, T. O., 87
THOMPSON, Virginia A., 48
THOMPSON, W. H. H., 77
THOMPSON, Wm. O., 49
THOMSON, Harrison G., 58
THORNTON, Beulah, 22
THORNTON, Frank, 22
TIMBERLAKE, E. G., 52
TIMBERLAKE, Elizabeth Ann, 52
TIMBERLAKE, G. R., 52
TIMBERLAKE, J. W. (m), 93
TIMBERLAKE, Lizzie L., 93
TIMBERLAKE, S. J., 52
TIMBERLAKE, W. P., 52
TIMBERLAKE, W.G.P., 52
TINKLE, Amos, 45
TINKLE, Earl H., 95
TINKLE, Elizabeth, 45
TINKLE, Harvey L., 95
TINKLE, John B., 45
TINKLE, Pratt, 45
TINKLE, W. T., 45
TOMLIN, Amanda Caroline, 33
TOMLIN, Elvira Bruce, 33
TOMLIN, John H., 33
TOMLIN, John L. H., 33
TOMLINSON, B., 93
TOMLINSON, C. E., 93
TOMLINSON, Frances, 10
TOMLINSON, Georgia, 94
TOMLINSON, Ike C., 10
TOMLINSON, J. A. (m), 10
TOMLINSON, J. R. T., 93
TOMLINSON, James A., 97
TOMLINSON, Martha E., 101
TOMLINSON, Mary, 97
TOMLINSON, S. T., 93
TOMLINSON, Sallie Pope, 10
TOMLINSON, Thomas D., 101
TOTTEN, A. W. U. (Hon.), 63
TOTTEN, Alice, 63
TOUHEY, Catherine, 39
TOUHEY, John, 39
TOUHEY, Kittie L., 39
TOWLER, Wm. P., 3
TREADWELL, Robt. A. (C.S.A. TN Cav.), 30
TRICE, E. J., 114
TRICE, Edward J., 114
TRICE, Jane, 114

TRICE, Laura Virginia, 114
TRICE, M. J., 114
TRICE, Martha Jane, 114
TRICE, Mary E., 114
TRICE, Nancy J., 114
TRICE, Thomas G., 114
TRIMBLE, Elizabeth Helena Parkman, 17
TRIMBLE, J. H. (m), 17
TUCKER, S. W., 27
TURLEY, Wm. Payne, 40
TURNER, D. T. (m), 89
TURNER, E. A., 18
TURNER, Martha, 18
TURNER, Serena W., 89
TURNER, W. A., 18
TYSON, Ben, 20
TYSON, Fannie, 21
TYSON, J. W., 21
TYSON, Jeanette Campbell, 20
TYSON, Joe Will, 19
ULRICH, W. H., 20
UMPHLETT, Hamilla H., 25
UMPHLETT, Job, 25
UMPHLETT, Lewis Collins, 25
UMPHLETT, Lucy E., 25
UMPHLETT, Miriam S., 25
UMPHLETT, Rachel W., 25
UPTON, Anna, 13
UPTON, G. O. (m), 13
UPTON, Sadie L., 13
UTLY, Lella Wade, 13
UTLY, Mary Deleisseline, 11
VANDENBROOK, Geo., 12
VANDENBROOK, Herman J., 27
VANDENBROOK, Irene McCoy, 12
VANDENBROOK, J. J. sr.?, 13
VANDENBROOK, Newton, U.S.N., 12
VANDENBROOK, P. L., 13
VANDENBROOK, Rebecca, 27
VANDIVER, DeEtta, 119
VANDIVER, Ezzell, 119
VANDIVER, J. A., 119
VANDIVER, John, 119
VANDIVER, Martha, 119
VANN, Alice M., 23
VANN, John M. J., 23
VANTRESSE, V. C. (m), 114
VANTRESSE, Virginia T., 114
VAULX, Eliza B., 62
VAULX, James, 62
VAULX, James Junius, 62
VAULX, Jane, 63
VAULX, Julia, 63
VAULX, Margaret Akin Boyd, 62
VAULX, Margaret Ann, 63
VAULX, Margaret Garsides, 62
VAULX, Susan, 63
VENTRESS, Mary E., 52
VINCENT, Thos., 32
VOSS, Dossie (m), 46
VOSS, Lizzie, 46
WADLEY, P. B., 24

WAKEFIELD, John, 7
WALKER, A. J., 100
WALKER, A. J., 101
WALKER, Clarence, 100
WALKER, Elgin, 48
WALKER, Emma, 101
WALKER, Emma Laura, 46
WALKER, Emma Laura, 48
WALKER, Fannie, 99
WALKER, Grace, 104
WALKER, Hattie, 104
WALKER, J., 104
WALKER, J. C. (m), 99
WALKER, J. S. (m), 101
WALKER, J. W. (m), 104
WALKER, James C., 99
WALKER, Jesse May (f), 100
WALKER, Lessie P. (f), 100
WALKER, M. P., 100
WALKER, Mary P., 101
WALKER, Mattie, 101
WALKER, Mollie, 100
WALKER, Ora, 99
WALKER, Pinckney, 48
WALLACE, D. J., 90
WALLACE, David J., 90
WALLACE, Earnest, 90
WALLACE, Florence, 103
WALLACE, I. H., 90
WALLACE, I. M., 90
WALLACE, Ida M., 90
WALLACE, J. D., 90
WALLACE, J. H. (m), 90
WALLACE, John R., 90
WALLACE, M. B., 90
WALLACE, M. H. (m), 89
WALLACE, Mabel E., 90
WALLACE, Margaret W., 90
WALLACE, Mary E., 89
WALLACE, Mary E., 90
WALLACE, Mary J., 90
WALLACE, Matthew H., 90
WALLACE, Robert H., 47
WALLACE, Robert L., 90
WALLACE, Samuel H., 90
WALLACE, T. A. (Mr.), 90
WALLACE, T. A. (Mrs.), 90
WALLACE, T. A. (m), 103
WALLACE, infant (m), 90
WALLACE?, Idabelle, 90
WALLACE?, Lottie, 103
WALLER, N. B., 105
WALSH, Annette, 15
WALSH, Teliatha J., 15
WALSH, Thos. E., 9
WALSH, W. K. (m), 15
WARE, E. A., 42
WARE, Mary Thelma, 42
WARE, W. S., 42
WARFIELD, Wm. S., 51
WARLICK, David, 110
WARLICK, Nancy, 110
WARLICK, Philip, 110
WARLICK, Wm. Franklin, 110
WARMATCH, J. W. (m), 83
WARMATCH, Jennie, 83
WARMATCH, Marvin, 83

Index to Madison Co. Tennessee Tombstones

WARMATCH, Mattie, 83
WATKINS, W. H., 12
WATSON, Belle Young, 102
WATSON, Ira A., 80
WATSON, J. T., 80
WATSON, J. T. (m), 80
WATSON, Joseph H., 92
WATSON, Laura J., 79
WATSON, Louie Zelma, 80
WATSON, M. A., 88
WATSON, N. L., 80
WATSON, Nancy, 80
WATSON, Neal, 102
WATSON, P. J. (f), 92
WATSON, Thomas Emmet, 88
WATSON, W. J., 88
WATSON, W. L. (m), 79
WATSON, Wm., 92
WAYNICK, Lilla Adell, 100
WEAKES, J. R., 76
WEAKS, N., 104
WEAKS, W. H., 104
WEAKS, Will D., 104
WEAKS, Wm. Richard, 104
WEATHERLY, J. M. Orbio, 53
WEBB, Elnorah L., 104
WEBB, Milner P., 104
WEEKS, Ada, 76
WEEKS, Dellia, 104
WEEKS, Horace, 76
WEEKS, J. R., 76
WEEKS, M. A., 76
WEEKS, Will D., 104
WELSH, Archie Lee, 91
WELSH, D. L. (f), 91
WELSH, Eliza, 91
WELSH, J. P. (m), 91
WELSH, Maggie B., 91
WELSH, Pat, 91
WHEELER, Edna, 48
WHEELER, Mattie, 99
WHITAKER, Elizabeth, 18
WHITAKER, Flora, 18
WHITAKER, L. W. (m), 18
WHITAKER, Lillie Williams, 18
WHITE, G. R. (Dr.), 69
WHITE, J. H., 57
WHITE, John A., 7
WHITE, N., 69
WHITE, Wm. Stewart, 21
WHITFIELD, Fannie, 32
WHITLOW, Bess, 5
WHITLOW, Elizabeth, 5
WHITLOW, Kate J. Rogers, 5
WHITLOW, Nathan, 5
WHITLOW, W. (m), 5
WHITMAN, Bennie, 67
WHITMAN, Henry, 67
WHITMAN, J. H. (m), 67
WHITMAN, Lena, 67
WHITMAN, Mary A., 67
WHITMAN, Mary L., 67
WILBON, J. R., 17
WILBON, May, 4
WILDBERGER, Ora, 63
WILDBERGER, W. P. (m), 63
WILDE, August, 11
WILDE, Chas., 11
WILDE, Chas. F., 11
WILDE, Lena, 11
WILDE, Mary, 11
WILIE, Lilie Mae, 11
WILIE, W. R., 11
WILKERSON, Dolopes Moody, 64
WILKINSON, J. K., 69
WILKINSON, J. R., 50
WILKINSON, Saida Lee, 50
WILKINSON, Sarah Elizabeth, 50
WILLIAMS, Almedia, 92
WILLIAMS, Chas. H., 28
WILLIAMS, Dorothy, 28
WILLIAMS, Eliza Strother, 7
WILLIAMS, Emma, 28
WILLIAMS, J. H. (m), 44
WILLIAMS, J. L., 28
WILLIAMS, Jane M., 44
WILLIAMS, Joe H., 56
WILLIAMS, John Jay, 7
WILLIAMS, John L. sr., 28
WILLIAMS, Katie, 13
WILLIAMS, Lillie, 18
WILLIAMS, M. S., 68
WILLIAMS, N. B. (m), 13
WILLIAMS, N. M. (m), 92
WILLIAMS, Newton Milton, 92
WILLIAMS, Pleasant Daniel, 51
WILLIAMS, R. B., 43
WILLIAMS, R. H., 28
WILLIAMS, Sophia R., 52
WILLIAMS, infant (f), 28
WILLIAMSON, Drucilla, 88
WILLIAMSON, J. J. sr., 22
WILLIAMSON, J. T. (Mrs.), 22
WILLIAMSON, Malissa A., 54
WILLIAMSON, Thos. G., 88
WILSON, A. R. (Rev.), 18
WILSON, Addie Cathey, 46
WILSON, Chas. B., 3
WILSON, Comer May, 7
WILSON, Emily, 18
WILSON, F. A. (m), 7
WILSON, Fannie J., 12
WILSON, Fay, 7
WILSON, Francis Marion, 7
WILSON, J. A. (m), 12
WILSON, Jennie Crawford, 46
WILSON, Jennie L., 46
WILSON, Katie Bell, 44
WILSON, Little Jennie, 46
WILSON, Little Vernon, 46
WILSON, T. T., 46
WILSON, Thomas T., 46
WINDROM, Eugene, 43
WINDROM, Florence E., 43
WINDROM, N. R., 43
WINDROM, Nancy R., 43
WINDROM, T. D., 43
WINDROM, Thomas D., 43
WINSLOW, G. G., 107
WINSLOW, Laura P., 78
WINSLOW, S. M., 78
WINSLOW, T. H., 78
WINSTON, J. B., 105
WINSTON, Mattie, 105
WISDOM, Ann, 51
WISDOM, J. L., 51
WISDOM, L. K., 51
WISDOM, Mahola, 14
WITHERS, J. R., 63
WITHERS, M. F., 63
WITHERSPOON, Angie Hays, 2
WITHERSPOON, Elvira, 17
WITHERSPOON, Elvira, 2
WITHERSPOON, Katherine B., 2
WITHERSPOON, Ross, 2
WITHERSPOON, Wm., 2
WOMACK, Eliza, 66
WOMACK, Eliza, 66
WOMACK, Elizabeth Lee, 21
WOMACK, J. G. (Dr.), 21
WOMACK, James G., 66
WOMACK, James Green (Dr.), 21
WOOD, Carey, 99
WOOD, F. B., 99
WOOD, Frank D., 99
WOOD, H. A., 99
WOOD, Hester A., 99
WOOD, J. D., 99
WOOD, Mary Elizabeth, 99
WOOD, Sarah S., 61
WOODS, Elizabeth, 26
WOOLFOLK, A. J., 73
WOOLFOLK, C. B., 68
WOOLFOLK, G. N., 73
WOOLFOLK, J. C.?, 73
WOOLFOLK, J. G. (m), 100
WOOLFOLK, J. R., 73
WOOLFOLK, Jennie, 73
WOOLFOLK, Jessie J. (f), 68
WOOLFOLK, John G., 100
WOOLFOLK, John R., 57
WOOLFOLK, Julian R. (Dr.), 68
WOOLFOLK, Mollie B., 100
WOOLFOLK, Neal, 73
WOOLFOLK, Sue E., 100
WOOLFORK, L. F., 97
WOOLFORK, Ruby, 97
WOOLFORK, W. B., 97
WOOLLARD, James W., 55
WOOLLARD, Julia R., 56
WOOTEN, Annie D., 117
WOOTEN, J. P. (m), 67
WOOTEN, M. A., 117
WOOTEN, Mary, 67
WOOTEN, W. S., 117
WORD, Elizabeth, 111
WORRELL, John D., 42
WORRILL, Birdie Lua, 62
WORRILL, J., 62
WORRILL, Lua, 62
WRIGHT, Anna, 11
WRIGHT, Christiana Hogsett, 17
WRIGHT, Felix, 11
WRIGHT, Isaac Pleasant, 50
WRIGHT, J. F. (m), 11
WRIGHT, J. K. (m), 50
WRIGHT, James Kelly, 50
WRIGHT, John, 4
WRIGHT, John Morgan, 11
WRIGHT, Lillie A., 50
WRIGHT, Mary Susan, 50
WRIGHT, Nancy Jane, 4
WRIGHT, Nellie D., 44
WRIGHT, Z. N., 17
WYATT, J. W. (m), 114
WYATT, Nelia A., 114
YANCY, F. W. (m), 25
YANCY, Isabella, 25
YANCY, Robt. J., 25
YANCY, Susan R., 25
YANDELL, G. T. (m), 115
YANDELL, Geo. T., 115
YANDELL, Maud H., 115
YANDELL, Maud H., 115
YARBRO, Lizzie A., 104
YORK, Nancy E., 38
YORK, Nannie J., 38
YORK, Sam, 38
YOUNG, Belle, 102
YOUNG, John, 23
YOUNG, May J., 23
ZACHARY, Mattie Elizabeth, 69
ZARICOR, Albert G., 41
ZARICOR, Ethel B., 41
ZARICOR, Juanita, 41
ZEISER, F. W. (m), 37
ZEISER, Minnie, 37
____, Julia, 6

www.ingramcontent.com/pod-product-compliance
Lightning Source LLC
Chambersburg PA
CBHW081133170426
43197CB00017B/2843